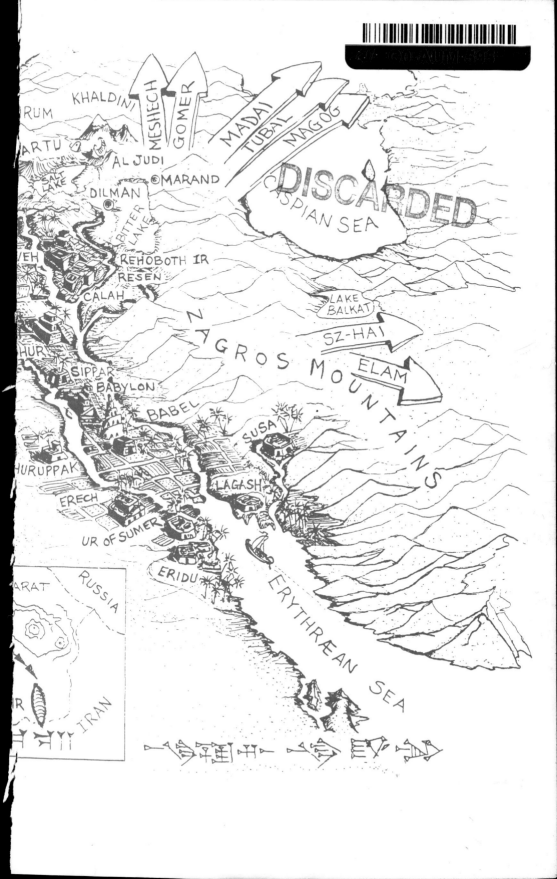

The Ark of Noah

The Ark of Noah

DAVID FASOLD

WYNWOOD™ Press
New York, New York

Scripture quotations identified KJV are from the King James Version of the Bible.

Scripture quotation from *The Living Bible* Copyright © 1971 by Tyndale House Publishers, Wheaton, Ill. Used by permission.

Scripture quotations identified NIV are from the Holy Bible, New International Version. Copyright © 1973, 1978, 1984 International Bible Society. Used by permission of Zondervan Bible Publishers.

Chinese characters reprinted from THE DISCOVERY OF GENESIS, Copyright © 1979 by Concordia Publishing House, St. Louis. Reprinted by permission.

Hieroglyphic text from *The Egyptian Book of the Dead* by E. A. Wallis Budge, Dover Publications, © 1967.

Library of Congress Cataloging-in-Publication Data

Fasold, David.
    The ark of Noah.

    1. Noah's ark.   2. Ararat, Mount (Turkey)
3. Excavations (Archaeology)–Turkey–Ararat, Mount.
4. Turkey–Antiquities.   I. Title.
BS658.F37   1989   222′.11093   88-20437
ISBN 0-922066-10-8

Printed in the United States of America

This adventure has been shared by my under-standing wife, Anna. During my three years of expeditionary research, which involved many months away from home, she was where I needed her most—raising our two sons, Nathan and Michael, who I hope will view the Ark one day.

And in the dear memory of my loving sister, Elizabeth Fasold Herron, who shared in my excitement, one day at a time, until she was carried home in the ark of our salvation on August 3, 1987.

Contents

Preface

In an attempt to establish the origin of modern man and the seed that has germinated into the flourishing of civilizations, the archaeologist has lifted his brush from the sands of time to paint a portrait of the ancient Near East splashed with colors of enlightenment. For his devoted labors in illuminating these areas of understanding, we are grateful. But it remains a painting poorly executed, for the artists of anthropology have not yet succeeded in producing within that balance of shadow and light any expression of harmony that allows the viewer to envision from whence he came.

This painting remains muddled by a modern-day myth that the legends burned into the memories of the ancients and impressed onto tablets of clay were not actual records of an historical event. Thus the historians have failed to reclaim from obscurity that dark "land of the crossings" from which the settlers have come, survivors of an advanced culture that was cleaved by an event of such catastrophic proportions as to literally divide history and the development of man into a new age. This experience of an overwhelming deluge still remains as the most solemn and awesome recollection of the human race.

My portrayal, then, is the fertile crescent born anew, a rejuvenation of civilization reawakened from a slumber of the dead by the descendants of this past age, borne upon the survival ship that traversed the eras in a voyage of circumstance and necessity, the descendants of Noah and progenitors of modern man.

In the attempt to retrace our ancestors' footsteps to the door of the Ark itself, however attractive such a mission might appear, I have failed to interest the academic community at large in participating. Understandably, such a proposal raises serious doubts. But when an invitation is extended to view the tangible remains of the antediluvian vessel high upon the mountains of Urartu, the response of science should be investigation pure and simple, not ridicule and scorn.

Perhaps reluctance on their part is the only safe ground, for should this prove to be the most controversial artifact ever recorded, the legend is exonerated and the biblical Flood is true. Even their high towers of "qualifications" will not save them from the deluge of error.

Does the theory that man has come from the lowest depths of humanity to his present elevated position have validity? Is it time for the history of man to be rewritten, this time with more foundation and truth?

Or is it time to return to the original accounts, and read them with the seriousness they deserve?

For those who have always believed, I claim no discovery and my story is of little classical value or scholarly merit. But it is my hope that it will be greeted as representing the first confrontation with a startling new body of evidence and a sense of what the discovery has meant to those explorers who experienced it.

To those for whom a devotion to truth and understanding bring a spark of life . . . welcome aboard the mother ship of mankind, built to bridge two worlds, which rode upon that cataclysm of old and bore us to our new beginnings.

DAVID FASOLD

Introduction
by Charles Berlitz

Has Noah's Ark finally been found?

The location of the legendary Noah's Ark on Mount Ararat has been reported a number of times in antiquity and in the Middle Ages by such travelers as Marco Polo and other merchants and pilgrims following the caravan trails. It has been reported seen in modern times by mountain climbers, shepherds, fugitives, and explorers, religious and laic. Some climbers claim not only to have seen the Ark but to have touched it and even taken wood from the giant hull. Since World War I it has sometimes been sighted by aircraft pilots from military or private planes. It has been reported on the mountain in World War II and in the subsequent Cold War period.

The problem has long been how to positively identify it, inasmuch as climbers or viewers of Mount Ararat may be influenced by seeing something where the Ark is supposed to be. Pictures of something which might be the Ark have been taken from a space capsule at seven hundred miles altitude over the mountain, but the shape loses its cohesion when subjected to magnification. Other photographs taken from planes seem to have been lost, sometimes in mysterious circumstances. Further, photography from the air or on the side of the mountain near the Russian border, where the Ark is supposed to be frozen most of the time under the ice, is presently not only difficult but, like reported photographs from high-altitude spy planes such as the U-2, dangerous.

When one climbs to the upper reaches of Mount Ararat one risks being struck by lightning, falling into deep crevasses through thin ice over glaciers, blown off the mountain by unexpected winds, hit by stone avalanches, attacked by wolves or wild dog packs, or shot by bandits or rebels. The dedication of the climbers, many of whom feel they are on a religious mission, is a definite manifestation of the power of the belief that Noah's Ark is waiting to be found on Mount Ararat. But the Bible never mentions Ararat specifically, rather "the mountains of Ararat," Ararat being a form of the old word for Armenia – *Urartu*. The fixation upon Mount Ararat itself is anciently based on Saint Jacob's testimony. He said that an angel carried him up the mountain to show him the Ark, and then took him down again.

Explorers and searchers for the Ark must face the element of popular disbelief in the very presence of such an artifact on Ararat as, "How can you find something that does not exist?" The popular legends concerning Noah's Ark, the enormous size of the ship allegedly built by Noah and his three sons, the gathering in and feeding of the horde of animals that were summoned, two by two of each species, and finally, the illogicality of a flood that could cover the whole earth, may be based on the memories of a great flood but are certainly difficult concepts for the nonbeliever to accept.

But there are startling indications of a catastrophe which affected the whole earth ten or eleven thousand years ago. This was a combination of earthquakes, volcanic eruptions, cosmic storms, sudden changes in sea level and climate. We are now able to ascertain that catastropic flooding occurred in different parts of the earth as large areas of the land and water changed places. To many of the earth's inhabitants, the world seemed to be drowning in a great flood, from which only a few "chosen" people escaped.

The legend of the Flood and the Ark is older than Greece, older than Egypt, older than Babylon and the cultures that preceded it. The memory of the Flood, as this world disaster appeared to most of the ancient peoples inhabiting the earth at that time, is still preserved in national and tribal traditions throughout the world.

Only the name of each local survivor varied in prehistoric northern Europe, East Asia, the American continents, Africa, and the Pacific. In the ancient Middle East, although the name

Noah was antedated by other local names, the story is the same. Noah's name, common to the great religions of Christianity, Judaism, and Islam, is now the most famous name among the ship captains who survived, as is the place of salvation – the mountains of Ararat.

Not only is the finding of the ancient Ark important to archaeology and the history of civilization, which would thereby be extended backward thousands of years, but it also is of tremendous importance to religion. The Ark is the first biblical mention of an incident and an artifact that may be scientifically verifiable. Of the first ten books of Genesis, common to Christianity and Judaism, the first five chapters are devoted to the creation of the world, the heavenly bodies, man, and the animals, and the next five to Noah, his family, and the Flood. The shape of the Ark, as well as the cross and a fish, were the first symbols of Christianity.

During the last few years, the search for the Ark of Ararat, on the high icy plateau, in crevasses, and even under the ice, has been intensified. The usual pattern for searches to take place only on Mount Ararat has been changed by the exploratory investigations of David Fasold, a deep-sea diver and holder of a master's ticket in the merchant marine. Fasold has dedicated years of his life and considerable personal funds to long explorations of the Ararat area, with the premise that Noah's Ark has already been found. The true Ark, he claims, was photographed from the air in 1959 after a mud slide uncovered a stone formation closely resembling a ship. This stone shape of a ship is not on Ararat but twelve miles away on a lower range.

The dimensions of the ship are almost identical to the biblical description of the Ark: approximately 450 feet long, 75 feet wide, and 45 feet high – except for the height – but the stone ship is still rising from the enveloping solidified mud. Fasold claims the stone form is a real ship, not fossilized but made of reeds covered with cement. As we now know, cement was used thousands of years before Rome in different parts of the Middle East.

During his years of on-the-spot research, Fasold has been assisted by scientists who include a Los Alamos specialist and a radar field technician. They have used the most sensitive radar devices that can detect formations *and* mineral content, not only under water but under land, up to a depth of forty feet, as well. Starting with frequency generators to determine metal concentration of spikes inside wooden beams, he traced thirteen bow-to-stern interior divisions and nine interior bulkhead-to-bulkhead supports. A more detailed search with subsurface interface radar revealed clear outlines of closed sections, beams and cross beams, collapsed decks, iron and other metals used in clamps, and pins at approximately eighteen- to twenty-inch intervals. The discovery of the inner plan of the stone shape of a gigantic ship could not have been ascertained without digging into the shape except by using the subsurface radar. Here we have an example of advanced technology revealing history that has not been generally accepted as such, obscured up till now by the mists of legend and time.

The huge drag stones used on ancient ships have been found on a plateau several miles away, possibly dropped there when the ship started to go aground. The Ark survived because of its cement covering and lay under layers of frozen mud until it surfaced in 1948.

The discovery of this stone ship and ongoing tests over and soon inside the vessel have created a world sensation, not only in archaeology but also in Middle East politics and the study of the world's lost history. If this is indeed the Noah's Ark of the Bible, its complete appearance and identification may cause many to entertain somber reflections. Colonel James Irwin, an astronaut who walked on the moon and who has long searched for the Ark, has expressed what many fundamentalists feel: ". . . the finding of the Ark could very well herald the return of the Messiah and the end of the earth." If the appearance of the Ark *is* a warning, one must admit it comes at an appropriate moment in world history.

The Turkish Ministry of Culture has now made the remains the focus of a national park, and Turkish archaeologists, hopefully with international collaboration, will continue the investigation. Meanwhile, a sign indicates the direction to the ship. It says: NUH'UN GEMISI (Noah's Ark).

It is an interesting coincidence and historic justice that the

ancient ship, unrecognized since 1948 by formal archaeologists and religious searchers, should finally be identified by a
fellow sea captain – a professional colleague and ideological
descendant of Noah.

The Ark of Noah

1

Boat on the Mountain

THE ASCENT

I let the pack fall from my shoulders and paused for a rest. I was already dizzy from the short climb, and for a sea-level man only a week out of sunny Florida it was becoming a tough trek.

Exploring the steppes of Anatolia in the lingering snows of March may not have been such a great idea, but my purpose for being there drove me on.

On the valley floor far below one could almost make out the armies of Alexander in the morning mists, or was it a returning caravan that had carried treasures of the Orient to the Bosphorus and beyond?

The shadow of Ararat, dark against the dead pastureland of retreating winter, raced across the landscape to reveal the multicolored images as heavily laden trucks carrying fruits of modern industry and the machines of war weaved eastward through the ancient garment of Turkey like a brightly colored thread to the worn fabric of her border into Iran.

In the ancient land of Urartu, Ararat dominates the land. Its massive weight depresses the valley floor for miles around, and the awesome heights create a weather system unto itself, shrouding the snow-covered volcanic peaks in the clouds of its own making. But the early-morning hours are crisp and clear, and those on the other side in Soviet Armenia are greeted by the peaks in the wake of dawn.

Ararat is a Painful Mountain, as its name declares, for in Turkish it is called Ağrı Dağ. Its slopes were becoming a barren battleground of warring theories for fundamentalist thought.

1

Ararat sinks into the surrounding crust of the valley, oppressed by the burden of proof to claim the Ark. Will it reveal the secret place and the Ark of Ages hidden within its folds, or only the untruths of its legend in time?

For Ararat is a relative newcomer, and its sister peak to the east younger still. The drainage patterns left from the Deluge seem well established until the time that Ararat was upthrust during some later period of upheaval, leaving the beds of long-established streams and tributaries dry on her shoulders.

But to those so motivated, to prove their particular and peculiar interpretations of Holy Writ, there can be no doubt that their research is factual and inerrant. The mountains of Ararat refer only to Ararat itself and it is not so much the question Is the Ark there? but When will it be found and upon whom will God bestow his blessing by revealing it?

Those who have claimed to see it there have been many and varied, less in quest of truth than in notoriety, fabricators of wild claims and tales for which their listeners had hungered. The Ark was intact and preserved for the ages, to be revealed in the last days as a bulwark of faith and belief.

Some who have hoped to vindicate these legends are sincere and dedicated people, scholars of science, historians, and even an astronaut who walked on the moon. They are men of great integrity with religious destiny that cannot be denied. But for the most part, the others have been self-proclaimed experts, victims of their own ignorance leading pilgrimages of the uninformed, lending credence to their mission with frequently larded reference to the Almighty. But God will not move the Ark to their mountain in answer to prayer.

Regardless of their differences, the explorers held some things in common: a malady of addiction to the story of the Flood as an actual historic event of cataclysmic proportions, and the hope that the remains of the escape vessel could be found. This was called "Ark Fever," and it was shared by us all.

Of course, it is recognized that this hope was something that was not shared by others and quite outside the order of acceptance among higher critics. Actually, I rather enjoyed the violent reactions to this quest for the Ark that could be goaded from almost any professional anthropologist with charges that

I was a misguided adventurer whose theorizing in such schol-arly fields was an emotional expedition of futility, rather than intellect. I was always a bit mystified that professionals so unanimous in their rejection of sinking continents could agree on a former land bridge from Siberia to Alaska. Knowledge and remembrance of a great Flood is not only recorded from Plato to Peter but is actually among man's oldest written records impressed upon clay tablets by the early Sumerians and on view for all to see in museums today.

Of course these stories are embellished, but are they in essence recording an event that actually occurred? If so, then the task of science is investigation pure and simple. Why then was I viewed as an outsider and a maverick by historians? Would a "ship on the mountains" seriously jeopardize uni-formly held opinion on the history of the world? Did they fear the Genesis account might be true?

Unlike my contemporaries, I had discounted all spurious accounts of seeing the Ark on Ararat that had been cranked out by the Armenian rumor mill and confined my investigations solely to pre-Christian records.

I found within the works of a Chaldean priest mysterious phraseology used in describing the "Magur," or god boat of the Deluge. To my way of thinking, it appeared rather to be giving a geographical location for it. That I should be able to solve this 2,250-year-old puzzle by unraveling this cryptic message I found strange in itself. I thought it stranger still when I met another explorer who had preceded me to the site.

Ron Wyatt was from Madison, Tennessee, an explorer of biblical truths. That he also should suggest his contemporary Ark hunters were on the wrong mountain was really hiking on thin ice. The object Ron was investigating at this late stage had been discounted by experts years ago. It had been written off by George Vandeman and Rene Noorbergen in 1960 as a freak of nature. It was not the wooden, barge-shaped Ark of Christendom. Furthermore, Wyatt's claim of discovery was countered by Noorbergen as simply asking a local cabdriver to take him near the spot where the object was locally well known. A photograph had even appeared in the September issue of *Life* magazine in 1960. It was called the Tendürek Formation.

But Wyatt was inquisitive, and he had returned on several occasions since that first visit to the site in 1977. Wyatt was suspicious that the mound held the remains of the great ship, but he could recover no hard proof. It was, to the others, just an out-of-date opinion.

Meanwhile, my interest in the Ark's location was now at a peak. It came nowhere near where the others had looked and certainly not on the Tendürek mountains. My cumulative information from Arabic and Persian sources was that it had been investigated around 880 B.C.E. and found buried so as to be described as being three stories deep. It would be found on the northwest slope of an area or place named Nisir, no higher than 2114 meters on a north/south axis alongside a large rock. According to my interpretation of Berosus' figures, it would be 515 minutes of the sun's arc west of the Aşaru, or prime meridian, of the Persian Empire. A rhumb line of 36° from the Amphalos, or geodetic navel at Persepolis, would intersect this longitude at 39°26'N on today's charts. Upon plotting this position on a War Office chart of Turkey, I had made an astounding discovery, an interesting notation that suggested this location was hiding the Ark.

I called James Irwin, astronaut and seasoned explorer, who had already led many expeditions to locate the Ark on Ararat. I suggested an area south of the mountain, but he cut me short. "Dave, if you don't believe the Ark is on Ararat, you should get together with Wyatt. Maybe you two should team up together."

Wyatt's interest was solely the site on Tendürek. "But it should be southeast of Doğubayazıt," I exclaimed, "not on the Tendürek range!"

"But I am east of the town," Ron replied, somewhat confused. "Listen," he said. "Everyone is giving the wrong directions. Even people who claimed to have been there before would head off the wrong way if I hadn't led them by the hand."

My trip to Turkey was slated for June. When I returned home from a meeting with a ground penetrating radar manufacturer in New Hampshire, there was a telephone message from Ron. He had business in Ankara. If I cared to accompany him, after business he was going on to his site. Would I like to get my bearings? He had already made a reservation for me. I said I already had reservations about going in th̶   ̶ws, but his friendly perseverance was hard to resis̶   ̶ chance to see if I was wrong before investing̶ and Ron's chance to prove to me he'd beaten eve̶ find, but it most certainly couldn't be on the Tendür̶ tains!

Samran was slight of build, very dark and handsome v̶ the smoldering eyes of a Bedouin that spoke a warning t̶ those who might underestimate him.

After eleven years in the merchant marine, I had acquired enough Arabic to carry on a simple conversation. Unfortunately, Samran had accumulated the same phrases in English. We had lengthy conversations, but nothing in depth. Samran was a likeable sort.

Dilaver, on the other hand, spoke no English whatever, and among us all we spoke very little Turkish. But with Dilaver, this posed no problem. I think he was able to read our thoughts. It was some time before I fully realized this. We all just seemed to move forward together in a union of silence toward our goal, each on his own private pilgrimage to our beginnings and the origin of man in this age. Dilaver dropped his pack as he approached and sat down for a rest.

"En kısa yol bu mu?" Dilaver's breath vaporized in the chilled morning air as he studied Ron and Samran struggling ahead in the deep snow. It might be the most direct route, but certainly not the easiest, I thought. I gestured off to the right. "Let's go this way." Dilaver's response was always the same: "İnşallah !" One could feel very close to God in this country, as in all Moslem countries everything was in submission to the will of Allah.

I stood up while slinging the camcorder over my shoulder and reached down to grab the frequency generator with my free hand. Bearing compass, altimeter, and snow goggles dangling from my neck spun in slow circles as I reached for the canteen of hot Çay.

Yes, İnşallah, if God be willing, I would break my fast and drink hot tea with my friends on the Ark today – God be willing, and if this wasn't some kind of a cruel joke, I thought.

I hurried to catch up.

KURDS: GUARDIANS OF THE SECRET PLACE

It is hard to say who was most startled by our abrupt meeting. We had been climbing in silence for about an hour up the north slope, while a small group of Kurds had been heading down out of view. We met at the rise of a hill, face-to-face at twenty feet. There were three of them.

Dilaver rushed forward to intervene, bending slightly in explanation of our intrusion into the area. Polite Koranic greetings were exchanged while the Kurds cautiously eyed us. But theirs was the stare of a hardy people who had just barely weathered the isolation of the harsh winter in the desolate highlands of their forefathers.

This was my first encounter with the Kurds, about whom I had read so little. What information I could glean from other climbers and authors was that they were for the most part Moslems of the Haifi sect who preferred to live alone unmolested, confining their squabbles among themselves and their numerous family clans. Outsiders did not intervene, nor were they welcome, and Kurds had a quaint habit of shooting at strangers. They guarded their turf unchallenged, yet, they had consented to be Turkish, or from their viewpoint preferred the stability of Turkey and therefore were accepted as Turks. They guarded the borders of their homeland well.

The identity of the Kurds is still one of the unsolved problems of ethnology. They are recorded as having claimed these mountainous areas since at least 2000 B.C.[1] Their brothers to the south were split into other sects, or Mezhep, of Islam, belonging to the Sunni and Safi groups, quarreling with the Farsi (Iranians) who were fundamental Şii, or Shi-ites.

It was in the mountains of the Korduaians, or Kurds, where Berosus had said the remains of the Ark could be seen. These people would know and keep their secret well, as in ages past during Achaemenian times[2] they were among the privileged

---

[1]Henry Filmore, *Pageant of Persia* (New York: Bobbs-Merrill Co., 1936).

[2]A period of about two hundred years that closed with the conquest of Persia by Alexander the Great and the murder of Darius III in 331 B.C. It was the time of Plato, Socrates, Aristotle, and Herodotus.

guardians of the temples of the Magi. Were they guarding the secret resting place of the Ark?

By now we were only some two miles from the Iranian border, and during Dilaver's explanation of the purpose of our visit, the Kurds eyed us suspiciously. We were trespassing on their land and it would have been useless to continue without their permission. Soon a cautious look of recognition spread across the face of one mountain man as he approached Ron, took his gear, and slung it over his back. The Kurds would forego their trip to the plain below and escort us through the area in safety.

I would make it a point to know these people well. They represented three major families of these parts and their names were Memet Özer, Ahmet Sarihan, and Memet Eraslan, from the village of Üzengili.

The snow was becoming soft and we hurried our ascent, staying to the west of the snow-filled fissures of the flow area, as our seven shadows slowly diminished in the morning sun. Ron was in the lead with the guides and approaching the top of a hill with Dilaver and Samran close behind.

I looked up and saw Samran transfixed at the crest of the hill. Slowly he raised his hands above his head in disbelief. It was 0610, March 27, 1985; the moment of truth.

"Bis-mil-la-hir-rah-ma-nir-ra-him. . . ." Samran's prayer was lost in the wind. "In the name of Allah, the Beneficent, the Merciful. All praise is due to Allah, the nourisher of all worlds. The Merciful, the Compassionate. Master of the Day of Judgment."

I was completely stunned! Christian and Moslem paused on that crest in reverence of what lay below them, dark brown against the snow. Wracked and distorted, yet preserved for the end of the age, were the walls of a ship projecting upward some twenty feet out of the earth. It seemed we stood there in silence forever, each in his own thoughts, searching the heart for a meaning to it all. For me it felt like the end of life's journey in the learning of the human mind, where sometimes the most terrifying events are forgotten, a memory blotted out and displaced deep into the unconscious strata of the mind.

The sight before me awakened a faint recollection that suddenly rushed forward, the memory of a past event so terrifying and violent as to be unimaginable. It is an instinctive fear indelibly imprinted in the genetic makeup of modern man that has been transmitted through inheritance from the survivors of the Deluge and can be awakened by the sight of the Ark. A memory of the judgment of man and a fear of the judgment that is to come upon the world. It comes full circle within the mind when confronted by the tangible remains and reality of the event.

I descended the hill to the flow as if in a dream, passing through the ages, and as a pilgrim, to the beginning of time. I was Japheth returning to the Ark before migrating north to replenish the coasts and the isles with the seed of my children. One more look, to see if it had all really happened.

I carefully placed my foot on the snow-covered rise of the stem, with the wind howling in my ears, and felt a surge of life.

I left my fears on the threshold. *Every word of yours is pure, Lord,* I thought, *and a shield unto those who put their trust in you.* Then I stepped inside.

FIRST LOOK

There was a curious form to this end of the vessel. Ron had said he suspected that this end had been dragged out. To me it appeared as if the ends had been great uplifted structures, similar to the Egyptian Solar Boat, that had now fallen flat outside the hull for approximately thirty feet. Walking upon this projection I entered the hull proper, which loomed up through the snow like the staves of a broken barrel.

My first impression was that the Ark had been an enormous double-ender, long and sleek, and appeared very modern in design. This was a bit unnerving. In 1984 Ron had already had an analysis done at Galbraith Laboratories on some samples of detector hits from the sides. The results presented yet another problem.

The analysis suggests that the object contained an aluminum and iron alloy, or that metal residues were absorbed into the sample materials from a nearby and as yet unidentified source, or that two adjacent materials became mixed

during the deterioration process. He also had found some
nodules containing eleven elements, of which 84.14 percent
was pure manganese dioxide. These he had turned over to the
Culture Ministry along with the reports. Ron was playing it
by the book. In Turkey it's their game, and you abide by their
rules. We couldn't be there if we didn't. We would confine our
research to surface investigations and measurements only.

The interior of the vessel sloped downward from the gunwales toward the center, as if the deck was still attached to the
sides, but carrying a terrific weight had collapsed it in the
middle under a mound of broken above-deck structure. The
sides on the exterior came almost straight down into the
surrounding alluvial flow. They seemed to be canted in a bit,
and it was impossible to say whether I was seeing the hull or
an above-deck multistoried structure, resting on a hull that was
still buried many feet below.

I studied the altimeter carefully, taking into consideration
the width of the needle until I was certain. It read 6,240 feet
(1901m) at the lower north end. I began to walk uphill inside
the structure.

I couldn't get over the feeling of how massive and strong it
appeared. Surely it was frail compared to the elements and
destruction during the final moments of the past age, but it
was not just something that had survived. Its strength, even
now, could be felt as in something that had overcome. It was
a sustainer of life, a place where those aboard and under the
covering passed from certain death unto life, and into a new
world. In one very broken cuneiform text of the Flood story, a
version of Atra-ḫasīs, the Ark is referred to as "naṣirat napištum," that is, "the lifesaver," and since the god Ea is the one
responsible for saving life, it seems an appropriate name.[3] I
heard my friends calling to me. Samran was putting on his
white Arabian "adress" with the red and white checkered head
scarf of his people for a photo, and I hurried to join them. They
were amidships about two hundred feet ahead of me.

The depression between the sides and the mound in the
center was filled with snow, so I walked on the exposed ends of

---

[3]W. G. Lambert and A. R. Millard, eds. and trans., *Old Babylonian Atra-ḫasīs* (Oxford: Clarendon, 1969).

the ribs, or columns, which were three to four feet wide. The mud matrix between them not only protected them but formed a footpath as well. I couldn't help thinking how the exposed "bones" of the Ark appeared as if they had been dipped in pancake batter and set out to dry. What was holding this structure together?

I was soon joined by more villagers. The morning was awakening the children, and they had scrambled down from their snug mud-bricked homes now belching clouds from dung fires as the windows were opened to the light of day. They ran giggling past me as I walked a precarious line to join Ron and the others.

AMOMUM . . . THE ROOT OF LIFE

Memet and Ahmet were gesturing for me to come closer and look at something growing inside the hulk of the Ark. There in a shallow depression, three or four stems stretched up through the snow, waist high, withered and dried with faded purple flowers near the top. The plant was covered with thorns. "This is something I've been meaning to show you, Dave," said Ron. "Could this be what the early pilgrims called 'amomum'?"[4]

Ron was aware, too, that Josephus[5] had written it was to be found in a district called Carron, which had excellent soil for its production and where it grew in abundance. This district or area wherein the amomum could be found also held the remains of the Ark–remains which, to his day, Josephus related, were shown to those who were curious to see them.[6]

I certainly was curious, and in true Key West tradition (where I had lived for five years) and treasure-hunting basics, I started to collect charts of my area of interest. I struck pay dirt, or hopefully the "excellent soil" Josephus had mentioned. It was on a General Staff War Office chart of 1941, well before

---

[4]An aromatic shrub. (Greek, *amŏmon*) root of an amomum plant.
[5]Flavius Josephus (historian circa 37–100 A.D.).
[6]*Antiquities of the Jews*, XX 24, 25.

the time I felt the Ark had come to light in recent years, and right on the line of Berosus.

The clue was in the form of a strange notation: "Devşirme Menekşe." The first word means "to pick up, gather, or collect." During Ottoman times it was a term connected with youth, or the gathering of youth for the Janissary corps, or a youth so recruited. The second word, "Menekşe," is from the Persian word *benefşe*. It was the Persians whom the aspiring apothecary of Europe consulted in his remedies, and is described as having a violet flower (Viola odorata). But it was the root (orris root) or kökü that was the subject of interest. Could it not then be considered "Gençlik Kökü," the fabled youth root?

> Let me uncover for you, Gilgamesh, a secret thing.
> A secret of the Gods let me tell you.
> There is a plant. Its roots go deep, like the boxthorn;
> its spike will prick your hand like a bramble.
> If you get your hands on this plant,
> you'll have everlasting life. (lines 266–270)

> I will carry it to Uruk of the Sheepfold; I will
> give it to the elders to eat;
> They will divide the plant among them.
> Its name is The-Old-Man-Will-Be-Made-Young.[7]
> I too will eat it, and I will return to
> what I was in my youth. (lines 280–282)

Sîn-leqi-unninni version[8]

I had utterly failed in my research to discover what it had looked like or its exact identity, yet it did not seem to be an unknown plant.

In the search for the origin of amomum, I learned that the phrase "iris root," or orrisroot, was from the European iris, and the underground stems that have a faint odor of violets. It is used in making sachets and tooth powders. The orrisroot industry now centers in Florence, Italy, where the roots are scraped, dried, and packaged. The United States imports about five hundred thousand pounds of the irregular, knobby sticks (about four inches or less in length) a year.

---

[7]The plant's name is *šibu issahir amēlu*, "a return to a man in his prime."

[8]John Gardener and John Maier, *Gilgamesh* (New York: Alfred A. Knopf, Inc., © 1984).

The iris itself comes from the Greek word for rainbow, which I felt could be significant to the Flood story. The root of certain of these bearded irises was indeed used in ages past for perfumes, powders, and medicines. Iris, in Greek mythology, was the golden-winged goddess of the rainbow and messenger of the gods, especially of Hera (Juno). She carried the commands of the gods to men, traveling on the path of the rainbow. Perhaps Iris is Isis, of the Ishtar cult. In one text of the Epic of *Gilgamesh* it says:

> Thereafter Ishtar drew nigh. Lifting up the jewels, which the god Anu had fashioned for her according to her desire, she spake, saying: "Oh! these gods! I vow by the lapis lazuli gems upon my neck that I will never forget! I will remember these days for ever and ever. Let all the gods come hither to the offering, save Bel alone, because he ignored my counsel, and sent a great deluge which destroyed my people."

So here, too, is the connection with the Flood. The Lord smelled the pleasing aroma and said in his heart: "Never again will I curse the ground because of man, even though every inclination of his heart is evil from childhood. And never again will I destroy all living creatures, as I have done" (Genesis 8:21 NIV).

In the Akkadian legend, Ishtar had come after Utnapishtim, had set up an altar, and made an offering upon the mountain:

> I poured out a libation. I set up incense vessels seven by seven on heaped up reeds, and used cedar wood with incense. The gods smelled the sweet savor.

So, too, had Noah done (Genesis 8:20), and then as Ishtar had lifted up her jewels from around her neck, she, too, vowed to never forget, as in Genesis:

> I have set my rainbow in the clouds, and it will be the sign of the covenant between me and the earth. . . . Whenever the rainbow appears in the clouds, I will see it and remember the everlasting covenant between God and all living creatures of every kind on the earth.
>
> 9:13–16 NIV

If this connection of Isis, who is identical with Hathor of Egypt, seems strange, the reader need only realize that the flower of the lily, a name sometimes used for the iris, is the French *fleur-de-lis* that represents the white iris, and appears as an emblem on the scepter of Egyptian rulers in 1500 B.C. and was carved on the brow of the Sphinx. I am quite familiar with this emblem, and had seen it constantly in my maritime experience, for it is the design used as a symbol for NORTH on a compass.

Still, I had found no direct link to amomum, although I toyed with the connection of "Amon,"[9] chief god of the ancient Egyptians. He was usually wearing a headdress capped by two large feathers. According to legend, Clovis I (an early form of Louis) used the fleur-de-lis in the early 500s A.D. after an angel gave him an iris for accepting Christianity. In 1376, Charles V chose three fleurs-de-lis for his coat of arms. This design had become a symbol of Christianity, like the crucifix, reaching Central Europe from Byzantium by the first millennium A.D.

Thus it was not on a hope and faint whim that I expected to find amomum at the Ark's site. The area of its growth might also be very localized where, as Josephus relates, "it grew in abundance." If this was a rare plant, it might be that its source was the Ark! It might be that its source was a staple carried aboard the Ark, not for fodder but one of a number of "root" vegetables—that is, plants whose natural means of propagation is by growing new stock from the fragments of the parent, and unless physically dug up and transplanted elsewhere, would be found only at the Ark site! The magic plant, which bestowed immortality and eternal youth on him who ate of it, appears to have been a weed, a creeping plant, with thorns which pricked the hands of the gatherer. Curiously enough, Gilgamesh seems to have sought it at the bottom of the sea.

One author has remarked upon this as possibly meaning an oyster, which, when the pearl was dissolved in wine, hopefully rejuvenated he who drank it. Although I consider this writer a cautious scholar, and I myself have no explanation for

---

[9]Amomum in Greek is *Amōmon,* thus Amon.

the plant in the *Gilgamesh* text being found underwater, I think
this is in the realm of speculation. It plainly refers to a plant,
which, due to its fragrance, was lost. Stolen by a serpent that
was attracted by its odor, it was eaten, whereupon the serpent
immediately shed its skin in a renewal of life. The quest for the
plant, flower, or fruit of life is referred to in many folktales. In
the *Máhabhárata*, Bhima, the Indian Gilgamesh, journeys to
northeastern Celestial regions to find the lake of the god
Kuvera (Kubera), on which grow the "most beautiful and
unearthly lotuses" which restore health and give strength to
the weary.

In Babylonia, as elsewhere, the priests utilized the floating
material from which all mythologies were framed, and impressed upon it the stamp of their doctrines. The symbolized
stories were afterward distributed far and wide, as were those
attached to the memory of Alexander the Great at a later
period. It was here that I found reference to our hero seeking
out the elixir of life on a mount called Musas [Mashti]. This
was in my area of interest, for opposite this slope, on the
southerly side into Iran, this very same mountain was named
Musa Dağı. I found the chances that the mount of the Ark,
carrying the name of the writer of Genesis, were well within
the realm of possibility.[10]

We moved to the high end of the vessel. It sloped upward
and appeared to be in better condition, with bulwarks intact
and a distinctive rise at the center. There on the projection was
the mayor of the village, surrounded by children. I joined him,
altimeter in hand, at the uppermost point. He raised his
walking stick high in the air and shouted for all to hear,
"Nuh'un Gemisi [Noah's Ark]." The words rolled down the
slope, startling the others. "Nuh'un Gemisi," chorused back
his little band of shepherds in reply. There was no doubt in this
man's mind what God had miraculously raised up out of the
ground, after centuries of being covered by the earth.

The needle read 6,350 feet (1935m), and from this vantage
point I could get a good compass bearing along the keel line. It
read 10° magnetic, with the highest peak of Ararat bearing 8°
far in the distance. I lowered the compass to find the kindly

---

[10]E. A. Wallis Budge, *The Life and Exploits of Alexander the Great.*

face and inquisitive blue eyes of an elderly man. "Nuh'un Gemisi?" he questioned, as if the compass should give me an answer.

THE CUBIT CONFIRMED

It was important to confirm, or attempt to confirm, my idea of the cubit used by Moses in describing the Ark. I stretched out the tape measure, starting at what I guessed might be the centerpoint of the sternpost at the higher south end, and worked my way back down the hull. It was 246 feet to the area where there was a rock intrusion through the western wall to the centerline of the ship. This had recalled Arabic tradition that the Ark would be found on a north/south axis alongside a large rock. Had someone seen it before it had been shoved into the rock itself and covered by the alluvial flow of mud that had buried it?

The beam at this point was measured at 121 feet, but where do you measure the Ark from, the inside dimensions or the overall width? I found that north of this stone outcropping the western wall was distorted and buckled out of shape, so approximated the centerline, all width measurements were then taken from the supposed keel line to the eastern wall only, and doubled for the approximate beam every 100 feet. I was surprised at the extreme width of the lower end, nearly 140 feet. All things considered, slack in the tape, and estimating the centerline, I felt I was getting the picture, and recorded in the field book all of my observations. It was difficult to know if the protrusion should be included in my overall length, and the inside of the hull seemed to close at 512 feet. Close enough, I concluded. It was the cubit of Moses the Egyptian, not Moses the Jew.

Ron agreed. "I had anticipated the same," he said. "Others had used the Hebrew cubit, and the object had appeared too long to fit the Ark's dimensions."

Bjorn Landstrom had worked with Ahmad Youssof Moustafa, excavator of the Pharaoh's boat at Cheops, and the author says the old Egyptian cubit was 52.5 centimeters. Therefore, 100 cubits equaled 52.5 meters. The Ark at 300 cubits would then equal 157.5 meters, or 516.73125 feet. (A meter equals 39.37 inches.) Landstrom was an undisputed expert on these vessels, and his calculations yield a cubit of 20.666929 inches. I could not agree entirely, as mine was slightly smaller at 20.61432 inches.

To understand Moses' dimensions we must first take into account his education. If I were educated in France rather than America, I might elect to use meters rather than feet in giving measurements. This should be obvious. What doesn't appear as obvious to other scholars is why Moses should be describing dimensions in Hebrew cubits. If Moses was raised in the house of Pharaoh and schooled in all the wisdom and knowledge of the Egyptians,[11] he would undoubtedly be using the Egyptian cubit. Now we have to be careful at this point that we are not saying the Ark was built by Noah on the Egyptian cubit. This of course would be wrong. I am suggesting that the Ark was built on a very special cubit given by the designer of both the Ark and the heavens and everything that is under heaven, and that this cubit, inherited by the descendants of Noah and known by the Egyptians, is the one referred to by Moses.

The Ark's cubit would not only be brought to Egypt by Ham's son but by Shem himself, a builder of the Ark and in my opinion the designer of the Great Pyramid. This of course would mean that the cubit used by Imhotep (Shem) would most certainly be that of the Ark.

I was troubled by remarks from brilliant scholars such as Edmond Sollberger (D.Lit., F.B.A.) of the British Museum who could state that the Flood legend was unknown to the Egyptians. He stated that it is indeed remarkable that the Nile Valley, where inundations are beneficial, does not seem to have produced any Flood stories. I could not agree, for there seemed to me to be the underlying knowledge of both the event and the persons involved plainly stated in ancient papyri and indeed in the very gods of Egypt themselves. The begetter of these gods was called Nu. A closer approximation to the Noe of the Genesis account is hard to imagine.

In this regard, Noah was the preserver of the seed of mankind, a popular notion among Sumerian and Akkadian ac-

---

[11]Exodus 2:1–10 and Acts 7:20–22.

counts. Noah, or Nu, being one with the original eight gods of the Egyptian pantheon also accounts for Nu being the progenitor of the father of their civilization. These eight were viewed as gods by having passed through the judgment and survived as well as their longevity, which their offspring did not inherit to the same extent. Naturally they were held in awe.

Nu   Father of the gods

begetter of the great company of the gods

Wallis Budge, late keeper of Assyrian and Egyptian antiquities in the British Museum, felt that Nu represents the watery mass from which the gods evolved—a perspective no doubt falling in line with the established theory that mankind evolved from a marine environment and some sort of primeval ooze! I would not discredit the Egyptians' knowledge of our beginnings with such modern-day ideas. The ancient Egyptian was without doubt a creationist.

If, however, one believes in the Flood as an actual historic event, then it takes little imagination to view Nu as directly connected with the watery mass of the Flood, and the "bark of millions of years" as the Ark from ancient times, with the "company of gods" as the survivors.

Ham would fit this category, with his son Miz'rāim being Menes, the Father of Egypt. Shem, Ham's brother, also perceived as a god in the Egyptian pantheon, is seen in the Book of Beginnings as a visitor to Egypt: "Hail to thee Sut, son of Nut, Aa-peh-peh (Apheti) in the bark of millions of years." The Nut referred to here is Noah's wife, the Nu in the feminine gender, or the goddess who accompanied Nu on the voyage. Just as Nu was the begetter of the gods in the masculine sense, Nut was the mother of all living, held in esteem among the gods and remembered as Isis.

Nut

	áp - tu	mut - k	Nut	en	átef - k	Nu
	Is decreed	thy mother	Nut	to	thy father	Nu

We are told in the Bible in both Exodus and Acts that Moses was schooled in all the knowledge and wisdom of the Egyptians. Egypt was the ancient seat of knowledge. Its center was located some ten miles northeast of Cairo today, and on the east bank of where the rivers divide to form the Nile delta. It was known to the Egyptians as Annu, "House of the sun" (Per Rā). ⌐⊐ ○ ⌐

This is a direct translation of the meaning found in Jeremiah 43:13: Bêth Shemesh, בֵּית שֶׁמֶשׁ

It is interesting to note that this great theological seat of learning claimed to have "the body of the aged one" interred at Annu.[12] If I may deviate from the learned professor's reserved opinions, I would suggest that this refers to Osiris, the Egyptian name for Nimrod, who was slain by Shem. It would appear that Shem had Nimrod tried, convicted, and executed in Egypt. Thus they say he was slain by the power of the ivory of Shem's tooth, or truth in the charges brought against him. Shem, who was known in Egypt as Sut, Set, or Apep, severed Nimrod's body into fourteen pieces with the bone of a fish, and sent them to the distant cities of the land that followed his worship.

Horus, son of Osiris (Nimrod), claims to have avenged his father and dismembered Shem in return. This is a doubtful boast in my opinion, but the papyrus of Ani (lines 10 through 68) state Horus gathered up the remains of Osiris:

> I have brought for thee thy bones into Re-stau, I have brought for thee thy backbone into Annu, gathering together his fragments there. I have repulsed for thee Apep.

Upper register plate XI, line 4

Thus, this act of Shem, having Nimrod put to death, is the basis of Set (Sut) falling from grace in the eyes of the Egyptians at a later period and his becoming Typhon, or the devil. The death of Nimrod is remembered through the Greek pantheon of gods and the festival of the Wailing for Bacchus. He is the Lamented One, the Tammuz of Ezekiel 8:14.

We first hear of this seat of learning in Genesis 41:45 אֹן, Genesis 41:50 אֹון, and again in Ezekiel 30:17 אָוֶן.

---

[12]E. A. Wallis Budge, *The Egyptian Book of the Dead* (New York: Dover Publications, 1967).

> And Pharaoh called Joseph's name Zaphenath-paneah; and he gave
> him as wife Asenath, the daughter of Potiphera, Priest of On.

If Annu existed from the time of Nimrod, and was still
functioning in the days of Jacob and Joseph down to the time
of Rameses III (circa 1225 B.C.E.), and was known to the Greeks
as Heliopolis, then Moses undoubtedly was schooled here at
On or Annu by the priestly instructors (of which there were
twelve thousand during the time of Rameses) in all of the
wisdom and knowledge one could offer from the house of
Pharaoh in physics, geometry, astronomy, medicine, chemis-
try, and even music.

As to why the Editorial Revision Committee of the Oxford
New International Version of the Bible should consider the
cubit of Moses a Hebrew unit of measure is a mystery, but
they could put their opinion in a footnote. To take the position
of infallibility by changing the text from 300 cubits to 450 feet
in Genesis 6:15 was a gross error in judgment.

To consider this cubit used in construction of the Ark as an
Egyptian cubit would be just as foolish an assumption as the
revisionists that, because they are translating Hebrew Scripture, the cubit in question is Hebrew (eighteen inches), implying that Noah was a Jew.

This cubit is neither Egyptian nor Jewish but is from another source. The clue that it is a celestial unit of measure is
found in the Book of Ezekiel 40:3 and 5, which makes it clear
it is a cubit greater than the Hebrew.

> . . . there was a man [Theophanies], whose appearance was like the
> appearance of brass, with a line of flax in his hand, and a measuring
> reed; and he stood in the gate. . . . a measuring reed of six cubits long
> by the *cubit and an hand breadth* (KJV, author's italics).

This angel appears to Ezekiel and, over the next nine
chapters, gives explicit instructions for the building of a temple. These chapters have posed numerous problems for expositors as to what temple it represents. I will reserve my comments here on what temple I feel is represented and move
directly to the prime misconception of biblical scholars such as
Dr. C. I. Scofield, who states:

> The ancient systems of measures and weights were not as precise as
> the standards known in later years. For example, the cubit measure
> was based upon the *length of the forearm*. . . .[13]

That the progress of human civilization, on which practically
all historians operate, is a theological doctrine developed by
church fathers, is something that was evident to Livio
Stecchini,[14] a specialist in the history of ancient measurements and quantitative science. To be more specific, he felt
that since these were early writers, scholars considered they
must have had infantile conceptions, and their concern for
precision in measurement was intellectually preposterous and
historically impossible. Stecchini was gradually forced to accept the fact that scholars of ancient history did not read
numbers in ancient texts or in research papers.

I felt the "cubit and an hand breadth" (Old King James
wording) of the angel of Ezekiel was the unit of measure of the
Grand Designer, and the Ark would be built to the same.

At this point I will propose to the reader that the measuring
reed of the angel of Ezekiel is nothing more than a well-
known ratio expressed in numerical terms. It is pi, used to
determine the circumference of a circle of any diameter. In
numerical form the distance around any circle is always
3.1416 times the diameter. This measuring reed can thus be
viewed in various dimensions of 3.1416 meters, 123.6 inches,
or 10.3 feet in length, all amounting to the same.

The length of the Ark can be viewed as exactly fifty times
this measuring reed, or pi, for 157.08 meters. When viewed in
inch measure, the resultant numerical series is phi, or 6180,
more commonly known as the Golden Section, mistakenly
considered unknown in architecture until its rather late redis-
covery in Greek times by Euclid and the Pythagorean sect.

Twice this 6180 leaves us with a numerical sequence composed of the first three integers, but it hints at more than this.
Peter Tompkins, in his *Secrets of the Great Pyramid*, suggests the

---

[13] *The New Scofield Reference Bible,* Notes 2 Chronicles (New York: Oxford University
Press, 1967).

[14] Peter Tompkins, *Secrets of the Great Pyramid* (London: Harper & Row, 1971),
Appendix. Notes on the relation of ancient measures to the Great Pyramid by Livio
Stecchini.

Egyptians used a right triangle with an angle of 36° which they called "mr." If this triangle has a longer side of 100, then the hypotenuse is 123.6068. Again we find this sequence in the length of the reed as 123.6 inches.

Since we are told the measuring reed is composed of six cubits, I assumed the cubit of the Ark to be .5236 of a meter. Since a meter is 39.37 inches, a cubit is revealed as being 20.6 inches in length. Thus the 300-cubit length of the Ark should be found to be a measure of 515.3533 feet.

To those fundamentalists adhering to Scofield's and other biblical scholars' interpretation of the cubit used by Moses as producing an Ark of 450 feet, it would appear that this object is too long and should be rejected as the remains of the great ship. I preferred to disregard the opinions of biblical scholars in my search for the cubit and the whereabouts of the remains of the Ark and submit to the reader that the mathematical design of the Ark will prove to be a marvel of marine engineering and not the product of primitive man.

Other authors had fortified my belief in this cubit expected to be found in the Ark's construction. In the work of José Alvarez Lopez of Argentina, *Physics and Creation,* he considered the cubit of 523 millimeters exactly half of what he called an "absolute meter," which he claimed occurred as a natural unit in the solar system. In his calculations, the planets of our solar system orbit in harmonic distances from the sun. These are multiples of a single unit of length and his absolute meter, an arrangement that is naturally decimal.

It was at this point in the early 1980s that I began to suspect the statement of Berosus, the Chaldean priest of Bel, actually suggested a location for, rather than a description of, the Ark. To my contemporaries, the thought that the ancients had the ability to relay this information in geometric terms was folly. Yet the basic idea of the ziggurat of Babylon was the northern hemisphere projected on flat surfaces, as done in map making.

This new concept of Berosus' statement was so startling in relation to current assumptions about the level of the ancients' abilities in mathematics that it could hardly be accepted. That is why the correct cubit used was imperative to my studies.

Stecchini points out how scholars are so bent on principle to interpret the history of measures and measurements in terms of the most crude primitivism that even in most works dealing with English measures, one reads that the English foot was originally set by the feet of an English king.

In another variant of this fairy tale, some historians tell us it was the distance from the nose of King Henry I (1068–1135) to his index finger with the arm outstretched that determined the yard of three feet.

I have not found it surprising that my contemporary Ark-hunting friends on the slopes of Ararat consider the cubit simply the distance from the elbow to the extended hand.

In a publication by Dr. Don Shockey, the latest in tales of eyewitness accounts of sighting the Ark on Ararat, his readers are enlightened that in Egypt, the cubit is based on the length of a newborn baby.[15]

All of the above is touted as "the real thing." The front cover boldly proclaims that artifacts from Noah's Ark have been found on Mount Ararat. Unfortunately, in over eighty photographs shown throughout the book, the author fails to produce a picture of even one of them.

THE FREQUENCY TEST

In my opinion, the length of the Ark conformed to the cubit of Moses. Since I had measured from the center of the point where the sides came together at the upper south end, I concluded that the 512 feet could easily have been the 515 I was looking for.

It seemed appropriate to use inside measurements, for I was trying to determine the space available within the Ark. That is all Moses was saying: The volume of the compartments available to provide the total space required was equal to a rectangle of 300 × 50 × 30, or a total of 450,000 cubic cubits. Other authors could compute this to consist of so many railway cattle cars, or how many tennis courts could fit on the deck. But these experts would have to leave their rectangular, square-cornered barge/Ark concept behind. I spent too many

---

[15]Dr. Don Shockey, *Agri-Dagh, The Painful Mountain* (Fresno: Pioneer Publishing Co., 1986), p. 22.

years at sea to ever buy that idea! But they could be of good cheer if they accepted this as the Ark, for it was bigger and better than they ever expected. A conservative figure of 2,275,630 cubic feet was now available for the needs aboard.

I sat down a minute to rest and opened the Thermos/ canteen for some tea. There were many false concepts that were going to tumble. I expressed this to Ron. "Don't be too sure, David. It's been a real uphill struggle for me," he replied, "and you can expect the same."

"Anyone who can't recognize this as a shipwreck either wouldn't know Noah's Ark if he was standing on it, or should have his 'theological cataracts' removed!" I answered in disgust.

"Don't look at me fella!" Ron said. "There have been some real impressive credentials and academic types out here who stood by and watched while they blew the sides out of it with dynamite, but they didn't have a marine background like you."

I sat there propped against the rock intrusion that had impaled the western side amidships, sipping my tea and thinking about how hungry I was. There wouldn't be lunch. We'd forgotten to bring any. "What's the matter with it, Ron, wrong color?"

"For them," he answered. "Wrong color, wrong shape, wrong mountain! Nobody likes to be wrong."

"Well, it's got to be in here somewhere," I said, rising and throwing out the lukewarm tea from my cup. "Nicolaus of Damascus said the remains of the timbers were a great while preserved, but there still remains a part of it. Let's see if the part that remains might not be buried and preserved under our feet."[16]

I broke open the frequency generator and Samran came alongside me, robes flowing white on white against the snow. He squatted comfortably to inspect the instrument as I placed the probes in the ground, and the villagers all squatted, too. I tried to do the same as I hooked up the batteries, but my double layers of pants prevented my knees from bending. *You've got to*

---

[16]Nicolaus of Damascus was quoted by Josephus in *Antiquities of the Jews*, Book I, chapter 3.

be raised in the east to do that, I thought as I went down in the mud with my face close to the wavering digits of the frequency counter. I'd forgotten my glasses as well as my lunch, and the numbers focused slowly as I dialed in the number for iron.

Tubal-cain was "an instructor of every artificer of brass and *iron,*" Genesis[17] had said (author's italics), and Plato in Dialogues told us:

> . . . men were rich then, as in the Golden Age of Chronos, and lived in plenty. . . . Then followed the Bronze age, a period of constant quarrelling and deeds of violence. . . . *Finally came the iron age . . .* while Zeus determined to destroy the human race by a great flood. The whole of the land lay underwater, and none but Deucalion and his wife Pyrrha were saved.

I know that anthropologists will argue it was impossible to have iron before the iron age. My answer to them is that intellectual brilliance is no guarantee against being dead wrong. Their iron age was of this age, not the age that was, or Plato's Atlantean Age. If it was a figment of his imagination, and that of Moses, too, then we would find out now.

I started at the western wall and walked slowly down the inside slope heading athwartships, when I got my first line. I let it pass, but soon got another several feet farther on. Then I got another, and another. "Hey, Ron! I've got something uniform here!"

"Let me try," Ron said, retracing my steps back to the inner wall. I grabbed the camcorder.

"You're live!" I shouted, framing him in the video monitor. "Start walking." If I ever had any doubts that it was the Ark, they were gone now!

"Ron, you are crossing longitudinal walls, or floor beams that contain decomposed iron fittings, maybe nails, or brackets of some kind." My voice was raising higher in excitement. "They are so evenly spaced I could measure the distance between them. What do you think they are, Ron?" I said, moving in for a close-up to catch the emotion of the moment.

Ron just stood there, grinning from ear to ear. "I don't know, maybe rows of cages . . ." he started to say.

---

[17]Genesis 4:22 KJV.

"Come on, Ron, do you think you're on Noah's Ark?"

"Hey, fella," he broke into a sigh of relief, "I always said this was Noah's Ark!"

I turned to find the mayor of the village with the question still on his face. "Evet [yes], Nuh'un Gemisi," I shouted in joy, and his eyes broke into a smile of tears.

THE REJECTION

My news was met with skepticism from my Christian brethren. I soon learned it was acceptable to be searching for the Ark and other biblical truths, but to return to say you had actually found them required a lot of faith on their part. There were few among them ready to listen for very long.

"Heard you were on the Ark," an acquaintance said upon my return. He stopped me after a few minutes of earnest listening and asked, "What did it measure out to?"

"From inside the bow to the stern, about five hundred fifteen feet," I replied.

"But the Word of God says four hundred fifty feet," he replied.

"Wait a minute," I said. "God doesn't say four hundred fifty feet. Bible scholars like Dr. Scofield say the Hebrew cubit, being approximately eighteen inches times the three hundred-cubit length and divided by twelve inches, equals four hundred fifty feet. Genesis, it is agreed by most scholars, was written by Moses, who was adopted by the daughter of Pharaoh, raised in Pharaoh's household, and instructed in all the wisdom of the Egyptians. That would make the Ark's length, in Egyptian cubits of twenty point six inches, longer at five hundred fifteen feet.

"Now, I also don't know at what point the Ark was measured, the waterline or the uppermost continous deck, but you have to admit," I said, trying to lighten the conversation, "that's still in the ball park, right?" Too late.

His eyes narrowed. He looked at me and declared, "Well, then, it's certainly too wide! It's not in the shape of a rectangle, either, is it?"

"Well, not really, but then I'm sure it contains the same

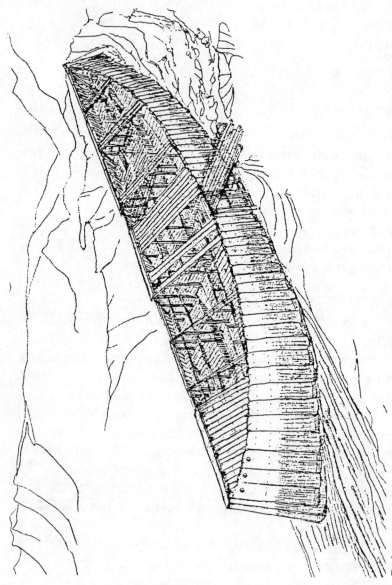

Preliminary attempt by me to resolve the method of construction based on visible remains of vertical structural members protruding from matrix. Conceived as enormous wooden timber sideboards interlocked into athwartship flooring, based on false concept that the vessel was constructed of wood.

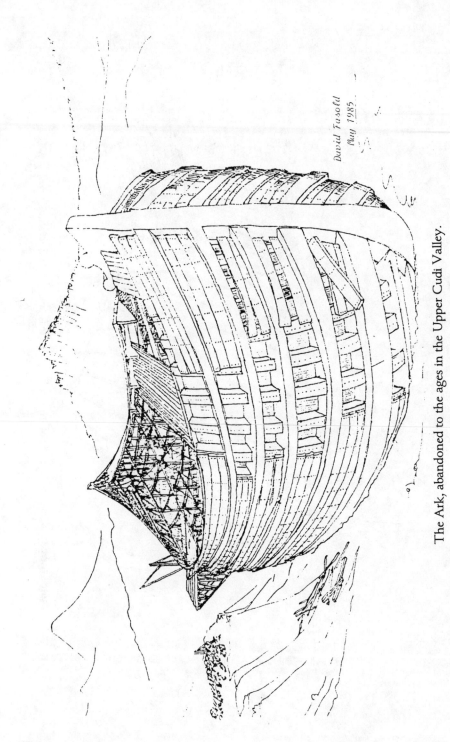

David Fasold
May 1985

The Ark, abandoned to the ages in the Upper Cudi Valley.

27

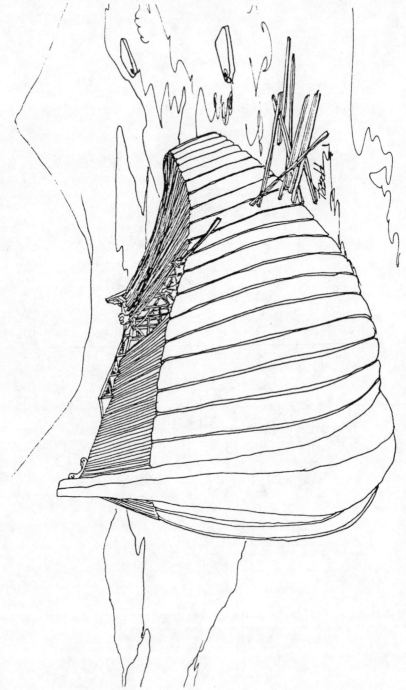

It was not until the expedition of June 1985 that it became clear what "gopher wood" really was.

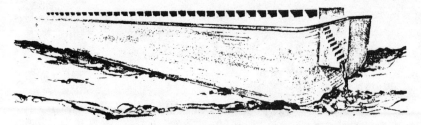

Original sketch of the Ark by artist Elfred Lee.

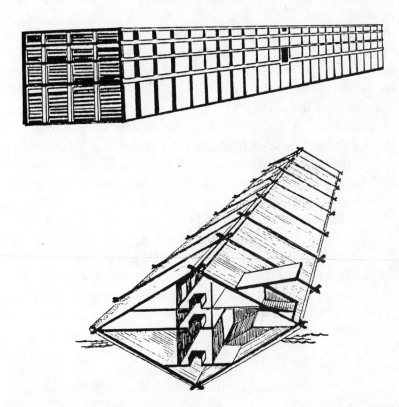

To be acceptable to the biblical scholar, the Ark must be portrayed as a rectangle. However, a model on display in Solomon's Palace in Jerusalem is worth mentioning. The concept of architect Meir Ben Uri required little more than a number of equal-sized triangular templates fitted together in a "prismatic rhomboid."

volume as the rectangle described in Scripture. Just because my house contains so many square feet doesn't mean I live in a square house!" And as quoted in Genesis 6:15, I pointed out, "This is the fasion which thou shalt make it of" (KJV). It may have been referring to volume, or capacity, and using a rectangle to convey the idea: after all, experts at the Institute for

Creation Research say the same thing. They're always referring to how many boxcars can fit in the Ark, or how many
tennis courts can lay on the deck.

"You're saying you can't take the Bible literally?" my
acquaintance asked.

"Well, what we found has a boat shape! We are looking for
a boat on a mountain, aren't we?" I finally said in disgust.

"I want it on the mountain the Bible says it's on," was his
ultimate retort.

I began to see the rejection symptoms based on experts'
opinions resurfacing, and they embittered and alienated me for
a time. The experts had been wrong, and now no one could
recognize the truth if they were standing on it.

Because Ron Wyatt and myself were not the first to investigate this site, it seems only fair at this point to give credit to
those who were the early discoverers of the Ark.

It all began in a flurry of excitement late in 1959. A Turkish
flier named Sevket Kurtis had photographed the area in a
government mapmaking program and the results were being
viewed by stereoplanigraphic projection. The cartographers
stared in disbelief as a boat-shaped object seemed to lift above
the landscape, quite out of place with the terrain. Captain
Ilhan Durupinar of the Turkish Army notified his superiors.

The report that hit the press stunned Rene Noorbergen,
globe-trotting journalist and longtime Ark enthusiast. Had the
Ark at long last been found? Soon he was forming an expedition to investigate. Enlisting the help of Dr. Arthur Brandenberger, respected professor of photogrammetry at the Ohio
State University in Columbus, a detailed study of Durupinar's
negative followed.

Upon closer examination it was deduced, however, that the
object exceeded the dimensions commonly accepted by the
experts from the Genesis account, and this proved enough for
most fundamentalists to write it off as a freak of nature and
stay home. But Noorbergen was fascinated. The lack of funds
to finance explorations has been the curse of discoverers since
long before Columbus, and the situation was not new to
Noorbergen. Soon his plans were usurped by another indi-
vidual who had the resources.

George Vandeman, prophetic evangelist of the Seventh-

Day Adventist Church, soon became the leader of the expedition planned for the early spring of 1960. Noorbergen, who had laid the groundwork for investigations, was now along as photographer to record the events. In retrospect, he probably would have been better off going alone.

In June of 1960 the team arrived in eastern Turkey with Vandeman in charge. The group consisted of two research assistants, Wilbur Bishop and Hal Thompson, Durupinar, Brandenberger, and Noorbergen. An archaeologist named Seigfreid Horn accompanied the group.

The first problem that arose was the object was not on Ararat at all. This was quite a blow to the group and those who consider the Bible to relate "mountains of Ararat" in the singular. With the object having a rather streamlined shape and exceeding the biblical interpreters' concept of the cubit as 18 inches (450 feet), the group reluctantly set out away from the traditional mount of the Ark toward a mountain slope mistakenly considered in the Tendürek mountains, and according to Noorbergen practically dragging Dr. Horn along with them.

It was obvious at this point that what resulted was a halfhearted attempt to refute the object as not being the Ark and quickly end the whole mistaken affair. Too many traditions of the Ark on Ararat made this site and object a rather poor candidate for the long-sought-after relic. With Major Baykal of the Turkish army and fifteen soldiers leading the Americans in tow, the group mounted up and pack muled into the mountains, with Noorbergen apparently the only optimist in the bunch.

The result of the investigations was gleefully summed up by the "Ararat or nowhere" groups and the "I told you so" fundamentalists who stayed home and labeled it the "Phenomenon Ship." One of these was Ark researcher Violet Cummings.[18]

Cummings' report is only one in a number of publications that appear to be trying to outdo one another in variations of spelling the name Tendürek! And all seem unsure of just

---

[18]Violet Cummings, *Has Anybody Really Seen Noah's Ark?* (San Diego: Creation-Life Publishers, 1982).

where this object they are reporting about is located. Cummings states:

> In the excitement and anticipation of the new discovery several important factors were overlooked. In the first place the Tenderick [sic] foothills where the object lay was not high over Mount Ararat as at first claimed at an elevation of 6,000 feet, but in a remote valley some fifty miles from Ararat itself.

This statement is not altogether correct. First of all there is not a Turk in the area who would ever agree that these mountains were the foothills of Tendürek, and the very peaks of Ararat and Tendürek are separated only by 29 miles, hardly the 50-mile distance she reports. The site is only 16 miles SW of Ararat and 17.4 miles from Tendürek's peak to the WSW. Charts of the area clearly mark the site as being on the Akyayla Dağı (High White Plain), quite removed from Tendürek, one of Turkey's most active volcanoes. What is behind Cummings' reason for suggesting the Ark is far removed from the area of Ark folklore?

To bring the reader up to date, there is much at stake here. Cummings has authored several books based on Armenian traditions of sightings on Ararat. Her publisher is the Institute for Creation Research (ICR), headed by Henry Morris, another expounder of literal interpretation. To these two, should the Ark be found without square corners or somewhere other than Ararat, the joy of the discovery would overshadow their common errors.

The groups that insist the Ark must be found in a rectangular box shape on Mount Ararat itself appear to still be having a field day debunking the site. As late as December 1985 an article by Bill Crouse, senior scholar with Probe Ministries, appeared in *Moody Monthly* magazine. Crouse followed tradition by stating the site is fifteen miles *east* of Mount Ararat, to which he then added:

> Turkish geologists also point out several similarly shaped formations in the area.

Of course fifteen miles east of Ararat puts one six miles inside Iran, but I do give this expert credit for coming up with yet another variation in spelling the misnomered site. He calls it the Tenderuk Formation! Although many claim to know enough about the site to discredit it, even claiming to have investigated it for themselves, no one seems to be able to give its correct location even today, some twenty-five years after it was first visited by Noorbergen. Even geologist John Morris, son of Henry Morris and now vice-president of ICR, follows suit with the same false location given by others in his reports, claiming he visited the site himself, and it is nothing more than a clay upswelling in a lava flow.

Now let's return to the original investigations by Vandeman's team of professionals. Arriving at the site, disappointment set in as the object exceeded the 450-foot length now found printed in most Bibles in place of the original three hundred-cubit measure. In the course of careful and thoughtful examination of what started out as possibly being the remains of the most sacred relic of mankind, the decision was made to blast the walls with dynamite to see if any wood might fly out. If it did prove to be the Ark, I presume they could then have begun to tear it apart in a more orderly fashion. So sure were these fundamentalists of their biblical interpretations of how the Ark should appear that they gleefully recorded the event and Cummings delights in relating how they "exploded the myth":

Everyone scrambled out of the way, and . . . . Bang![19]

Thus, on the basis of these questionable investigations, this team of professionals returned home proclaiming it was not the Ark but a geological formation or clay upswelling in a lava flow. Subsequent publications briefly mention the 1960 investigations, giving the dimensions as 492 by 157 feet and stating that some investigators, however, still believe the shiplike formation is the actual outline of Noah's Ark, buried beneath, obviously referring to Wyatt.[20]

Noorbergen's position as late as 1980 is summed up by

---

[19]Cummings, *Ark,* p. 68.
[20]Rene Noorbergen, *Secrets of the Lost Races* (New York: Barnes and Noble, 1977), p. 72.

stating that "the result of the group's investigations showed the object to be a natural phenomenon of interest to experts in tectonics,"[21] and further suggests the Ark would be found on Ararat as expected: "I have to conclude that George Hagopian did see the Ark [on Ararat], and it was in a remarkable state of preservation."[22]

"If all efforts of the Ark enthusiasts were only concentrated on erasing all doubt about the Hagopian account," states Noorbergen, "then we (Ark hunters) might get somewhere soon."

For nearly seventeen years the object lay wounded and rejected after Vandeman's probe, literally written off and forgotten with no one taking a second look.

Should I attempt to single out the one person most instrumental in rekindling an interest in the site, it could only be Ron Wyatt, whose claim that it was the Ark was met with skepticism by his contemporaries. It was not the dimensions of the Ark, or the location considered by the experts, and Wyatt was a heretic for suggesting otherwise.

Wyatt undoubtedly gleaned much of his early information from Noorbergen on the site itself, and had worked on other projects in the Middle East with Noorbergen in the late seventies. In August of 1977 Wyatt went for a look at the site on his own with his two sons, but after a cursory glimpse of the object, a serious confrontation developed with the Kurds. Soon it was a life-threatening situation, and he and his sons literally ran for their lives. But Wyatt had made some significant discoveries never before recognized by anyone. They were large stone sea anchors. He was not able to return to the area until 1979.

Working quietly so as not to arouse suspicions, Wyatt determined there were metal readings within the walls of the structure, but after numerous visits he was unable to recover any hard evidence other than some likely scenarios as to what he was looking at, and some unlikely ones as well. Convinced that it was the remains of the Ark notwithstanding the lack of more real evidence than that before him, in 1984 he had the

[21] *The Ark File* (London: New English Library, 1980), p. 128.
[22] Ibid., pp. 206, 207.

chance to show it to Colonel James Irwin, the NASA astronaut and veteran of several Ararat expeditions, followed
closely by Marvin Steffins of International Expeditions.

Steffins spent a few hours at the site and abruptly departed
for home. Arriving in New York, Steffins called a news
conference to clear up a misunderstanding that had occurred in
Ankara just prior to his departure. Of course all involved were
innocent of any wrongdoing, but the affair was sensational-
ized by the press and Steffins was voted as the discoverer of the
Ark.

Since Noorbergen's photos appeared in the September 5,
1960, edition of *Life* magazine, both Steffins and Wyatt would
be hard put to press their claim. Meanwhile Irwin, arriving
home shortly thereafter, painted himself a stranger to all the
publicity. Wyatt remained in the background while the Ararat
Ark groups lit the fuses once again, intent on exploding the
myth that the Ark could be anywhere but on "their" mountain, and defending against the possibility they could be
wrong.

This raised an interesting issue. If the formation had previously been investigated *and rejected,* then many years later
claimed by Wyatt, who then had discovered the Ark?

2

The Deluge Revised

THE TWO FLOOD STORIES

While researching the Flood story found in Genesis chapters 6 through 9, I became increasingly troubled by what appeared to be blatant contradictions in the chronological order of events, and the dates of their occurrence. When I attempted to relay this to my fundamentalist friends, their attitude was one of amazement that I should suggest a doubt concerning the inerrancy of the Authorized Version of the Bible. Some even seemed to suggest that if the English of King James was good enough for the apostles' understanding, it should be sufficient for me as well.

The very fact that the version read today is considered the authorized edition leads one to believe there were others, and indeed there were. What we have in the Masoretic text found in practically all Bibles today is the result of the rabbis who met at Jamnia in about 100 C.E. They "canonized the text" of the Torah and then set about suppressing the variant recensions of biblical books then present. If it were not for the Qumran scrolls we may never have been aware of anything different. This action further separated Judaism from the Alexandrian Christians and from the first-century Church, which in general had adopted the Septuagint, not the Masoretic, as their own Bible.

The Greek Septuagint that was read by the early Apostolic Church gave figures that calculated the period from Adam to the Flood totaling 2262 years rather than the Masoretic's 1656 years. We will discuss more of this later, but it should be noted that the Septuagint, in giving the fathers' ages at the time of the

36

birth of their sons, increased them by 100 years from Adam to
Enoch, with the exception of Jared. It then decreased by 100
the number of years each lived after becoming a father; so the
total life spans of the patriarchs are equal in both texts. An
earlier text, the Samaritan, written in palaeo-Hebrew script
and limited to the first five books (the Pentateuch), totals this
pre-Flood period as 1307 years. There are varying opinions on
this count.

Christendom in general adheres to the Masoretic text, while
the early Christians would have had arguments with the
Southern Baptists of today and those adhering to Archbishop
Usher's (1650) proclamation of gospel truth that Adam was
created in 4004 B.C.E. To those who count differently it is 4026
and the list is endless, but an important consideration is the
period from the Flood to Abraham which, if we are to accept
the Masoretic "standard," appears to be a short period of time
to repopulate the world!

First, I do not agree or accept the Masoretic's date for the
Flood. Usher's date is 2348. His date for the birth of Abram is
some 352 years later or 1996 B.C.E. I believe the view of
Muslim scholars, who have always held that Abram's epic
journey from Ur of the Chaldees occurred circa 2300 B.C.E., will
slowly be accepted.

For the basis of our discussion, however, the Masoretic text
in the King James Version is sufficient, and began with a
simple question as to the age of Shem when he begat his son
Arphaxad. All the scholars listed the life span of Shem as 600.
I continued to count 602. The result required a critical review
of biblical scholars' material and a reconsideration of their
present interpretations of the whole Flood account.

This discussion will result in a difference greater than two
years. I will propose the following as the "Fasold Concept" for
the critical analysis of my colleagues, and to my readers as a
most important discovery into a proper understanding of the
Flood account. The events in the biblical text are out of
sequence, and the reason is a false assumption that the year of
Noah's day was the same year we have today. To bring the
chronology of events back to where there are no contradictions results in overwhelming evidence that the year of this
earlier age consisted of only ten months of thirty days each, or

a solar (Dynamic Time Period) year of three hundred days. There are even subtle implications from other sources that this period of the solar year in earlier stages may have been closer to ten days less in duration, according to archaeological evidence.

This slow change in the length of the year may have been the effect on the earth of whatever it was that caused the Flood. After the Flood the length of the year was unstable until it settled to a period of 360 days, which remained in effect for over 2,000 years.

We will now begin a careful analysis of the two Flood stories found within the Authorized Version.

We begin with the birth of Shem. Biblical scholars and revisionists have had problems with him from the very beginning.

Numerous translators had rearranged the sentence structure of a particular verse, and I began wondering why. In order to come up with a new version for the buying public, it would seemingly be justifiable to render some difficult verses into something more understandable. But this was a simple statement, nothing complex, yet they seemed to be trying to resolve a problem.

It kept me puzzled until I discovered the root necessity for the change. Mathematically, the years were not adding up to the right number, and the problem begins back in Genesis 5:32 (KJV):

> And Noah *was* five hundred years old: and Noah begat Shem, Ham, and Japheth (author's italics).

This is how it reads in the original Hebrew, yet in the New International Version (NIV) a change has been made without even so much as a footnote to explain the reason for doing so. The same verse here reads:

> *After* Noah was 500 years old. . . (author's italics).

This is how the revisionists take a simple statement, change the Hebrew text, and make it ambiguous so as not to be pressured into solving the problem of something being mathematically impossible.

In my opinion, there are two reasons the NIV revisionists have done this. One is the question, How could Noah have begat three sons in one year from one wife, unless they were triplets? This is solved by changing the Hebrew that states this occurred when Noah *was* five hundred years old, into a period of begetting sometime *after,* possibly over the next few years. This is not what the Hebrew text says. If we can't take a simple statement at face value, then we must question the begets and begats from Noah back to Adam. The second reason for the change is to harmonize this verse with another giving the age of Shem two years after the Flood. This is the verse all the revisionists had trouble with, which I refer to as the "Shem Shuffle"!

THE REVISIONISTS
"SHEM SHUFFLE"
GENESIS 11:10

The King James Version states it as the Hebrew:
 A. SHEM WAS AN HUNDRED YEARS OLD
 B. AND BEGAT ARPHAXAD
 C. TWO YEARS AFTER THE FLOOD.

The New International Version apparently thinks it makes better sense if the statement is juxtapositioned:
 C. TWO YEARS AFTER THE FLOOD
 A. WHEN SHEM WAS 100 YEARS OLD
 B. HE BECAME THE FATHER OF ARPHAXAD.

The Living Bible paraphrased takes a more laid-back approach:
 B. SHEM'S LINE OF DESCENDANTS INCLUDED ARPACH-SHAD
 C. BORN TWO YEARS AFTER THE FLOOD
 A. WHEN SHEM WAS 100 YEARS OLD.

We must remember that these records are primarily being kept by the Jews to record the line of Seth through Shem, and not the Gentile nations; "Blessed be the Lord God of Shem" the record states in Genesis 9:26 KJV, and Shem was born when

Noah was five hundred years old. They were all born, as the Hebrew text states, when Noah was five hundred years old, but from *different mothers*. All the bickering as to who was the eldest among the brothers is so much needless argument among theologians, for it was only the offspring of the Sethite wife that would produce the progenitor of the Jews.

The problem the revisionists are wrestling with is that Shem cannot possibly be one hundred years old two years after the Flood for the following reasons.

The Flood occurred in the six hundredth year of Noah's life. At the onset, a rabbi argued with me that this was an ordinal number, but in Genesis 7:6 KJV there is a cardinal number: "And Noah was six hundred years old when the flood of waters was upon the earth."

Now if Shem was born when Noah was five hundred, and the Flood occurred one hundred years later, Shem was in the Ark for a year. Two years after the Flood, could Shem be only one hundred years old? Of course not, and this is what has caused the turmoil! Even Westcott and Hort got into the act in their New World Translation by evading the problem when they translated Genesis 5:32:

> And Noah *got to be* five hundred years old. After that Noah became father to Shem, Ham and Japheth (author's italics).

Of course, anyone who has studied how Westcott and Hort put their version together wouldn't really take this publication seriously to begin with.[1] The real problem rests with the revisionist concept of what Genesis 11:10 is stating. History was divided by the Flood.

Noah's descendants are stripping out the flooring for fuel. A great portion of the hull is still being used as a warehouse for the necessities of life. Metal fittings are being salvaged to be forged into tools for agriculture. Within the confines of the hulk are depleting stockpiles of material, weaving looms and lamp oil, medicines and grain for replanting, and seeds for the vine.

"Tell me the story again, Father," says little Arphaxad,

---

[1]The Watchtower Bible and Tract Society of New York, Inc.

surrounded by his numerous cousins, wide-eyed in wonder before the giant structure, now lying immobile and lifeless. On their journey back to their pastureland and herds, he would again hear the story of the event that divided history, and every new occurrence would be dated from that cataclysm.

"The Flood occurred in the six hundredth year, second month, and seventeenth day in the life of your grandfather, when I was one hundred years old," relates Shem to his son. "And then I begat you, little Arphaxad, two years after the Flood occurred." So the reader can see the text is relating the age of Shem to the event of the Flood, not to the birth of Arphaxad. Thus if Shem lived 500 years after he begat Arphaxad, then Shem died at the age of 602, not 600.

Before my readers question my purpose in all this, they might well ask the revisionists and their school of interpretive publishers the same question. If this is the inerrant Word of God, why does it need changing? Who is authorized to make the change from the Hebrew text *was* to *after?*

If the structure of a simple three-line statement can be juxtapositioned in three different versions, I think revisionists are trying to turn meanings around to their own particular understanding. Their opinions should be in a footnote. A change of the text itself eventually results in a Christianized version of Hebrew literature. These theologians and revisionists have already replaced so much of the original text through years of theological systems that they have propagated the concept of replacement theology, where the New Testament has replaced the misnomered Old Testament, Christianity has replaced Judaism, and the Church has replaced Israel!

Are even the earliest of revisionists guilty of the same? Have whole story lines of the Flood account been changed around as well?

The traditional view of both Judaism and Christianity has been that the first five books were written by Moses under divine inspiration. But the duplication of narrative in Genesis 7:7–10 alongside 7:13–16 led even Jewish commentators to raise questions as early as the twelfth century, that the first five books appear to have had more than one author. Biblical scholars have commented on this as well, and some have suggested scribal or priestly meddling.

I am of the opinion that the Book of Genesis had several authors and their works were compiled by Moses, after which there were revisions. The Bible never claims that Moses is the author or writer of Genesis. Many scholars of the late nineteenth century doubted that writing existed prior to the time of Moses. These thoughts were discounted by the discovery of Sumerian clay tablets describing the Flood, similar to the Genesis account. Those bent on destroying the Bible's credibility surmised the Genesis account to have been "borrowed" from early mythology. Ever since these discoveries in 1908, evidence is being uncovered that refers to writings before the Flood. It should not be considered unreasonable, in my opinion, that the original story of creation and the first nine hundred years of history was recorded by Adam himself.

Duplication in the Flood narrative needn't be scribal additions if one considers that Noah as well his sons may have written their own versions of the Flood account, all of which were in the hands of Moses at the time he compiled the account. Thus as in the New Testament, should the writings of Matthew, Mark, Luke, and John all be drawn into one story line, some repetition would result.

These early tablets may have gone through revisions in both language structure and word meaning changes as the succeeding generations made additions to history and passed on copies to the ever-increasing family units. Those listing the background of the Sethites through Shem may have been taken from Terah by Abram from Harran, been added to by Shem, a contemporary according to the Masoretic text and Midrash commentary, and then through Jacob into Egypt. Many other early tablets may have been at the University of On, where Moses studied. When Moses compiled this history he tried to accommodate all the minimal variations into one running story line that naturally resulted in some repetition.

In many cases, the repetition is only a statement from the end of one tablet acting as a flag word phrase which leads the reader to the next clay tablet continuing the narrative. But in at least one instance, these flag words are out of order. That Moses actually included these while copying the text onto parchment verifies how religiously he copied from the original. In compiling the creation story and the Flood account from these early records, he undoubtedly had to be very skilled in interpreting the various forms of writing as translators of cuneiform are able to do today. Perhaps since he was closer to the source, it was not quite so difficult. Some terms, if not readily translatable into the Hebrew of the day, may have been left in their original form, such as the term that confounds scholars today and has resulted in the misnomer "gopher wood."

Then in later times, scholars, not realizing the text of Moses was a compilation of different authors and eyewitnesses to the event, attempted to make them more readily understandable to their generation. Their main concern, again, was that the text was not mathematically correct. The time period the survivors were within the confines of the Ark was a year of 10 months of 30 days each, or a solar year of 300 days. Most certainly, to people living in a year of 360 days, the text was in error, but with a juxtapositioning of events, this error could be eliminated. However, the telltale signs of this change have remained in our handed-down account, causing some serious inconsistencies in the story line.

Just as the priests found a solar year of 300 days unacceptable during their time when a year was comprised of 360 days, so scholars of today find it difficult to conceive of a solar year of anything less than 365.

Following is the commonly held view of the chronology of events and the passage of time from the authorized accounts, with which I cannot agree as to the actual sequence of events during the Flood.

THE COMMONLY HELD VIEW OF THE AUTHORIZED ACCOUNTS

Sequence of Events	Genesis	Span of Time in Days
A. There were 40 days during which the rain fell.	(7:12)	40
B. Throughout another 110 days the waters continued to rise, making 150 days in all.	(7:24)	110
C. The waters occupied 74 days in the "going and decreasing." This was from the 17th day of the 7th month to the 1st day of the 10th month.		74
D. Forty days elapsed before Noah sent out the raven.	(8:6, 7)	40
E. Seven days elapsed before Noah sent out the dove for the first time. This period is necessary for reaching the total and is given by implication from the phrase "other seven days."	(8:8) (8:10).	7
F. Seven days passed before sending out the dove for the second time.	(8:10)	7

G. Seven more days passed before the third sending.   (8:12)   7
H. Up to this point 285 days are accounted for, but the
   next episode is dated the 1st of the first month in the
   601st year. From the date in 7:11 to this point in 8:13
   is a period of 314 days; therefore an interval of 29 days
   elapses.   29
I. From the removal of the covering of the Ark to the
   very end of the experience was another 57 days.   (8:14)   57
                                                                        ___
J. Total Days   371

THE 300-DAY SOLAR YEAR

While looking at the authorized account of the Flood story, it should be pointed out that there have been several assumptions made by the scholars that were necessary to obtain anything close to their hoped-for figure. The reader might well ask, why 371 days, if the scholars assume the solar year of Noah's time consisted of twelve months and a year of 365 days? Wouldn't that give a time period within the Ark as 375?

Doctor C. I. Scofield attacks the problem in a footnote of the Oxford NIV Scofield Study Bible: ". . . or 371 days in all, which figures agree when 7:11 is deducted from 8:14, 12 months of 30 days plus 11 days. The Jews count both the beginning and ending days of a sequence."

This is theological bunk! If Noah was a Jew, then we are all Jews! After telling us the months consist of days, and Noah the Jew is counting days, Scofield then reverts to telling us they were really counting nights, decreasing his overcount by reverting to a lunar calendar and concluding his argument with, "But the actual elapsed time was exactly a solar year."

So much for the ten days over the year as recorded in the account. The Flood begins in the six hundredth year, second month, seventeenth day.

It is my position that this statement should be taken at face value as the year, month, and day of the life of the patriarch and has nothing to do with calendar dates. Scofield likes to say it was the month of May. The Midrash agrees with Scofield's theory that it is the second month of the year, yet I will hasten to say, the text does not state it was the year 1656 from the creation of Adam. It would have been a simple matter for Noah to have given us that record, yet in its entirety it appears to be referring to nothing more than an event given in the day, month, and year in a period of the patriarch's age.

Genesis 7:13 relates it was on that *same day* that Noah entered into the Ark, and the Lord shut him in (7:16). Noah remained within the confines of the Ark until God called him out in his six hundred first year, second month, and twenty-seventh day (8:14, 15). This is a time period of ten days over a solar year.

It is interesting to note that another well-known biblical scholar, Henry H. Halley, author of *Halley's Bible Handbook,*[2] gives a period of one year and seventeen days.

The reader can see that the mathematical problem is still not solved. If the year consisted of 12 months of 30 days each, it results in a 370-day count, not 371, and if today's year of 365 is used, the result should be 375. The text is not referring to either of the above.

The text clearly states that the year consisted of ten months of thirty days each, not a twelve-month year.

In Genesis 7:24 KJV it plainly says, "And the waters prevailed upon the earth a hundred and fifty days." During this time period we are told that from the second month, seventeenth day, to the seventh month, seventeenth day, a period of five months has elapsed. It took another five months for the water to abate. Genesis 8:3 continues: "And the waters returned from off the earth continually: and after the end of the hundred and fifty days the waters were abated."

If the text is stating in the plainest terms possible that the period the floodwaters were upon the earth were two periods of five months each in the waters coming and going, we should expect to find a statement that the floodwaters had completely abated on the twelfth month, seventeenth day. But the record is strangely silent! However, ten days after that, on the twenty-seventh day, we read that the earth was dried (Genesis 8:14). In the following verses we see that on that day the survivors disembarked.

---

[2]Henry H. Halley, *Halley's Bible Handbook* (Grand Rapids: Zondervan Publishing House, 1965), p. 74.

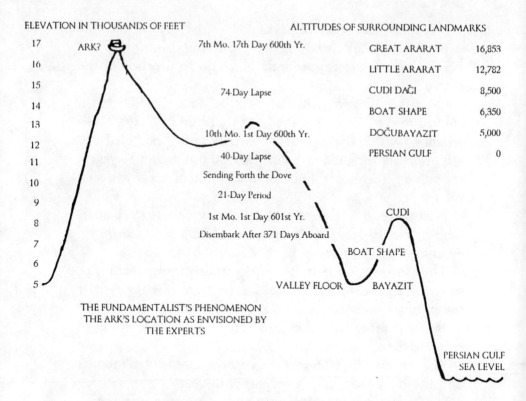

ELEVATION IN THOUSANDS OF FEET   ALTITUDES OF SURROUNDING LANDMARKS

GREAT ARARAT	16,853
LITTLE ARARAT	12,782
CUDI DAĞI	8,500
BOAT SHAPE	6,350
DOĞUBAYAZIT	5,000
PERSIAN GULF	0

17 ARK?
16
15
14
13
12
11
10
9
8
7
6
5

7th Mo. 17th Day 600th Yr.

74-Day Lapse

10th Mo. 1st Day 600th Yr.

40-Day Lapse

Sending Forth the Dove

21-Day Period

1st Mo. 1st Day 601st Yr.

Disembark After 371 Days Aboard

CUDI

BOAT SHAPE

VALLEY FLOOR   BAYAZIT

THE FUNDAMENTALIST'S PHENOMENON
THE ARK'S LOCATION AS ENVISIONED BY
THE EXPERTS

PERSIAN GULF
SEA LEVEL

Furthermore, in the preceding verse we read that Noah was already in his six hundred first year. What happened to the 11th and 12th months? They never existed, except in the minds of the biblical scholars.

But the mention of what Noah did on his birthday is recorded, substantiating my premise that this date keeping is in relation to only the days in Noah's lifetime. In Genesis 8:13 we read that he celebrated the day of his birth in his 601st year, 1st month, and the 1st day of that month, by removing the roof covering for light and fresh air.

Before I proceed with what I consider the proper biblical concept of the Flood, we must acknowledge the strange order of events that have, along with erroneous scholars' opinions, resulted in other Ark hunters searching for the remains of the Ark in the wrong place.

Following is a graph of what these Ark hunters are still basing their searches on.

It begins with an unbelievable act of seamanship when Noah maneuvered, or through the providence of the Almighty, the Ark came to rest on the very top of Ararat the exact moment of the peaking of the Flood on the 150th day.

Later, I will show through my research how only tradition put it there, and that Ararat as we see it today didn't even exist at the time of the Flood. If I suggest to my contemporaries that since Ararat is only approximately seventeen thousand feet high, this was the peak of the Flood, and there were many mountains in the world that were not covered, their immediate response is that those higher mountains were covered by the Flood as the Scriptures have stated, but they were moved up by tectonic upheaval shortly thereafter. There is good cause to accept a portion of their argument, but should one dare to suggest that Ararat itself was another of these latecomers, their reaction is close to violent. So, although Ararat is a rather young volcanic cone, geologically speaking, it is useless to suggest that it wasn't built until after the Flood when confronting the Ararat groups.

For the sake of continuing, I will give these people something to cling to by considering that the Ark is on the peak of Ararat and the rest of the world is completely covered by water.

In relation to these Ararat groups and the graph I have drawn, it would appear that from the peaking of the Flood in the seventh month, seventeenth day, the waters decreased by 4018 feet in a period of seventy-four days to expose Little Ararat (elevation 12,782 feet), so that in the tenth month Noah could relate, ". . . were the tops of the mountains seen." The Ark therefore is on the southeast slope. This is the brilliant deduction by Ark hunter Chuck Willis, an attending physician at a men's prison in Tehachapi, California. He proposes a cable car system to take people to a place where they could view the Ark under an oxygenated dome. Willis's site is at an elevation of 16,800 feet. To date, he has not found the Ark. I find it amazing the Ark could still survive there with all the volcanic activity, and at such a high altitude it must have been uncomfortable for Noah and the animals.

According to one observant investigator,[3] the shepherds

<hr/>

[3]Charles Berlitz, *The Lost Ship of Noah: In Search of the Ark at Ararat* (New York: G. P. Putnam's Sons, 1987).

bring their flocks no higher than 8,000 feet. After that the sheep begin to die, a phenomenon formerly believed to be because of the divine interdiction against climbing the mountain.

But the interesting point to be made about Noah's observation of the tops of the mountains is that it occurred on the first day of the tenth month. For the following verse states, "And it came to pass at the end of forty days, that Noah opened the window of the ark which he had made" (Genesis 8:6 KJV).

If this truly is the proper sequence of events, we might find this recorded as the eleventh month, eleventh day if the year consisted of twelve months as the scholars suggest, but the record is silent. It is also silent in explaining how Noah could have seen the tops of the mountains forty days before he opened the window!

If we are to accept the account as proposed by the biblical scholars, there has been an elapsed period of 114 days since the peaking of the Flood and the Ark's landing to the day that Noah opened the window. This is a suspiciously long period of time to stand idly by, locked within the bowels of the Ark.

7–17	Ark coming to rest, peaking of the Flood, an additional thirteen days for the month	13
8–1 through 30		30
9–1 through 30		30
10–1	Tops of the mountains seen, yet window not opened	1
	An additional twenty-nine days for the month	29
11–11	Window opened after forty days	11
	Total time period since coming to rest	114

The reader can see that the rate of the decreasing waters in just seventy-four days exposed Little Ararat, a drop of 4,018 feet from Willis's proposed site. Therefore, should this rate of 54.3 feet per day continue, we could expect to see at least two islands in the stream with Little Ararat exposed by 2,172 feet and Ararat itself, Ark Island if you like, projecting up some 6,190 feet above sea level. Quite a formidable piece of real estate.

However, it would also have exposed Arasgüneyi Dağ by 1624 feet, 102 kilometers to the west, as well as Köse Dağı by almost 700 feet, not to mention Tendürek Dağı 55 kilometers to the southwest and the peak of Koçbaşı above the waters by almost a thousand feet, all of which may not be visible from Noah's little window at Willis's site. The fact that other mountains were within view and clearly within flying distance of the dove seems to have escaped the viewpoint of these experts, for the greatest inconsistency in the text is this: "[Noah] sent forth a dove from him, to see if the waters were abated from off the face of the ground; But the dove found no rest for the sole of her foot, and she returned unto him into the ark, for the waters were on the face of the whole earth" (Genesis 8:8, 9 KJV).

To any serious researcher of Noah's Ark, red flags should be going up right now! How could the dove find no rest for the sole of her foot and the waters be on the face of the whole earth?

This contradiction was caused by early revisionists who meddled with the text. The clue to the change is in the flag word recorded in Moses' original account that was not removed. The flag word is *whole*. It appears only one other place, back in Genesis 7:19 KJV: " . . . under the whole heaven."

I propose that the bird sequence has been moved into a later portion of the narrative in an attempt to build an acceptable 360-day year out of the 300-day solar year of the original record.

OPENING THE WINDOW

It's time that we open the window of the Ark to take a fresh look at the Flood account without doggedly researching the material of others.

Why haven't biblical scholars ever asked themselves this: Why didn't the dove simply fly to the tops of the mountains that were seen previously, and what forty days was the account referring to? How about the forty days of rain! It's obvious the scholars and Ark hunters are not grasping the situation. Put yourself in Noah's place.

If the Lord had said, seven days before you entered the Ark, " . . . and I will cause it to rain upon the earth forty days and forty nights," wouldn't you be counting those days and expecting them to stop at the appointed time? And if the incessant rain had been pounding on the roof covering for over a month, wouldn't the silence be deafening when it stopped? Quick, what would you do?

"And it came to pass [as the Lord had spoken] at the end of forty days [of rain] that Noah opened the window of the Ark which he had made." *And he looked out,* as anyone would do in a similar situation. What happened next is related to Gilgamesh by Utnapishtim, the Babylonian Noah, in a first-person narrative from the earlier clay tablets before the compiler of the Book of Genesis was born, before there was a Jew, and before there were revisionists and theologians.

> The storm was over and the rain of destruction had ceased. I looked forth. I called aloud over the waters.

So it is evident by earlier sources that the storm of destruction ceased after its allotted time, and as could be expected, the window was opened for the first time. After the forty days of rain Noah peeked out to see if he alone had survived. " . . . and every living thing that I have made will I destroy from off the face of the earth," the Lord had said, and the earlier tablets record it to be true:

> But all mankind had perished and turned to clay.

And when Noah had opened the window, was it 74 days since he had seen the tops of the mountains, or 114 days since he had come to rest? No, for the Babylonian account of the Flood continues:

> Then I opened *wide* the window of the ship, and the sunlight suffused by countenance. I was dazzled and sank down weeping, and the tears streamed down over my face. Everywhere I looked, I saw *WATER!*

This then is when the waters were upon the *whole* earth and under the *whole* heaven!

The opening of the window and the sending forth of the raven and the dove do not occur after the "coming to rest" but before, and within the first 150-day period of the Flood. They have been pulled from the earlier portion of the text and inserted in a later portion of the text to *add days to the account!*

This is how they did it:

The true time period within the Ark was	310 days
Remove the statement about Noah opening the window after the forty days of rain from following 7:18 as well as the bird sequence, all of which occurred before the coming to rest.	
Insert it after the coming to rest and the tops of the mountains seen for an additional	40 days
Add now the three flights of the dove	21 days

For a new time period of 371 days in all.

For the proper sequence of events, I have prepared the following:

THE FASOLD CONCEPT

Sequence of Events	Genesis	Span of Time in Days
A. There were 40 days during which the rain fell.	(7:12)	40
B. At the end of 40 days, Noah opened the window.	(8:6)	
C. It is at this time the birds were dispatched.		
D. The waters prevailed upon the earth 150 days.	(7:24)	
The Ark has come to rest (not aground) on the 7th month, 17th day.	(8:4)	110
E. To 8th month, 17th day.		30
F. To 9th month, 17th day.		30
G. To 10th month, 1st day. Tops of mountains seen.	(8:5)	14
H. From the above, to the end of the tenth month.		29
NOTE: The narrative never suggests more than ten months!		
I. 601st year, 1st month, 1st day (grounding). . . . behold, the face of the *ground* was dry.	(8:13)	1
J. From the above to the 2nd month, 1st day.		30
K. Until the 2nd month, 27th day was the earth dried.	(8:14)	26
Total Days		310

The amount of days in accordance with the Scriptures is exactly 310 days, the days from the 600th year of Noah's life, 2nd month, 17th day, to the 601st year, 2nd month, 27th day.

Noah was within the confines of the Ark for exactly ten days over a solar year of ten months of thirty days each.

		Flood day	
Year 600	2 mo. 17th day:		beginning of the Deluge
	3 mo. 17th day	30	
	4 mo. 17th day	60	
	5 mo. 17th day	90	
	6 mo. 17th day	120	
	7 mo. 17th day	150	
	8 mo. 17th day	180	
	9 mo. 17th day	210	
	10 mo. 17th day	240	
year 601	1 mo. 17th day	270	
	2 mo. 17th day	300	ending of the Deluge
	plus 10 days	310	earth was dry

HOMO IGNORAMUS

There are other inconsistencies in the authorized account that are easily explained by this new sequence of events. The crow and the dove take on more significant roles and are explained in a later chapter. Where the olive leaf came from which obviously could not have drifted, taken root, and sprouted in only seven days, and the purpose of the seven-day wait between the sending forth of the dove, the period of time between the coming to rest and the ground being dry, is also answered by discovery of the drogue anchors.

But could the idea of a earlier period comprised of a shorter year be acceptable? Attempting to reconcile the pre-Flood era and that period of time shortly thereafter with our present system of $29\frac{1}{2}$-day lunar months and a solar year of $365\frac{1}{4}$ days may not be realistic. Immanuel Velikovsky compiled vast material from various cultures that concludes there have been occasions of perturbations in the vault of the heavens and the earth, during which the moon has receded to an orbit of 35 to 36 days' duration.

The Flood was the result of an event that changed everything! Peter relates the ancients' understanding that for the most part the world is turning its back on today regardless of the evidence.

> For this they *willingly are ignorant of,*
> that by the word of God the *heavens were of old,*
> and the earth standing out of the water
> and in the water. . . . But the heavens and the
> earth, *which are now,* by the same word are
> kept in store, reserved unto fire against
> the day of judgment . . . .
>
> 2 Peter 3:5, 7 KJV author's italics

Are we willingly ignorant that the old heavens as viewed from our planet have passed away with the land that was standing above the water of the prediluvian period? Portions of that landmass sank beneath the waters and through tectonic upheaval little of the old world remains beneath our feet, while the heavens that are above us now in this new elliptical orbit of

$365\frac{1}{4}$ days is reserved for a future time when it, too, will change. John speaks of this in a foreseen future event when there fell great stones out of the heavens preceded by an earthquake "such was not since men were upon the earth, so mighty an earthquake, and so great" that "every island fled away, and the mountains were not found" (Revelation 16:18, 20 KJV).

Peter precedes these comments by stating that we should know this first, that there shall come in the last days of our present system scoffers, saying, "Where is the promise of his coming? for since the fathers fell asleep, all things continue as they were from the beginning of the creation" (2 Peter 3:4 KJV).

It is here that Immanuel Velikovsky begins to take a rather hard look at Homo Ignoramus. The sun rises in the east and sets in the west. The day consists of 23 hours, 56 minutes. The year consists of 365 days, 5 hours, and 49 minutes. The moon circles the earth changing phases, crescent to full to decrescent again. The earth's terrestrial axis points in the direction of the polar star. After winter comes spring, then summer and fall. These are common facts, but are they invariable laws? asks Velikovsky.

What single spectacle impressed itself upon the mind of man that evoked the astonishment of the survivors but a change in the order of the universe, and it caused the Flood!

Today, the willfully ignorant discredit traditions of upheavals and catastrophes by the shortsighted belief that no forces could have shaped the world we live in that are not now at work. In my opinion, this belief, which is the very foundation of modern geology, may have been a proud ship at her launching, but it is now full of so many holes it doesn't float!

There is no law of celestial mechanics that says the earth must have this particular rate of rotation. The earth's equator is inclined to the plane of its elliptic at an angle of 23.45°. This causes the change of the seasons during the earth's annual revolution around the sun. It is not necessarily a general law that a planet must be so, and from my reading of the account in Genesis, there had been a change.

For the theologian, the reason for the Flood and the cause of the Flood are two entirely different matters. The mechanics of the event may never be fully explained as to an outside influence disturbing the earth, which caused the tilt and change in orbit, resulting in a total breakup of the crust, or if the earth received a direct impact, as the Book of Revelation predicts, it will in the future form the star Wormwood.

An immediate change in the atmosphere is noted by Noah at the first sighting of a rainbow and his mention of seasons of heat and cold. In the years thereafter there appeared to be a decreasing of longevity, especially in the succeeding generations, and an abrupt change during the days of Peleg. The oldest account of this phenomenon is recorded by Emperor Ho-ang-ti who, according to the chronology of China, was a contemporary of Reu. In his medical book he proposed an enquiry "whence it happened that the lives of our forefathers were so long compared with the lives of the present generation." All was not peaceful on the earth when Noah stepped out of the Ark. The readjustments of tectonic plates caused by the oblation of the earth at its new equatorial zones since the axis shift may have still been causing havoc during later generations.

If we are to accept the Masoretic text as accurate, my figures would have Peleg living from 101 post-Flood to the year 340, but I have doubts as to this early date. Nahor, Terah's father, died approximately the same year, so there may be indications of another catastrophic event. Genesis 10:25 relates that during Peleg's day the earth was torn asunder by a violent upheaval. He may have met his death during this event.

Peleg's name is not in itself a proper name. It means "a division." There are about thirteen verbs translated "divide," each with a different shade of meaning. The popular explanation is that the world was divided among the various companies of peoples and that this coincided with the dispersal from the Tower of Babel. If this was the meaning, the verb used, to "divide by sharing," would be *chālak*. But the name is derived from *pālag,* "to divide by cleavage."

The Egyptians, too, have recorded this event when the earth's crust was rent during Peleg's time as the work of the Lord (Thoth) Tehuti pens ta, "cleaver of the earth." During more stable times he was remembered as Thoth-Hāpi-Tem neb Xut, "lord of the horizon."

This brings to mind Isaiah 24:1 KJV: "Behold, the Lord maketh the earth empty, and maketh it waste, and turneth it upside down, and scattereth abroad the inhabitants thereof." Babylonian tablets record actual dates such as "the thirty-third day of the month" during that period.[4]

The abrupt decrease in longevity, according to the Masoretic text, can be seen by the graph on the following page.

In summation of this chapter, I am proposing that the solar year prior to the Flood was undergoing a slow change, something that is alluded to in the study of the calendar at the Tiahunaco ruins on the Alti Plano in South America, which in my view must now be considered the remains of a pre-Flood city.

I have attempted to show that the solar year of the Flood as described in the Genesis account is referring to a year of three hundred days. In the following chapter about the pre-Flood kings, my proposal coincides with the biblical account of the reigns of the ten patriarchs as listed in the Genesis account before the Flood.

Could it be possible that the orbit of the earth was disturbed by outside influences passing through our solar system, causing a change in the earth's orbit around the sun to an elliptic path of a longer year? Would the axis shift be a result of this disturbance, or would the shift itself be the cause of the change?

If all things have remained the same, what then are we to make of the orbiting satellite, whose distance from the earth was 5.9 terrestrial radii, that made 447 revolutions around the earth in a year comprised of 290 days during the prehistoric times of the ancient Americans? If the interpretation of these ancient calendars is valid, then perhaps we should apply a shorter year to the pre-Flood accounts of the Mesopotamians.

---

[4]*Babylonianische Zeitordnung,* p. 191, note.

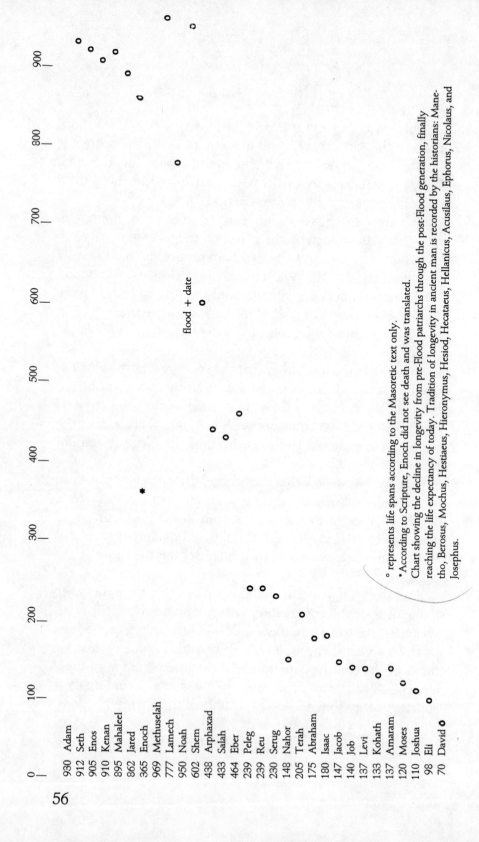

900 — 800 — 700 — 600 — 500 — 400 — 300 — 200 — 100 — 0 —

flood + date

930 Adam
912 Seth
905 Enos
910 Kenan
895 Mahaleel
862 Jared
365 Enoch
969 Methuselah
777 Lamech
950 Noah
602 Shem
438 Arphaxad
433 Salah
464 Eber
239 Peleg
239 Reu
230 Serug
148 Nahor
205 Terah
175 Abraham
180 Isaac
147 Jacob
140 Job
137 Levi
133 Kohath
137 Amaram
120 Moses
110 Joshua
98 Eli
70 David

° represents life spans according to the Masoretic text only.
*According to Scripture, Enoch did not see death and was translated.
Chart showing the decline in longevity from pre-Flood patriarchs through the post-Flood generation, finally reaching the life expectancy of today. Tradition of longevity in ancient man is recorded by the historians: Manetho, Berosus, Mochus, Hestiaeus, Hieronymus, Hesiod, Hecataeus, Hellanicus, Acusilaus, Ephorus, Nicolaus, and Josephus.

56

3

The Antediluvians

THE PRE-FLOOD KINGS

In this chapter we shall consider the ancient chronological reigns of the ten kings who ruled before the Flood. The life spans of the patriarchs found in the account of Genesis and the reigns of the antediluvian kings from the so-called king lists of the Sumerian and Babylonian cuneiform texts do not appear to agree, yet they have similarities which I believe should be investigated in light of my proposal that the pre-Flood era had a solar year of three hundred days.

Since the scope of these investigations is limited by the subject of the events leading up to the Flood, only the antediluvian portions of the lists can be considered in this work. That we are only reviewing the list of Berosus is not an attempt to oversimplify the problem. There are numerous lists that have considerable variation in their contents in so far as the order of the kings and their cities. Berosus' list, however, conforms to the tradition in general which records between eight and ten kings reigning for between 186,000 and 456,000 years.

The list of Berosus in comparison to an earlier list, that of the Weld Prism of the priest Nur-ninsubur, follows.

To Berosus, the Flood was but a chapter in the history of man, and he was the first to set down the Babylonian account of it in a European language.

Berosus, whose name could mean "Bel is his shepherd," was not a historian in the true sense of the word that Josephus was some three centuries later. Berosus was a scholar of the classics and the very fact that he was able to draw his history of the world from the numerous texts in the Sumerian and

AN EXAMPLE OF AN EARLIER KING LIST IN COMPARISON WITH THAT GIVEN BY BEROSUS

Berosus, Babylon 281 B.C.E.

King	City	Years
Aloros	Babylon	36,000
Alaparos		10,800
Amelon	Pautibiblon	46,800
Ammenon	Pautibiblon	43,200
Amegalaros	Pautibiblon	64,800
Daonos	Pautibiblon	36,000
Euedorachos	Pautibiblon	64,800
Amempsinos	Laragchos	36,000
Otiartes	Laragchos	28,800
Xisouthros		64,800

Nur-Ninsubur, Larsa 2170 B.C.E.

King	City	Years
Alulim	Eridu	28,000
Alalmar	Eridu	36,000
Emenluanna	Badgurgurru	43,000
Kichunna	Larsa	43,000
Enmengalanna	Badgurgurru	28,000
Dumuzi	Badgurgurru	36,000
Sibzianna	Larak	28,000
Emenduranna	Sippar	21,000
Uburratum	Shuruppak	18,000
Zinsuddu	Shuruppak	64,000

The names given by Berosus are but a graecized form of the Sumerian. In the Weld Prism and Nippur Tablets, the vowels should be given their Latin values. There is no *o* in Sumerian or Akkadian.

Akkadian tongues inscribed in cuneiform signs upon thousands of clay tablets at his disposal from the Temple Library at Babylon points to a scribal education. Furthermore, his dedication of the work for the instruction of Antiochus I leads one to believe he was probably a member of the Seleucid court.

We might date the birth of Berosus circa 350 B.C.E. While attempting to place the date of his composition within the reign of Antiochus I (commonly accepted as 279–261), I would like to point out that we should not take these dates too seriously. Since the folks who made up the Julian and Gregorian calendars about 700 years later now admit that Jesus was born 4 B.C. (Before Christ) and that there is a 200-year discrepancy in a 400-year period just before the birth of Christ, Vendyl Jones, a scholar friend of mine, and I prefer to use the term B.C.E., meaning "Before the Common Error"!

Berosus claimed to be a contemporary of Alexander the Great and a priest of the god Marduk (Bel) and interpreter of Belus. He lived in Babylon, but by the use of the phrase "to genos, and natione" identified himself as a Chaldean in origin. He was an astronomer and no doubt one of those consulted by Seleucus I and his predecessors, a member of the Magi, the group who some three centuries later would seek out the birthplace of Jesus by the GP (Geographical Position) of the star over Bethlehem.

Berosus may have been moved to write his history and present it to Antiochus over his deep concern for the Greeks' lack of appreciation for the culture and civilization the Chaldeans had brought to the world. By the completion of his work, it had been fifty years since their Greek "liberator," Alexander, had burned Persepolis to the ground. This was the first time Mesopotamians had been conquered by outsiders, and they were finding that Greeks and Greek thoughts were totally alien to them.

Berosus wanted to impress the Greek student that Babylon was ancient. He emphasized that these kings before the Flood were Chaldean kings and not Greek, and that it was they who were responsible for civilization. If this was an attempt to gain respect from their conquerors for their contributions and accomplishments of the past, Berosus' work may not have achieved its purpose. For the most part, it remained a closed book except for those few students of Mesopotamian affairs and scrutiny by the Jews, for whom Babylonian traditions held a particular interest. Berosus retired from Babylon to take up residence on the Ptolemaic island of Cos, where he gave formal instruction to the Greeks into the mysteries of Chaldean astrology.

When one comes to the study of Berosus' "Babyloniaca," or as referred to by Josephus, "the Chaldaiaca," he is not studying the original. In its original form, this work is lost. Ancient writers who profess to be quoting his works appear to be relying on an abridgment made in the first century by a Greco-Roman scholar named Cornelius Alexander Polyhistor. There can be little doubt that even Josephus relied on Polyhistor's knowledge of what Berosus had written. According to the careful reading by these early scholars of the fragments that remained, there was little doubt that it had been written in extremely poor Greek, emphasizing a Chaldean concept of creation and an essentially unexplainable mystical doctrine. Since these early times, only Polyhistor's abridgment was accessible, so another attempt to restore this work was made by Eusebius of Caesaria in the fourth century, relying on an adaptation of Polyhistor's work completed two hundred years earlier by Abydenus. Regretfully, even this text is lost except for excerpts preserved in a Byzantine chronicle from the ninth century. There is also an Armenian translation of the Chronica of Eusebius that has accumulated the errors of centuries. So considering the above, there is the possibility that much of what Berosus was attempting to relay in the Greek of his day, which was not his mother tongue, it must be remembered, together with his interpretation from the cuneiform, down to what we understand him to mean today, we find there is considerable source for error and corruption.

To begin with, I do not believe that Berosus said the Ark was five by two stadia. That would be 3,000 feet long, and 1,200 feet wide. Nor do I believe that Berosus was saying, as modern-day scholars suppose, the antediluvian era consisted of the reign of ten kings for a period of 432,000 years. I prefer to suggest there is some misinterpretation here rather than write Berosus off as a fool!

There are biblical fundamentalist scholars who would consider these figures and variables found in other king lists as proof they are unreliable. However, the Christian scholar is on rather shaky ground himself, for there are three texts of Christendom that disagree as well.

The latest or newest text found in most authorized versions of the Bible today is the Masoretic text. This totals the period between creation and the Flood as 1656 years. The text the early Christian Church followed was the Septuagint that places the period between Adam and Noah's "lift-off" as 2262. The earliest text, the Samaritan Pentateuch, gives this period as 1307 years.

The chronological order of these kings in relation to the patriarchs of Genesis occupy the interest of the Christian scholar, then, while the lengths of reigns are looked upon with disdain. To the humanistic-minded student, a pre-Flood period allowing the "evolution" of man to progress over a period of some 450,000 years, Berosus' figure of 432,000, is not perceived as intolerable. But to consider that Aloros (Adam), who is allotted only 930 years in the Genesis account, could maintain his position as king for an incredible period of 36,000 years, strains the credibility of even the most optimistic of historians.

Some of my readers, then, may find it objectionable and futile for me to attempt to reconcile these figures with the Masoretic text. I acknowledge the objections to the Masoretic, which I feel in the post-Flood period does not allow substantial time for the repopulating of the earth down to Abraham, and the fact that this text in its present form is 350 years later than the earlier Samaritan (408 B.C.E.).

The question here is not really which text is correct, an antediluvian era of 2262 years, 1656, or 1307, but how on earth Berosus ever came up with the figure of 432,000 years. Let me say I would be most happy had Berosus said 496,800. The fact that he didn't leads me to understand that Aloros was 216 years old when he began his reign.

Berosus wrote in terms of the Saroi, Neroi, and Sossoi. These terms are presently considered 3,600 years for the Saros, 600 years for the Neros, and 60 years for the Sassos. Berosus' antediluvian time period of 120 Saroi (the Sumerian Sar) is then thought to be a period of 432,000 years.

I propose that the Saros is a period of 3,600 *days!* But here an important consideration must be made. I have relayed in the previous chapter that the problem of the contradictions within the Flood text can be resolved if it is understood that it was compiled during an era when Dynamic Time was a 360-day period.

The period of the Flood *as recorded* was 150 days up and 150 days down, plus the 10 days. The year consisted of only 300 days. It was then necessary to rearrange the chronological order of events so the entire sequence covered a day count that supported an era of 360 days. Further erroneous and futile explanations in Bible footnotes by theologians only compound the problem when they attempt to make the text fit within the framework of our solar year of today.

I propose that the Saros of 3,600 days divisible by the 300-day solar year is still within the sexagesimal system as a period of 12 years, and that the reigns of Berosus' kings indeed covered 120 Saroi, or 1440 years. The pre-king era consisted of 18 Saroi, 216 years, when Aloros was considered father of all living. Alaparos, his son, was 86 when his father proclaimed himself "shepherd of his people." It must be remembered that these periods of Saroi refer to reigns and not life spans of the patriarchs.

Could the day count of the year have been different in pre-Flood times? The Bible (2 Peter 3) says that the heavens that were of old perished along with the land that was above the waters in the Flood.

Immanuel Velikovsky in his *Worlds in Collision* is the only researcher I have found to suggest this. In his argument for a serious acceptance of a 360-day solar year after the Flood he buttresses his arguments with such abundance of proof that I find it incredible the academic world has not accepted this in the thirty-eight years since he proposed it. He then hints at the same concept of my theory that the age which preceded the Flood had a shorter year than the 360 days. He says, "In a much earlier age, when the year was of an entirely different length, one revolution of the earth was equal in time to ten revolutions of the moon. We shall trace this period in history in a succeeding volume of this work."[1] On this thought,

[1] *Worlds in Collision* (New York: Pocket Books, 1977), p. 350.

Velikovsky neither elaborates nor follows up. It is quite possible that he had realized the calendar data of Tiahuanaco showed a solar year of 291.2 days and thus a ten-month solar year of lunar cycles.

I adhere to the theory that an axis shift was the cause of the change in the order of things. The earth may have rolled as much as 27° at the time of the Flood. This would be followed by a period of precession over many years following the shift, required in returning the axis to an equilibrium position.

Something of this nature occurs when a gyrocompass loses power on a merchant ship. It was always a mad dash to the gyro room from the bridge when the power failure alarm rang, for if the gyro was not locked in during its down period, the rolling of the ship would cause the axis to swing as well, requiring a longer period of precession and return to a normal function.

To apply this gyroscopic action to the earth, should some outside source disturb its equilibrium, such as a close encounter with another large body, the same gyroscopic theory would apply. There are three changes that would take place. During the precession, the spin axis tilt will usually decrease (although hypothetically, it could increase). During this period, the spin axis location can move and the velocity will always increase slightly.

Applying this to the earth, we can see that after the tilt at the time of the Flood, the axis could have regressed to something closer to our 23° plus of today. That the axis location has changed in the past is no longer scientific debate, as evidenced by numerous examples of out-of-place fauna and carcasses of temperate zone animals found preserved in the Arctic regions.

Our point of interest is the velocity increase which resulted in the earth's spin rate changing from 300 to 360 revolutions in completion of its orbit around the sun. We cannot be sure that the orbit did not become elliptic as well.

The post-Flood result, after a period of precession that probably lasted into the times of Peleg, was a year of 360 days. As Velikovsky concludes, should this not have been the case that the year truly was 360 and not the 365 days of our year today, it would have been noted by perplexed astronomers and by those who worked the land, for within a short period

of only forty years – a period a person could readily observe –
the seasons would have become displaced by more than two
hundred days. During this era the calendars of the Hindu,
Persian, Chaldean, Assyrian, Chinese, Greek, Roman, and
Mayan all had this 360-day count. Then something mysterious began to happen.

It is my opinion that something affected the earth again, this
time, however, without the associated calamities. Cultures
widely separated, indeed, in some cases unaware of one another's existence, began to reform their calendars, changing
the day count to 365.

The Chaldean king Nabonassar (747–734) and his astrolo-
gers/astronomers developed a new calendar, correcting the
existing one. The Hebrews followed suit sometime during the
seventh century B.C.E., which became fixed in the fourth century C.E. The Seleucid calendar, that which existed during
Berosus' time, was based on the Syrian, which only several
centuries earlier had seen the need for a change. Seleucus
Necator, one of Alexander the Great's generals, founded an
empire that stretched from Asia Minor to India on this new
count for the year. That is not to say that Europe was unaware
of a change in reckoning. Numa Pompilius, king of Rome
around 715 B.C.E., became tired of adding days to the earlier
calendar ascribed to Romulus and made it 365 by adding
January and February. That is why September, October, November, and December no longer represent the seventh,
eighth, ninth, and tenth months of our year.

Egypt, too, had changed its 360-day count to one of 365 in
the eighth century B.C.E. Generally speaking the farmers and
nomads of Africa had unwritten calendars, but they soon
recognized the solstices and equinoxes were not keeping time,
and they adopted the new. It was farewell to a year of 360
days, by which they had chiefly kept time in an era that
stretched back to 5493 B.C.E., or the founding of Egypt, according to the Abyssinians. Those of the Julius Africanus
thought it began in 5413 B.C.E.

But what of the astronomers in southeast Asia who based
their reckonings back to the ancient Kali Yuga, an era that
began in 3102 B.C.E., and the Chinese, whose calendar is the

longest unbroken sequence of time measurement in history, that to them began in 2953 B.C.E.?

Their measure of time, which was adopted by the Koreans and Japanese, was suddenly changed. The circle of their astrologers changed from 360° to that of 365°15′ in the fourth century B.C.E. In a remote and as yet undiscovered area of the globe (we are led to believe), the New World counterpart to the Chaldeans, the Mayans, suddenly made a drastic alteration in the counting system between 500 and 300 B.C.E., at about the same time our own calendar came into existence. Their era had stretched back to 3113 B.C.E. and the original system of daily counting the 360 through the solar cycle (which archaeologists erroneously refer to as the "short count") served them well enough to calculate the solar and lunar eclipse and to include the planetary cycles of the solar system in their calendar as well. Now with the change in the year realized, the old system was abandoned and a new, very complicated calendar was constructed based on what archaeologists now refer to as the Mayan "long count."

I would not want the reader to presume I hold the present-day opinions of anthropologists studying the Mayans or their archaeological knowledge of them (something to which I wish I had had the opportunity of dedicating myself) in low regard. But they must surely realize the Mayans knew how to count the days in the year. If they counted 360, it should be obvious. This short count and long count is bunk! The length of the year had changed.

I find it amazing that the Mayan Grolier Codex can be touted as ranking among "the supreme intellectual achievements of human history" by these academics, as the world's first and only known calendar of Venus ever produced by any civilization which, according to Spinder and Makemson's correlations, place the date back to 3374 B.C.E. Archaeologists still hold the Mayans used the short count because it was easier to compute with even numbers, or they had actually had a false idea for the past three millennia!

Here again the earth had undergone a change in the spin rate by increasing from 360 to 365 plus. We should look for changing weather patterns, abandonment of populous areas, and migrations to have occurred during this period in history, about the time of calendar reform.

We should not find it surprising, then, that the cataclysmic event that caused the earth to roll, lifting the tectonic plates in new equatorial zones of oblation and emptying ocean basins of their waters to flood the earth, should not cause an increase in velocity to the spin rate according to the gyroscopic theory, and a sixty-day increase of rotation during one complete orbit about the sun.

Nor should we find it unreasonable to assume that the ancients kept a day-by-day count of the rotation of the planet throughout its orbital cycle around the sun, just as the Mayans did by their long count in our era. In the 360-day era that count would be shorter, and in antediluvian times, shorter still. Before the Flood, every day count of 3,600 was a Saros of 12 years.

Before we look at Berosus' account of the ten pre-Flood kings, we have to ask ourselves, who would Adam be king over during the early period of filling the earth with his offspring? During these first generations, he might be considered as only the father of all living. It might be interesting to calculate the population figures for a pre-king era that preceded Berosus' list, but first, from whence came Adam himself?

To begin with the assumption that Adam, or "man," was a created being, and did not evolve, can be taken by humanists as purely a Christian fundamentalist concept. But in actuality, virtually all mankind professed a belief in creation. Eminent Egyptologists have come to the opinion that the dwellers in the Nile Valley from earliest times knew and worshiped one God, nameless, incomprehensible, and eternal:

> God is one and alone, and none other existeth with Him—the one who hath made all things—a divine spirit, a hidden spirit—God is from the beginning, and He hath been from the beginning. He hath existed from old, and was when nothing else had being. He existed when nothing else existed, and what existeth He created. God is life and through Him only man liveth. He giveth life to man, He breatheth the breath of life into his nostrils. He fashioned men and formed the gods (angels).[2]

---

[2]E. A. Wallis Budge, *The Egyptian Book of the Dead* (New York: Dover Publications, Inc. 1967).

These excerpts from the *Book of the Dead* date from the period of Menä (Mizraim, son of Ham; Genesis 10:6), the first king of Egypt.

Ham, of course, came through the Flood. Ham's son, Mizraim, was not that far removed that he didn't know the truth. It was Mizraim's brother's son Nimrod, through Cush, who really turned people back to idolatry as the world had been before. The Hamitic, or descendants of the line of Cain, ruled the earth. Paul spoke of this early era (Romans 1:21, 23): "Because that, when they knew God, they glorified him not as God, neither were thankful. . . . And changed the glory of the uncorruptible God into an image made like to corruptible man, and to birds, and fourfooted beasts, and creeping things."

But man was not always out of harmony with God. According to the biblical account, the angelic host, or sons of God in the heavenlies or extraterrestrial sphere, shouted and sang for joy as the earth was forming into a life-support system for the living creatures that would inhabit it.

Male and female, who owed their very existence to a direct creative act of God, were placed in the garden earth and blessed: "Be fruitful and multiply, and replenish the earth, and subdue it." Here in the term *replenish* (found in the KJV) is insight into a past catastrophe that appears to have extinguished all life forms from a prior age (*see* Jeremiah 4:23–28). I realize this is a bone of contention among theologians, but I think it deserves consideration. It most certainly cannot be explained away because we don't know how to deal with it. It is one of the few points on which I agree with Dr. Scofield that there is not wanting the intimation that beings were on the earth in an earlier era (*see* Ezekiel 28:13–16) and Adamic man was a new order upon the earth to replenish it.

If this is true, then the first verse in Genesis may be taken as a statement of fact followed by the second statement that the earth "became without form and void" as relating to a prior fall and judgment, with the following being in effect a re-creation.

I can only touch upon the idea that Adam may have seen the bones of dinosaurs protruding from the earth in his day. If the Ark was covered with asphalt tar, a fossil fuel, how could this be possible prior to the Flood as espoused by Whitcomb and Morris? Rather than taking a dogmatic and extreme fundamental view that all fossils in the strata were laid down in the Flood of Noah, shouldn't we consider that prior to Adam the earth was covered by water as well?

Adamic man, we are told, made male and female and having carnal knowledge of the flesh, conceived and bore their firstborn on the earth, named Cain. The King James Bible retains enough of the Hebrew in its original form to see that Adam did not know Eve, his wife, *again,* nor does it say that she *conceived* again but that she *again* bore his brother Abel (Genesis 4:1, 2). Cain and Abel were twins. Only the separation of the narrative into verses makes this easy to miss. Chapter 3 and verse 16 tell us that multiple births and sorrow in conception may not have been the original plan but a result of the fall into sin.

Even excluding multiple births, it is easy to calculate by the chronology supplied us in Genesis 4 and 5 that Abel was murdered just prior to the birth of Seth. Since Adam was 130 when Seth was born we might consider that the murder had occurred the prior year. We don't know for sure just how many children Adam and Eve had, but Josephus relates that by tradition, Eve bore Adam thirty-three sons and twenty-three daughters.

There is no reason to believe that Adam could not have started to replenish the earth through Eve immediately upon the directive to do so, bearing children yearly. The sexes seem fairly equally divided. If these offspring paired off at eighteen years of age to produce children of their own, by the time of Abel's death, Adam could have had nearly three thousand grandchildren. But that's not all. Carry this figure past the ninety thousand great-grandchildren to the fourth power, and the world population could have been almost half a million people!

Cain's expression of fear that "anyone that findeth me will slay me" can now be understood as no small concern for his safety from this sizable mob, seeking retribution for his evil deed.

Is it any wonder then that God marked Cain (and possibly his descendants) with a mark of protection? I have stated before my belief that Cain and Abel were twins. The King James Version has little in common with these verses in the

Hebrew where the term *littered* is used. The Hebrew says that Cain was born with his sister. Afterward, Abel issued forth with his two sisters. Therefore Cain may have possessed the birthright of the firstborn by just minutes, which might give further insight into the disagreement between the two brothers. Abel also may have had two wives.

The name *Cain* carries with it numerous meanings in both Hebrew and Chaldee. It is the name of the first child with a primary root "to own or possess." It also means "to strike quickly" (Strong's 7013, 7014, and 7069), which he did. In all fairness, Abel may not have been the easiest brother to get along with. His name (Hebel) is from a primary root "to be vain in act, word, or expectation."

Cain and his descendants migrated eastward to the land of Wandering (Nod) where he knew his wife; she conceived and bore Enoch. Cain built the first city with protective walls and named it after this son. It should not be taken to mean Enoch was his first or only offspring but possibly the first since expulsion.

The line of Cain continued to prosper until the time of the Flood, and throughout this period there were seven succeeding sages. The biblical account lists them as follows: Cain, Enoch, Irad, Mehujael, Methusael, Lamech, Tubal-cain.

The name *Enoch* (Chanowk) is from a primary root meaning "to initiate discipline," as the beginnings of civilization and city building implies. *Irad* (Iyrad) means "to be made a fugitive" or "to confiscate (sequester)," and may allude to him as the first collector of taxes for a city-state. *Mehujael* (Mechujael), "smitten of God" also implies a political chief and might. *Methusael* (Methushael) means "a man who is of God." His son Lamech is the name of two antediluvian patriarchs from an unused root of uncertain meaning. But the last king, Tubal-cain, carries both the meaning "to bring forth or produce" and "a lance or spear." The Genesis text clarifies this by stating Tubal-cain was an instructor of every artificer in bronze and iron. His name also implies wealth.

I will mention an interesting passage from the Epic of Gilgamesh that I believe refers to this past Cainite civilization. It has already been suggested by earlier writers that the life and exploits of Gilgamesh could parallel those of Nimrod. Gilgamesh is now recognized as an actual historical figure whose name appears on a king list of post-Flood leaders of early city-states.

The Bible correctly identifies these first cities built after the Flood as Babel, Erech, Accad, and Calneh. The city of Gilgamesh was Erech (Uruk), now found under the modern-day city of Warka, Iraq. This city is roughly datable to 3100 B.C.E. Some scholars consider him the twenty-eighth postdiluvian ruler reigning for 128 years, according to one king list, but we know him to be the son of Lugal-banda and the goddess Ninsun by tradition and thus he would be the third post-Flood King (Ham, Cush, Nimrod) or the second, according to the Uruk Apkallu List.

The city of Gilgamesh, we are told in the epic, was rebuilt upon the remains of a pre-Flood city discovered after the Deluge. Gilgamesh has rebuilt the walls upon the original foundations:

> Touch the stone threshold, which is ancient; draw near the Eanna, dwelling-place of the goddess Ishtar, a work no King among later Kings can match . . . as for its foundation, was it not laid down by the seven sages?

It is here, within the remains of the foundations and most likely from the tablets of the library in the Eanna that Gilgamesh had recovered, where he saw things secret, opened the hidden place . . . and found the copper tablet box. He had loosed the ring bolt made of bronze and opened the mouth to its secrets. He drew out the tablet of lapis lazuli and read it aloud: Gilgamesh, the lord of wisdom, who knew everything, carried back word of the time before the Flood.

I propose that the seven sages are none other than the seven patriarchs in the line of Cain, that Erech was built over the remains of a Cainite city, and that Gilgamesh, indeed all of the Sumerian people who refer to themselves as the "Black Headed People," are the descendants of Cain. I propose that their language is not Semitic because they are not from the line of Seth, and that the mother of Ham was Tubal-cain's sister Naamah, who was deified as the Sumerian Inanna and the Ishtar of Babylon.

As we return now to the days of Adam, the father of all living, three distinct lines have come forth: Cain, Abel, and Seth.

Cain's line possessed the birthright by virtue of his being the firstborn, and as we have seen, Cain means "possession."

The descendants of Abel still grew and prospered. I propose that Japheth represents this line.

But as found so many times in Hebrew literature, the firstborn does not always carry the blessings of his father. The right of possession did not follow the line of Cain as supposed, nor was it automatically transferred to the descendants of Abel. A new line was to receive the blessing of Adam, and that was the line of Seth. Shem represents this line.

A comparison of the names given the offspring of the lines of Cain and Seth as found in the KJV shows marked similarities, but not so many as supposed. In the Hebrew the names are quite different, the only exceptions being the names of Enoch and Lamech. This could allude to a serious squabble as to just who is in charge! The biblical account has little to say that would give us insight as to the accomplishments of the other lines but is most helpful with the line of Cain, listing its contributions toward civilization in city building, animal husbandry, music, and the forging of metals (Genesis 4:19–22).

The son born unto Adam after the murder of Abel was named Seth (Shayth, or Sheth) which means "substituted." This could mean "in place of Abel," but I rather think it applies to the birthright. The blessing of Cain as the firstborn would now be substituted. Seth's name also comes from the primary root "to appoint," to set or place above all.

Seth may have been a little bewildered as to what to make of the world situation during his time. The Cainites appear to have regarded their progenitor, Cain, as still possessing the birthright regardless of his murderous act and ultimate fall from his father's grace.

Seth begot his son at the age of 105, when Adam was 235 years old. He named his son Enos (Enosh), meaning "melancholy, desperate, sick, frail, and feeble," but most of all, woeful of the situation at hand.

It is at this point that my interest in the varying king lists peaks because while it would appear that this "sick, frail, and feeble" personage might not assume a reign as long as the others, Berosus gives him 13 Saroi or 156 years. To assume that the list of Berosus is correct above all the other lists would be groundless and in fact, due to the original being lost, should be in doubt. The other lists, baked on clay tablets impervious to time, or those carved on stone such as the Weld Prism, might be more accurate.

The only point I can be sure about is that the varying lists, when my theory of the day count is applied, show this period between 620 and 1520 years. These all fall within the Masoretic text and the era of 1656 years from Adam to the Flood.

Berosus gives only three Saroi or thirty-six years to the second king he lists. This may be not Seth but his son Enosh, the figures having been transposed in copying.

I mentioned in the beginning of this chapter that there was most likely a pre-king era that could have been as much as 216 years. If this is true as stated, we would find Adam, the Aloros of Berosus' list, proclaiming himself leader of the people about nineteen years before Enosh was born.

Berosus records the following:

> Aloros, a Chaldean from Babylon, was the first king of the land and he reigned for ten Saroi. They say that he spread the story about himself that the god appointed him shepherd of the people.

We can read a lot into the above statement. First it should be obvious why Berosus would like to link Aloros, the first king, to the Chaldeans of his day. The substitution of Babylon for Eridu as his city has also raised much comment.

It might also appear from the above that with the world's population what it was and everyone being quite aware of how their offspring are begotten, some may have viewed Adam's claim that he was *created* as someone special, a doubtful tale! Even Berosus seems to be hedging a bit at this point. It can be seen that the earliest generations may have doubted Adam's claims. It might have been Cain himself who thought it in his better interest to cast a shadow on the past. While Aloros tried to shepherd all of the people, apparently he only succeeded in reigning over the descendants of Seth.

But Aloros may in fact have assumed this position much

later in time. There is an enlightening discovery toward the end of this chapter should we propose that his reign may have begun some 26 Saroi since his creation, at age 312. I am more concerned with when this pre-Flood kingship ended than when it began. Aloros (Adam) reigned for 120 years.

Enosh begot his son Kenan (Cainan in the KJV), who would now "build and occupy" the land, as his name suggests. Aloros was already thirteen years into his reign and the land the Sethites were to occupy had been established.

There followed Mahalalel, meaning "praise of God" after the reigns of Alaparos, Amelon, and Ammenon. Berosus calls this patriarch Amegalaros. Jared is called Daonos, and Enoch becomes Euedorachos.

Enoch carries the same name and meaning as Cain's first-born, which I find most puzzling. Certainly they had not begun to run out of names so early on!

Enoch, listed as coming from Pautibiblon and Larak as shown on the two lists, is usually assigned as coming from the city of Sippar in other texts. He was accorded special prominence in late Babylonian tradition as one who had a divinatory technique by which the gods spoke to him. He was of course a Chaldean king, according to Berosus. Chaldee was Semitic as well as Akkadian and even Nebukadnezzar I claimed Enoch as his ancestor. The life of Enoch is a subject of much interest. He begot his son Methuselah at age sixty-five. In Hebrew *Methuselah* means "flying dart," missile of attack, sword, or weapon and there are some who claim it means "in his day it shall be sent."

There are apocryphal texts that lean toward this interpretation. These early books were read by the Apostolic Church and a portion of one is even quoted by Jude in verse 14.[3] It may be that Enoch had received warnings of the coming event that would cause the Flood. As long as Methuselah was alive the world would be safe. In his day (death) it would come.

Many of these works found in Coptic literature are fabrications of earlier works crammed full of erroneous teachings. A case in point is the Book of Enoch. In the Ethiopic version the book consists of five sections. Although some ten or more

---

[3] A direct quote from Enoch 1:9, 5:4, and 27:2.

fragmented copies were discovered at Qumran (IVQ) section two, the "Similitudes" on the son of man were mysteriously missing. Judging from the contents and the fact that it is missing from the earlier versions, this portion must be seen as a counterfeit produced by a first- or second-century Jewish Christian who revitalized the earlier writings to gain acceptance for his own ideas and gave the whole composition its present form. This late redactor condensed the portions on Enoch's journey to other worlds and a reckoning of the movements of the sun and the moon with so little interest that it is scarcely intelligible.

That is not to say that some of the earlier portions presently excluded from today's authorized versions are not resource for thought-provoking ideas. It is the originals or the closest thing to them we are after. I consider it a privilege to have worked under the direction of Joseph Patrick of the Hebrew University in excavating caves at Qumran in hopes of recovering more.

One of the more interesting traditions of these early writings relates that during the time of Jared, Enoch's father, the "watchers" descended from the heavenlies, approximately two hundred in number. Their leader Azazal was accused of having scattered over the earth the secrets of heaven. This event is spoken of in Genesis 6:4 KJV:

> There were giants in the earth in those days; and also after that, when the sons of God came in unto the daughters of men, and they bare children to them, the same became mighty men which were of old, men of renown.

At first this portion of Scripture is seemingly out of place in the narrative but should be seen as an overview of the condition of the earth during these antediluvian times. The statement is preceded by the thought that man is "flesh" in the earthly and carnal sense. The angels of God were not.

The mention of these "Nephilim" seems to be of interest to writers of late and needs clarification. Most expositors are unconsciously misled by the unfortunate translation "giants." *Nephilim* does not mean giants. It is from the Hebrew root *naphal,* "to be cast down as a fugitive from judgment." The giants were the "awful progeny" resulting from their union with the daughters of men! These offspring were known by various names but collectively as Rephaim.

The Bible leaves little doubt that fallen angels left their first estate (the spiritual realm in the heavenlies) and were successful in hybridizing a new race outside the original plan.

The record of these abominations is followed by this summation in Genesis 6:5 KJV:

> And God saw that the wickedness of man was great in the earth and that every imagination of the thoughts of his heart was only evil continually.

We have looked into the probable cause of the Flood and the mechanics that produced it. The above, then, was the reason for it:

> And it repented the Lord that he had made man on the earth, and it grieved him at his heart. And the Lord said, I will destroy man whom I have created from the face of the earth . . . for it repenteth me that I have made them.
>
> Genesis 6:6, 7 KJV

The Bible plainly declares that in pre-Flood times, and also for a brief period after the Flood, the earth was visited by extraterrestrials. They took up residence on the earth, having direct dealings with man. If the comment by Jesus in Matthew 24:37 ("as the days of Noah were") can be taken in this regard, then we might be looking toward a close encounter with the Nephilim in the near future.

During Enoch's day the extraterrestrials are said to have been revealing eternal secrets which fallen man was not meant to discover. This, and their hybridizing of the human race, eventually brought about a host from the heavenlies to remove them from the earth. Despite Enoch's accusations against the Nephilim, he was approached to mediate on their behalf. When the angels that "kept not their first estate" were confronted with their like that had not fallen, the Nephilim were reproached by the new arrivals who stated that angels were created to intercede for man and not the other way around.

This appears to have been an ongoing battle during pre-

Flood times, when the Nephilim were constantly being removed from the earth, for . . .

> . . . God spared not the angels that sinned, but cast them down to hell
> and delivered them into chains of darkness, to be reserved unto
> judgment.
>
> 2 Peter 2:4 KJV

The Epistle of Jude further clarifies their sin as taking up
residency on the earth:

> And the angels which kept not their first estate, but left their own
> habitation, he hath reserved in everlasting chains under darkness
> unto the judgment of the great day.
>
> Jude 6 KJV

For the Sadducees among us (Acts 23:8) who believe there is
no resurrection or angel or spirit, it is not unworthy of notice
that records of the Sumerians tell of gods descending from the
stars and Sanskrit texts where the ancients record "gods"
begetting, with women of earth, children with the supernat-
ural learning abilities and skills of their celestial fathers. Berosus lists them as well, and names them. They are called the
Apkallu, and his account is but one of many. This was so
important to Berosus that his concept of civilization *before* the
Flood was a result of revelation from divine messengers, over
time, and not human action to be explained in naturalistic
terms.

And all the days of Enoch were 365 years, states the biblical
account, and Berosus gives him a reign of 18 Saroi, or 216
years.

We now come to Amempsinos or Methuselah, "in whose
day (death) it shall be sent." Although Methuselah is the oldest
living patriarch, given an age of 969 years in the Genesis
account, Berosus gives him a reign of only 10 Saroi, or 120
years. His son Otiartes reigns 8 Saroi, or 96 years, and is
Lam-ech, father of Noah, the Xisouthros of the Berosus account in whose reign the Flood inundated the land.

The Babylonian counterpart of the biblical Noah, the just
man who was spared the fate of wicked mankind, is called in

the Akkadian tongue Utnapishtim. The name seems to mean "I have found life" or "he who has found life."

In earlier versions, Noah is given the epithet of Atra-hasîs, meaning "exceedingly wise." Thus the Xisouthros of Berosus is simply the graecized form of our original Flood hero of the earliest Sumerian accounts, Zi-u-sudra, or "life of long days."

This Zi-u-sudra is listed as the last pre-Flood king of the earliest Sumerian king lists, the son of Ubar-Tutu. He was given a reign by the Sumerians, according to scholars, of 36,000 years. But taking this figure and applying my theory of the 300-day solar year prior to the Flood, it can be seen that this period of 10 Saroi is 120 years.

Thus the biblical account of Genesis 6:3 KJV (author's italics) takes on its full meaning:

> And the Lord said, My spirit shall not always strive with man, for that he also is flesh: yet his days shall be an *hundred and twenty years.*

We can now see that it was at the very beginning of the reign of Zi-u-sudra, the Akkadian Utnapishtim, that "he found life" or salvation from the impending judgment, for as Noah found grace in the eyes of the Lord, he became enlightened to the fate of mankind and "exceedingly wise" to the coming event. Utnapishtim, at the direction of E'a, "the Lord," or "word God" (John 1:1–14), prepared himself an Ark of salvation for the saving of himself and his house. This Ark is called in one account *na-si-rat na-pis-tu,* the "life saver."

Subtracting 120 years from the Flood date, we can see that Noah was 480 years old when he began his reign as king and patriarchal leader of the Sethites. This is a period of 144,000 days. Although his father, Lam-ech, is listed by Berosus as Otiartes, the king preceding the last in whose day the Flood came, there is a discrepancy from the Sumerian list that needs explanation.

The Sumerian lists Zi-u-sudra (Noah) as the son of Ubar-Tutu. This is not Lam-ech but Methuselah. This is confirmed by both the Sumerian list and the list of Berosus, giving both Ubar-Tutu and Amempsinos a reign of ten Saroi. Why then does the Sumerian list omit Lam-ech by stating that the last surviving king prior to the Flood was Ubar-Tutu? Because according to biblical chronology, Lam-ech had died five years before the Flood. Thus Methuselah was the last surviving king. He was not the father but the grandfather of Zi-u-sudra, who "in his day it shall be sent."

According to my hypothesis, Methuselah died exactly seven days prior to the Flood date, which may account for the statement in Genesis 7:4, "For yet seven days, and I will cause it to rain upon the earth," referring to seven days of mourning. A better interpretation might have been, "When he is dead, it shall be sent," and the death of Methuselah in the six hundredth year of Noah's life, second month, tenth day, sealed the fate of unbelieving mankind. Noah was directed to load the Ark and prepare for the end (Genesis 7:1–5).

In seven days the effect of the astral vistor's approach to the earth began taking its toll and the reigns of the antediluvians were over.

It will be noted by the careful scholar that the Sumerian lists Zi-u-sudra's reign as 10 Saroi. This exactly coincides with the biblical account of 120 years. However, the list of Berosus gives Xisouthros a reign of 18 Saroi. This seeming contradiction presents no problem when it is remembered that the reign of the last king was *interrupted* by the Flood. Noah reigned 10 Saroi before the Flood, as did his grandfather Methuselah, and continued to shepherd his family and their offspring for 8 Saroi after the Flood, as did his father before his passing. The Saros, if we could consider the earth stable at 360 days to the year during this early period of precession (which I find difficult to accept), could still contain the same day count of 3,600, but this would be a passing of 10 years rather than 12. Berosus states: "Cronus appeared to Xisouthros in a dream and revealed that on the fifteenth day of the month Daisios mankind would be destroyed by a flood."

Scofield lists in his biblical notes that the Flood occurred on the seventeenth of May. I find both judgments difficult to believe. For one thing, Daisios or May being the fifth month today should be in question if assuming it to be Dystrus of the Macedonian calendar. Instead it would appear to be Daesius, the eighth month. The problems are compounded by the Babylonian calendar that celebrated the New Year in March or April, while the Macedonian celebrated the New Year in

October. The calendar during the time of Berosus was the Seleucid, which varied among different ethnic and religious groups. The Greeks celebrated the New Year in Greece September 1 while the Greeks in Syria celebrated on October 9. Personally, I find it about as important as carrying a dead reckoning position to five points past the decimal, and I am satisfied that it occurred in the second month, seventeenth day, in the six hundredth year of Noah's life. I only wish Noah had mentioned what year it was!

Berosus appears quite positive about the astronomical event that caused the Flood and about a future event.

> Some suppose that in the final catastrophe the earth too will be shaken and through clefts in the ground will uncover sources of fresh rivers which will flow forth from their full source in large volume. I, Berosus, interpreter of Belus, affirm that all the earth inherits will be consigned to flame when the five planets assemble in Cancer, so arranged in one row that a straight line may pass through their spheres. When the same gathering takes place in Capricorn, then we are in danger of the Deluge.

Prior to this event, possibly on the very day of his establishment as the head of the Sethites, Noah received the revelation of this coming upheaval and found himself in a position to provide the labor and material for construction of the Ark and devise the system to regenerate the complete genus of man for the new age. His three wives would represent the line of Seth, the line of Abel, and the line of Cain. It is my conviction that Naamah, sister of Tubal-cain, was the mother of Ham, Japheth was the ancestor of Abel, and Shem was the ancestor of Seth.

It may be that the other wives of Noah did not come aboard, and some of his own unbelieving children. The Koran (23:28) states, " . . . and the members of your household, except those of them already doomed. Do not plead with me for those who have done wrong: they shall be drowned. And when you and all your followers have gone aboard. . . . "

The Koran explicitly mentions members of Noah's family who would not board: "Noah cried out to his son, who stood apart: 'Embark with us, my child,' he said. 'Do not stay with the unbelievers!' He replied: 'I shall seek refuge in a mountain, which will protect me from the Flood.' . . . And thereupon the billows rolled between them, and Noah's son was drowned" (Sura Houd 40).[4] But the sons that did board are spoken of as representing nations or distinct lines . . . "blessings upon thee and on the *nations* with thee" (Houd 50).[5]

The three sons of Noah who did board then represented the nations or lines of Cain, Abel, Seth, and other distinct racial groups that existed before the Flood.

Tablet XI, column i of the Sîn-leqi-unninnī version (line 85)[6] says that even "the children of all the craftsmen I drove aboard." According to Babylonian texts, the Ark was to be loaded with grains and provisions, furniture and riches. Other versions call for Noah to forsake his riches and leave them behind. Obviously, much of his wealth would serve no purpose in the new world. He was to bring his men servants, maid servants, and their young. Although Berosus records that Xisouthros was to embark with his kin and closest friends, another researcher has turned up a Persian document that restricts those having pointed teeth from coming aboard![7]

The Scriptures imply there were only eight aboard, though that hardly seems likely given the size of the vessel and the tasks involved in manning it, not to mention caring for the animals. The story seems to have taken on further embellishments since the earlier texts. While the King James Version seemed satisfied with simply "all the cattle that was with him in the ark" (Genesis 8:1), modern expositors and revisionist committees seem bent on making the word *be-hay-maw,* a dumb beast, fit all categories. The reference to every living thing, which the NIV regretfully chooses to translate "wild animals," may not have been anything of the sort to conjure up images of the San Diego Zoo but the beasts of the field such as game animals, ibex, elk, and wild hog; for the most part,

---

[4]N. J. Dawood, *The Koran* (Bungay, Suffolk, Great Britain: Chaucer Press Ltd., 1956).

[5]A. J. Arberry, *The Koran* (New York: Macmillan Publishing Co., Inc., 1955).

[6]John Gardner and John Maier, *Gilgamesh* (New York: Alfred A. Knopf, Inc., © 1984).

[7]Charles Berlitz, *Doomsday 1999* (New York: Doubleday & Co., Inc. 1981).

domesticated animals for milk, hide, meat, and wool, as well as fowl for the palate and the unclean scavengers for necessity.

There are numerous texts naming others aboard that pre-date the writings of Moses in several cases, naming their functions. The Babylonians refer to Buzur (a good name for a sailor), and Uragal, who both helped in handling the anchor lines for the "braking stones." There was the boatman from the epic of Gilgamesh who brought aboard the shars of oil, who may be Urshanabi, the boatman who stayed with Utna-pishtim in his old age. Other indicators found today, such as the tomb of Noah's sister in Syria and the tomb of Noah's mother in Iran (Marand), indicate there were more than eight, so a dogmatic approach toward the crew and passenger list and the types of animals carried aboard should be avoided.

Much of the Hebrew folklore on the voyage is responsible for later misconstrued concepts of this actual event and for the children's books depicting the Ark as a floating zoo. The Jewish notion that Og the giant saved himself by clinging to the roof is just one more fable that should be viewed with amusement. In closing, the lengths of reigns listed by Berosus and his chronology is a creditable document in this regard when my hypothesis is applied, buttressing Moses' version, which I still feel is a more accurate account.

Regretfully, the publishers of the NIV[8] furnish the Bible reader with the erroneous conclusion that this is the Greek legend according to Berosus, when in fact we have seen it to be the Babylonian account, furnished *to* the Greeks.

THE CHINESE CONNECTION

Other cultures have a similar number of mythical kings or legendary rulers prior to the Deluge. In India we meet the nine Brahmadikas who, with Brahma, their founder, make up the ten petris, or fathers. Are they referring to the ten patriarchs in

---

[8]Oxford New International Version Scofield Study Bible (New York: Oxford University Press, 1984), footnote p. 11.

the line of Seth, as do the Arabs with their ten kings of the Adites?

We should not find it surprising then that the Chinese had their ten emperors as well, partakers of the divine nature (longevity?) before the dawn of historical times. Hemmed in by the largest ocean, the highest mountains, and one of the most extensive deserts in the world, the Chinese have remained isolated from their neighboring barbarians to boast an unbroken line of history for over forty-five hundred years. Sealed off from outside influences, China was known as Tien-hua, "under the heavens," and blessed by the one god, the supreme heavenly ruler known as Shang Ti, remaining monotheists with a strict moral code and no idols for some two thousand years.

Who are the Chinese? Where did they come from? These questions and more were brought to the front by C. H. Kang in his 1950 publication, *Genesis and the Chinese,* and are now revealed in a most interesting study of the Chinese ideographic system of relaying written information. In collaboration with Ethel R. Nelson,[9] the work provides convincing evidence that within the pictographic characters is the same Genesis story found in Judeo-Christian traditions.

八 + 廾 + 一 + 共 + 氵 = 洪

EIGHT + UNITED + EARTH = TOTAL .... + WATER = FLOOD

Selecting just two examples within the Flood account, it can be seen there were thought to be *eight* survivors within both words for the Ark and the Flood itself.

舟 八 口 船

VESSEL + EIGHT + MOUTH = BOAT

According to Sir William Jones, other undisputed sources of authenticity suggest the Chinese considered the Flood a world-

---

[9]C. H. Kang and Ethel R. Nelson, *The Discovery of Genesis* (St. Louis: Concordia Publishing House, 1979).

wide event, not a local flood. It so devastated the land that after several generations some descendants of the survivors regressed to living like beasts, eating raw flesh and knowing their mothers but not their fathers, a trait not exclusive to the ancients or the Chinese, remarks Durant.[10]

Although Kang and Nelson adhere to today's strict interpretations of the Bible's chronological dating of the Flood circa 2450, I would suggest another option. The Dresden Codex, best preserved of the four Mayan manuscripts, is considered a calendar of events of this fourth age beginning in the year 3113 on 09/09 (Nancy K. Owen). Other calendric data suggests the year 3114 on 08/11. There is some dispute about this date, which some scholars consider as late as 3104, but all appear to be in the general area of agreement. If this is a true period for the Flood, it fits nicely for early Sumerian cultures and pyramid building in Egypt. In my chronology, the dispersal from Babel occurred in the days of Peleg (101 to 340 post-Flood), most likely between Peleg's age of 150 to 160.

This would coincide with Fu-Hsi's arrival into Sz-hai, "within the four seas" in precisely 2852 B.C. The Chinese place his entry near Lake Balkat, a short distance from the Caspian Sea.

---

[10]Will Durant, *Our Oriental Heritage* (New York: Simon & Schuster, 1954).

4

Return to the Ark

RESHIT

My second look at the Ark came in June of 1985. The snows were gone and the hills were alive in color. Water could be heard gushing everywhere in the fissures of the flow. The remains of the Ark, held fast in the earth's grip through the centuries, diverted these waters again around her streamlined hull. Erosion of the alluvial cover, which had hidden and protected her throughout the ages, appeared to be making the giant form rise above the landscape. Even from a great distance one's eye was drawn to the strange sight of a ship on the mountain.

The words of a farmer named Reshit came to me again: "It is not a stone formation! I know a ship when I see one."

Many have claimed to have found the Ark. Years ago, a flamboyant character named Prince John Joseph Nouri from Trichur, India, calling himself the Archdeacon of Babylon, reported that he had located the holy relic on his third attempt. In the typical Barnum fashion of his day, representing himself now as the Archbishop of the Christian Nestorian Church, he stunned his listeners at the World Parliament of Religions in Chicago in 1893 with his vivid account of his climb on Ararat. He had made his discovery of the long sought-after Ark on April 25 some six years before.

His listeners took a rather dim view of his tale as he related its length of nine hundred feet. Had he conducted more research and described his find in more traditional values, he most likely would have met with success in soliciting funds to salvage the hulk and display it at the coming World's Fair.

Thus the double-edged sword of Christendom fell on him who would claim to have found a biblical truth, but alas, outside its inerrant measure. The story died quickly after publication in the *Zion's Watchtower* article of August 15, 1894, only to be resurrected by Eryl Cummings as a credible witness to the Ark's being seen on Ararat. The Ararat climbers of today still continue their search.

With the coming of the whoppers that followed, namely the Roskovitsky and Hagopian eyewitness accounts related in Cummings' continuing research, the short but interesting story of Reshit pales in significance. No one even knew his full name.

According to Cummings, the Turkish newspapers had made the report on November 13, 1948, of a man named Reshit who had seen "the petrified remains of an object which peasants insist resembles a ship high on Mount Ararat." But to me, Reshit's statements appeared to be saying it was *not* on Ararat!

I read the story again more carefully. The reporter, Edwin Greenwald, had gotten his story from a sixty-nine-year-old farmer named Shukra Asena. This was his report as told by Cummings:

> A Kurdish farmer named Reshit about two months prior had been climbing, two-thirds up the 16,000-foot peak, when he noticed something he had never seen before, although he had been up the mountains many times. A ship's prow protruded from a canyon down which tons of melting snow and ice had been rushing for more than two months.

There were of course suggestions that Cummings had taken certain liberties in relating what the article had actually said. The obvious question as to why a farmer should feel compelled to climb Ararat at all, or claim to know these dangerous canyons well, is a bit mystifying.

But then a statement from the old farmer, Asena, who was relating the story to the reporter, was even more mystifying.

> There is no folklore there about the Ark and persons who saw Reshit's find came away in great surprise.

Why should Shukra Asena relate such a statement from the villagers that they were surprised to find the Ark at that location? Of course the folklore of the Ark being on Ararat was well established. Could this be a clue that Reshit's find was not on the mountain of legend? Had the reporter just assumed that Asena had meant Ararat?

An expedition was sent out from the United States to the north slope of Ararat the following spring. Cummings' narrative suggests that the villagers were suspicious and uncooperative, responding simply by saying nothing to these outsiders. Climbers of Ararat in search of the Ark seem to be continually running into these situations which they perceive as conspiracies of silence frustrating their Christian cause due to Moslem intent on keeping the location a secret, preventing the holy relic from being defiled by infidels and the like.

Although the villagers had said they knew of no such person named Reshit or any new discovery, the expedition returned home firm in their belief that the Kurds were hiding something and the Ark lay high on the slopes above.

This still appears to be the root of their problem! No doubt Reshit was faithfully waiting on the north slope of Akyayla, some twenty miles south of the expedition, with hot tea and yogurt. It must have been very painful for him to discover that Christendom isn't interested in the Ark's being anywhere but Ararat.

I stood there with Reshit's words rolling over in my mind. This was indeed two-thirds up the mountain from the valley floor below. The media, or someone, had embellished the story. Believing the Ark to be on Ararat, naturally they envisioned a deep canyon down which tons of ice and snow would be melting, but even that would be suspect at only slightly over thirteen hundred feet. That would be two-thirds of the way up from the valley floor.

And wouldn't a farmer be in his fields? Why would he be climbing Mount Ararat several months prior to the onslaught of winter? Shouldn't he be down on the plains? The contour of the *earth,* Reshit had said, indicated the *invisible* part of the object was *shaped like a ship!* That was one of the things the fundamentalists held against this object. It wasn't rectangular.

Reshit had described a boat-shaped object *outlined* or *contoured* in the earth! He insisted it was not simply a rock formation.

Could this be Reshit's find? Perhaps when it first appeared it was not so prominent, and wasn't it still being called a rock formation by the doubters?

In the trips that were to follow, I would always suggest this. I had no proof, but I had always wondered just when it did make its appearance. The timing could have great implications. And I wondered if Reshit could ever be found.

It would be exactly a year later that I would seek him out. I would guess at his surname and be correct on all counts.

THE UPPER VALLEY

Even though there is much to spark one's interest in the flow area itself, the rushing waters drowned out all but my thoughts as I continued the climb to the Ark again. The acute angle of the slope was such that just keeping my eyes straight ahead was enough to decide the proper course to take through the fissures from the quake that had exposed, here and there, broken shards of a bygone day. They stood out, red in the sun, then darkened in the fleeting shadows of the birds soaring silently overhead. I found myself suddenly dwarfed by the unnatural sight of the bows of a great ship thrust from the loam in defiance of age and erosion. The remains are an awesome sight to the unexpecting.

But my anger toward those who reject it is mirrored by its jutting protrusion. How badly I wanted the others involved in the search to share these moments with me. Didn't they understand that no one would find the Ark on his own? It hadn't been lost but was hidden, to be revealed in the timing of him who orchestrates all such events in the history of man.

The amomum grew in such profusion that I bent down to inspect it more closely. When I first saw it, it had been nothing more than a strange dried stalk with long thorns. Now it grew in such abundance and vitality that it was difficult to pass through the area without getting barbed.

Surely this had not been brought aboard the Ark as fodder

for the animals. I tried unsuccessfully to pull it out to inspect the root, but as was written almost five thousand years earlier, it "pricked the hand of the gatherer."

Suddenly a young Kurdish boy stood by me with a knife in his hand and a smile. "Diken!"[1] he exclaimed, and deftly knelt down, cutting it loose from the ground. Placing the sole of his boot against the barbs he stripped the stalk, washed it in water nearby, and handed it to me. I paused cautiously. "It won't hurt me?" "Tamom!" he replied encouragingly, sticking out his chest and patting his bicep.

I ate willingly. It was not an unpleasant taste but certainly hard to describe. I had never tasted anything quite like it before. My little friend was named Musa, and that day he was given the job of searching out the grandest stalks and stripping them down with his knife. I consumed them on the spot, reflecting on how I had succeeded in finding that elixir of youth that had eluded such great figures as Alexander himself.

Who knew, I thought, perhaps in the winters ahead, erosion would reveal the Ark in spite of man's unwillingness to see it. The mud encasing the columns would fall to the ground in the heat of summers that followed, and I would be there to see it. It could take many seasons, but I would return. Man's quest for the truth is as timeless as the Ark is ageless in itself, and I had eaten of the plant of Utnapishtim, the "old man will be young," and I hoped it would be so.

The weather was perfect and would permit us to explore the area until we were exhausted. I was anxious to see many of the things Ron had described to me during our visit in the snows of March, but due to the cold and the ground cover we were unable to investigate.

Ron's scenario was that the Ark had originally landed at a higher elevation in a valley above the flow. And there, so he claimed, was to be found the remains of a settlement for the pilgrims who had journeyed to the holy site in ages past. Whether or not Ron had actually been there before to see this was not clear and he hedged around this discovery as though it were a secret of sorts.

A clue I had uncovered that might lend credence to this idea

---

[1]Meaning "thorny plant."

was a point on the escarpment above this valley called Ziyaret Dağ, which meant "voluntary pilgrimage" mount. I had noted this while working out Berosus' position for the Ark, but it was some 3.5 miles from the site and almost 2 miles from the valley above the Ark to the east. However, this was of great interest to me, for not only had the Kurds been recorded on video during our last trip saying "Meshur" (well known and famous) when Ron pointed up the mountain but Ron had also seen building blocks in the small village near the Ark site which he believed had come from the settlement above. While having tea in his guide's house he had noticed a block in the wall with some strange writing on it, and placing his host just to the side of it had taken movie film of both without making an issue of it. If this material was from the valley above and there were more to be seen there, then one might suggest that to be the place where the Ark had originally landed.

But first things first. I wanted to see the anchor stones that Ron had pointed out to me across the flow. There was also to be seen there, he claimed, a monument with stick figures representing Noah and his family. Ron certainly seemed to have the whole bag of evidence wrapped up.

Accompanying us on his first trip to Turkey was Dr. John Baumgardner, a card-carrying scientist from New Mexico. His area of expertise was, among other things, geophysics, considered high in the pecking orders of science. With the precise analytical instruments and computer banks at Los Alamos National Laboratory, John had a lot to offer the project. I do not know what originally motivated John to come look at this object himself. He had already purchased his ticket and was going on his own when he phoned Ron to ask if he would be there as well and said he would like to meet him. At Ron's request, I had juggled my flight to meet him in Germany, and as it turned out, Ron was able to get a leave of absence from work so we could all go to the site together.

I was very pleased that a scientist of John's standing would take the time on his own to investigate the possibility that the Ark had been found. Although he was an amiable person, I must admit his motive may have been to debunk the site as others had in the past. He certainly was along for a critical and hard look at the evidence, if there was any, and I might add, quite ready to go it alone if not with us. He said that a brief look at the topography in the area might settle the question quite quickly.

There were not many men like John in scientific circles. Most of them would not consider that abhorrent term *catastrophism* being used again in the twentieth century. Usually it was brought up in classrooms of uniformitarianism to inject a little humor. Those who interpreted much of what they saw in the geological record to be the results of a flood reminiscent of the Noachian Deluge were considered on the lunatic fringe of science or espousing revealed truth of the fundamentalists.

Although these thoughts carry religious overtones, John's decisions are based on objective data and rational processes and his view is that truth is truth – in whatever realm.

But in fact, John's views were really not so out of date. Much of the research of the nineteenth century is as good today as it was 150 years ago. Baron Georges Cuvier, one of the greatest naturalists of all time, wrote in 1817:

> These repeated advances and retreats of the sea have neither been slow nor gradual; most of the catastrophes which have occasioned them have been sudden; and this is easily proved, especially with regard to the last of them, the traces of which are most conspicuous. . . . Life therefore, has often been disturbed on this earth by terrible events. Calamities which, at their commencement, have perhaps moved and overturned to a great depth the entire outer crust of the globe . . . numberless living things have been the victims of these catastrophes.

So despite the Darwinian/Lyellian mind-set of today and the knee-jerk defenses to the term *catastrophism,* some brilliant scientists, such as paleontologist David Raup, are reawakening the scientific community with the ancient spirit of speculation.[2]

While I agree that extraterrestrial causes for these events cannot be ruled out, and indeed submit that they were the cause of the Flood, Baumgardner feels that it needn't be so. In 1977 Al Fischer, professor of paleontology at Princeton Uni-

[2]David M. Raup, *The Nemesis Affair: A Story of the Death of Dinosaurs and the Ways of Science* (New York: W. W. Norton & Company, 1986).

versity, and his associate, Mike Arthur, considered the ultimate driving force within the earth itself, having to do with
unknown cycles of convection in the earth's interior rather
than an outside influence. Baumgardner, also of Princeton,
became interested in this correlation with the biblical Flood
and the mechanics that may have caused it. He was able to do
his doctoral dissertation at Los Alamos. There he developed a
three-dimensional spherical hydrodynamics code ideally
suited for stimulating global tectonic upheaval by applying the
code to the problem of thermal convection within the earth's
mantle, which would appear to be sustaining continental drift
to some slight degree.

All of these theories are quite interesting in light of the fact
that even as late as the 1960s, Wegener was an anathema to
the American geology student. His theories of plate tectonics
now prevail.

I must admit I was a bit envious of Baumgardner's background, and in my ignorance, wary of yet another geological
opinion. Ships, I felt, were the domain of those with nautical
backgrounds and in all my years in the marine salvage industry I had never needed the guidance of a "rock doctor." But
then, I wasn't an expert on Noah's Ark either! Perhaps there
were none—just three people with varying degrees of ignorance anxious to accelerate archaeological inquiry into our area
of interest.

Baumgardner was quite awed by his first encounter. "It
most certainly doesn't appear to be natural," he said. I was
pleased with his first impression. I liked John already!

That is not to say there weren't disagreements from the
start. The first issue was the flow. Ron had this fire-
and-brimstone scenario which John cut short by asking where
was the lava or the fissure that produced this outflowing. It
appeared to be only an alluvial slippage from above. I was not
close enough to geology to render an opinion but suggested
that perhaps with thunder clouds forming across the valley
and the chance of rain in the afternoon we should take this
opportunity to climb the slope now and if cut off later in the
day we could confine our explorations closer to the Ark and
civilization. So we began our trek with the possibility in mind

that the original strike point of the Ark might have been at a higher elevation and at some point in time it had been brought down to this secondary position, caught on the outcropping, and became covered with mud.

We began this trek by a circuitous route in search of a large five-ton stone with stick figures on it and anchor stones Ron had pointed out to me in the snows of March some distance away that we were unable to investigate on the first visit.

After a considerable length of time wandering about in circles, I was becoming convinced that either Ron was endowed with a terrible sense of direction or he had never been to this area before and was only hoping that something of interest could be found there.

I remember mumbling something about O. Henry's, "true adventurer who goes forth aimless and incalculating to meet and greet his unknown fate," when Ron whirled around with the answer to my question that due to his keen interest in the objects at an earlier time, they must have been spirited away by the Kurds!

I was beginning to see that it was rare indeed to encounter anything but a firm conclusion from Ron, and we pushed on up the flow, looking closely for anything resembling a debris trail of the Ark's structure and his lost city in the clouds.

The Kurds accompanying us were a bit puzzled as to what we were searching for. To them the object of interest lay below, so I made rumbling sounds like an earthquake and depicted the Ark riding down the slope to their village, then pointed up to the source of the flow and the peak of the escarpment high above. "Cudi" (Judi), replied the village elder with a smile. I literally reeled from the significance of his response.

Dilaver pushed to the front and excitedly repeated the word. "Cudi," he almost demanded from the old man. "David," he said, as if to begin an explanation, then remembering he couldn't speak English, he turned away with a grin of satisfaction and engaged the Kurds in a pandemonium of excited conversation.

I gave a thumbs up and a "Çok Güzel." It was very, very good! It was the mount of the Ark of the Koran.

A voice cried out: "Earth, swallow up your waters. Heaven, cease your rain!" The floods abated and Allah's will was done. The ark came to rest upon Al-Judi.

Houd Sura 11:44

JUDI, JUDI, JUDI

The fact that the western peak of this escarpment above the Ark was called Judi (spelled Cudi in Turkish but pronounced the same) by the local Kurdish/Turks of the area posed more problems rather than eliminating the uncertainty surrounding the name.

Samran Al Mutary, who was no longer with us for this June expedition, had met with the same problem at home. When Ron and I had visited him at Tabuk, in the northwestern section of Saudi Arabia, we were met with objections from his Islamic brethren that the Ark could not possibly be in Turkey, for the Mount Judi of the Koran and the final resting place of "Safina et Nuh" (Noah's Ark in Arabic) was in Arabia. It would appear that the world is full of "flint-headed fundamentalists," and I can imagine the theological debate between Arab and Turk as to whose country contains the true Mount Judi. Arabia had one, now Turkey had four!

My position on the true location of Judi was simple. Since Musa (Moses) was considered a true prophet of God by Mohammed, his writings or compilations of early records stating that the Ark came to rest in Urartu (Ararat) narrowed the choice down to two mounts in Turkey. The present state of affairs now suggested four sites in Turkey, as we shall soon see.

To the Christian fundamentalist, however, these pose no problems whatever, for there is only one site of the Ark, and that is the great Mount Ararat itself.

I settled this question long ago, but I must relate to the reader a classic piece of bungling by the Ark hunters before me. It is told here not to belittle the efforts of others in seeking the Ark but to serve as an example of the logic employed by the experts in evaluating the facts that have kept them from finding the Ark!

It begins with a popular story among the Ararat group that is still considered by them an eyewitness account of a sighting of the Ark during World War I. It is related by Cummings as yet another example of how the forces of evil continue to thwart all efforts to locate the Ark on Ararat. The cause is not so diabolical as they imagine, but simply poor research and reasoning. Violet Cummings, in her book *Has Anybody Really Seen Noah's Ark?* begins the fascinating account of how her husband, Eryl, the "father of Ark hunters" of our time and the most experienced researcher of them all, came across a letter describing the event.

It seems that in 1945/46 a Turkish newspaper had released a story of a proposed American expedition bound for Turkey in search of the Ark. Five Turkish war veterans read the news item with interest. These Americans would be in need of guides. It was agreed that they should offer their services in the form of a letter, to spark the Americans' interest, and present it to the American Embassy. The contents of the letter are given by Cummings as follows:

> When returning from World War I, I and five or six of my friends passed by the Ararat. We saw Noah's Ark leaning against the mountain. I measured the length of the boat. It was 150 paces long. It had three stories. I read in the papers that an American group is looking for this boat. I wish to inform you that I shall personally show this boat and I request your intervention so that I may show the boat.

It is clear that this letter was written some thirty years after their "discovery" of the Ark, and kept secret by all five, or was it six, the writer tries to recall, awaiting the right moment to spring it on the world, if only they were allowed to personally lead the expedition to it and receive their just reward. The description was verifiable by the Genesis text, sure to have its desired effect, and with local folklore a fanciful piece could be constructed before the foreigners arrived.

The proposed expedition never reached fruition and the letter languished in the files for years until August 1966, when by chance Eryl Cummings saw it. Cummings was ecstatic. He accepted the letter and its contents as genuine, and felt it fully corroborated the sighting in Colonel Alexander's account of Roskovitsky's discovery of the Ark high on Ararat around the same year.

Cummings, however, was a little puzzled by the fact that Mount Ararat in 1915 was in Russia!

What the Turkish soldiers were doing passing across the peak of Ararat on their journey home from Baghdad to Adana, where by chance they noticed the Ark "leaning against the mountain" did not seem to disturb him. "There seems no reason to doubt the authenticity of their discovery," noted Eryl Cummings.

Now let's look at some historical facts. In the winter of 1915 the British captured Baghdad and threw the Turks into a hasty retreat. The Russians, allies with the British, fortified their southern borders. These five or six Turkish soldiers, miles behind enemy lines, simply strolled across Ararat on their detour of 1,680 kilometers, crossing the border twice on their way home *in the dead of winter!*

It is pointless to reiterate more of the story except to say that by now, some twenty years after the letter was written and fifty-one years after the event, Cummings was hot on the trail, doggedly seeking out the soldiers who claimed this remarkable discovery.

By 1966, all the soldiers were long dead, but Cummings succeeded in locating the scribe who had composed the letter. The scribe, now in his seventies, recalled the details of the story so vividly, he was sure he could lead a party to the Ark even though he had never actually been to the site. In corresponding with this elderly gentleman, one of Cummings' translators noted that the scribe was not referring to Ararat but to a hill called Cudi. This contemporary translator further explained it is stated in the Koran, the Moslem Holy Book, that Noah's Ark came to rest on Mount Judi.

With this vital piece of information, Cummings made an astounding statement in light of the fact that he was considered by others a creditable researcher:

It is known of course, that these words – and also Al Judi – are interchangeable, and all mean the same thing. At the time it took a lot of persistent digging to ferret out this choice and important bit of information.[3]

Only those who persisted in putting all sightings on Ararat could reach such a conclusion. The letter of 1946 did indeed prefix the name of the mount with "the," not generally done with the name Ararat but common with the Arabic term Al Judi.

Other researchers before me have convincingly debunked Cummings' documented eyewitness accounts as unsupported. John Montgomery labored through a literary labyrinth of sources and correspondence with relatives of those involved to discover prime characters were not even in the Caucasus during 1916 but were living in Paris from 1902 through the Second World War. The myths were exploded as early as 1972,[4] yet Cummings persists. It is an embarrassing reality that the original Roskovitsky story was a complete fabrication by one Benjamin Allen, used to raise supportive funds for the Sacred History Research Expedition (SHRE) back in the early forties. Even today this piece of fiction continues to draw interest from those who would fund contemporary Ark hunters with vivid imaginations on an all-expenses-paid mountaineering vacation at Christendom's expense.

The particular story I have related was discarded by me soon after reading it in 1983, through the use of a simple road map. My assessment of the soldiers' true homeward trek can be followed on the map by a dotted line. Here we discover the source of the confusion.

The soldiers, in passing by Silopi, a little town south of Şirnak, are now only 682 kilometers east of Adana, and home. Can the reader see the name of the mountain they passed by? It is called Cudi Dağı, the Al Judi of the Koran (in the minds of the Moslems from this area). But if one is inclined to have the mount of the Ark in his area, then further to the west, some 342 kilometers, just below Urfa, is another Cudi Dağı. Now if

---

[3]Violet Cummings, *Has Anybody Really Seen Noah's Ark?* (San Diego: Creation-Life Publishers, 1982), p. 107.

[4]John Warwick Montgomery, *The Quest for Noah's Ark* (Minneapolis: Bethany Fellowship Inc., 1972).

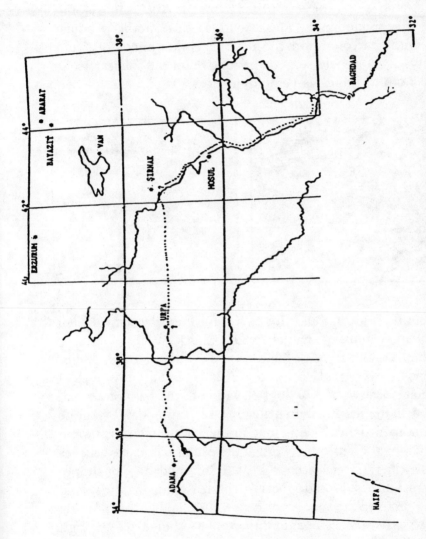

Fasold theory: the trek of the Turkish soldiers in 1915 was from Baghdad to Adana, but an indirect route was necessary to avoid capture by the enemy. For explanation of question marks, see maps on page 98.

97

one is good, then two are better! Unfortunately, both are as
bare of remains of the Ark as Ararat.

At this point, I believe the reader will admit that some of my
predecessors haven't done their homework. Did the soldiers
pass by Al Judi? Yes! And probably twice! Did the group pass
by Ararat, where they happened to see the Ark leaning alongside the mountain in *Russia?* No. Is this another credible
eyewitness account from the files of Eryl Cummings, or an old
army joke? I would suspect the motive for the soldiers' letter
was nothing more than employment.

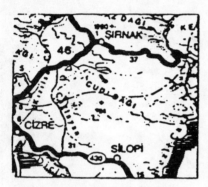 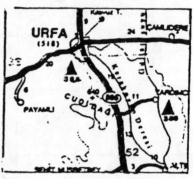

But this only accounts for two of the four sites named Cudi
in Turkey today. Thanks to Dr. Chuck Willis of Fresno,
California, another Ark hunter, we now have a third. Willis'
proposed hiding place for the Ark is slightly lower than
Ararat's peak at 16,947 foot elevation at the base of a small
knob on the southeastern plateau. To accommodate everyone
he has named this ridge Al Judi, further confusing the issue and
alienating the Turks by giving it the Arabic name. He believes
this means "Great Place," "Great Accommodator," or simply
"Great Cliff." It would appear by this reasoning that he should
have prefixed the spot with the word *Akbar,* but the meaning
of Arabic words seems as unimportant to Willis as Cummings'
idea that all names mean "Ararat." Willis claims the Ark is
buried at the base of this cliff at 16,800 feet. To fortify his
position, he simply gave it the name himself. To date, Willis
has failed to come up with any hard evidence to substantiate
his theory, which among them all is the least convincing.

Thus, with these three sites all named after the Koranic

landing place of the Ark, all are the wrong locations. It would appear that both Christian and Moslem traditions are in error, but here lies the paradoxical situation. Both Moses and Mohammed were correct, and in my opinion, the traditions of Islam shed a more accurate view on the layout of the wreck. According to Moslem tradition the Ark is on a hill, not a mountain, upon the mountainous range of Urartu and on a north-south axis with the body on the west side of a hill. This is the exact situation at our site. Cummings should have been aware of this. The scribe, Sakir,[5] even described it as such. Even with the reported damage at one end and alongside a large rock, Cummings and others failed to make the connection.

The Ark of the misnomered Tenderick Formation (sic) researched by Cummings as well, had a keel line bearing of ten degrees, a close approximation to the scribe's north-south axis and does indeed lay on the western portion of the hill, not only alongside a large rock but impaled by it as well.

The scribe's description was nothing more than Arabic tradition of the layout of the site *before* it had been pushed sideways onto the rock by the alluvial flow that slid down to the east of it, resulting in the Ark's being almost completely covered. As we shall see later on, this is the strange sight that greeted the Assyrians at a later date circa 800 B.C.E. They called it Varuna's House of Clay. They entered it at the surface. It was three stories deep in the ground; thus an underground fortress came to be known as a "vara."

Why should the Arab have knowledge the Christian does not have? It should be remembered that Abram fathered Ishmael through Hagar at age eighty-six, then Isaac through Sarah fourteen years later, his name now changed to Abraham. The Midrash sheds more light on just who Hagar was. Her name is gar, meaning "stranger," and Hagara, the strange woman, meaning she was a stranger to the house of Israel. She was Egyptian, not of the house of Jacob, and as pointed out by Vendyl Jones,[6] she was not just some gypsy handmaiden to Sarah, but in truth, one of the daughters of Pharaoh who,

---

[5]Cummings, *Ark*, pp. 106–108.

[6]Vendyl Jones, Institute of Judaic-Christian Research, Arlington, Texas.

loving Sarah, requested to accompany her as her handmaiden
when they left Egypt. Her real name was Katura, and the same
who became the wife of Abraham after the death of Sarah,
bearing the old patriarch six additional sons. Thus it is an
erroneous assumption that the Semitic peoples outside the
Hebrews could hold little traditional knowledge as to the
whereabouts of the Ark. We must also remember that Shem
was a contemporary of Abraham and his many sons
throughout his lifetime, and in fact outlived Abraham by
thirty-five years, according to the chronology of the Masoretic
text.

This is not to say that others make mistakes and I don't. As
we continued climbing, at another rest stop I thought I should
clarify once again that the tip of the escarpment locally was
called Cudi. To confirm once again that we were not on the
Tendürek range, I said "Tendürek Dağ, nerede?" and the old
man pointed west-southwest.

"And Ağrı Dağ?" I queried. "Büyük Ağrı, Küçük Ağrı Dağ,"
he responded by pointing at the two peaks of greater and lesser
Ararat.

"And here," I questioned. "Meşhur [well known and fa-
mous]." "Hayır [no]!" he corrected me. "Mahşer, Mahşer!" he
repeated. Again this brought Dilaver into the discussion. Now
another Kurd of the party began saying "Mahşur." I assumed
it was the difference between Turkish and Kurdish pronunciation until I heard the elder say, "Mahşer Günü." I had been
wrong. It was not "Meşhur" but "Mahşer"! The phrase was
Koranic, an Arabic loan word like Judi, that meant "the Last
Judgment," and expressed with a *u* as Mahşur, it meant "raised
from the dead"! I couldn't believe it. Twenty-five years after
the first Ark hunters had a look at the site it was discovered
that the name of the area was "the last judgment day." With
Noah's Ark at the bottom of the slope, it was surely justified.
And the Ark itself? I would find out later how truly it was
raised from the dead.

It was from this point on that Ron Wyatt and I, and John
Baumgardner, too, became known as the doomsday team.
Dilaver was so excited that he and the Kurds wanted to stand
before the video and make a speech. They all lined up in front

of the camera and repeated the words. It was joyfully documented.

Soon we were standing at the top of the flow in the center of an opening. There were depressions like footsteps filled with standing water in a blanket of flowers, spreading out over the soft valley floor. The croaking of thousands of frogs was not interrupted by the party of pilgrims beholding the magnificent view before them.

Following the flow downward with the eye, several more depressions filled with water were visible, and the whole valley mouth showed signs of recent slippage. There were fissures of earthquakes here as well. I looked down from the valley to the wide plain below that separates this range from the Mount of Ararat. The distance to the foothills was easily twelve miles, but the slope angle is such that the Ark site cannot be seen.

From this position the very peak of Ararat bears 10° magnetic, and rotating clockwise the valley mouth closes off at 67°. At approximately 100°, although not visible from this location, at seventy-three hundred feet, the eastern end of this sloping escarpment juts from the green of the hills some distance away. If Al Judi meant nothing more than the "high place," as I interpret it, then at 135° and closer to us is the spot. It is not the most spectacular end of this ridgeline upthrust, but certainly the west end is highest, and by historical definition might be the place where Noah built the altar for the first sacrifice in the new world.

As mentioned before, the eastern portion is called Pilgrim Mount, or literally translated "voluntary pilgrimage." The closer of the two ends is on the map as Yiğityatağı. It translates as "hero's bed" but means the habitat of heroes, or where the heroes call home, or come from. This, too, I felt related to the site.

Noah and his sons, by coming through the judgment and the longevity they carried with them into the new age, were naturally regarded as heroes. Although the Mesopotamians regarded them as gods, it was unseemly that the mounts should retain names expressing them as gods, though in the past they may have done so.

But the name "hero's bed" was acceptable to both Christian and Moslem alike. There are more striking similarities encountered in the place names of the immediate area, to be shared with the reader in following chapters. I don't want to digress from this peak of Judi, so I will continue by saying it was unfortunate that I was unable to get to this point for investigating the possible remains of an altar of sorts. The graffiti of pilgrims and the broken shards of offerings in remembrance of the first sacrifice may litter the place, but any attempts of future explorers to attain the heights should be tempered with caution, for unfortunately this ridgeline follows the sinuosities of the Turkish-Iranian border, and one would literally be taking his life in his hands to attempt scaling the escarpment during these politically unstable times.

In fact, the mountain men were a little skittish about going too far into the valley itself. They would make pantomime gestures of bullets bouncing off their chests, and I tried to make them understand that with the trajectory employed at this distance, the velocity at this range would be so underpowered that they would only wound us at best, and furthermore, we would probably not be hit by their first shot.

Nobody moved. "The first near misses we'd hear whizzing by would give us ample time to make our descent!" I continued. At this point their mouths dropped open, and some turned away as Dilaver began laughing heartily. He knew my sense of humor by now, and they all laughed with him, but they were relieved to see we had no intentions of making the climb.

We sat down to rest. We had brought some cheese and bread which we attempted to pass around, but no one would share it. *Now I've gone and done it,* I thought. I had pushed them too far. They wouldn't even drink from my canteen.

"Tsk!" The old man made the local noise for attracting attention through his teeth, and directed my glance toward him. "Ramadan," he said, and smiled. They could take a joke. They were abstaining totally from food and drink until sundown. They were observing the Moslem fast.

I continued my notes on other points of interest. At the same bearing of 135°, and another at 155°, are some interesting outcroppings, but apart from these definite features only steep, soft hills encircled to 350° where the valley opened again to the view of Mount Ararat.

As the group packed up, I thought how incredible it was that these people, so hardy for their ages, could go without water after such an arduous climb. "Why don't you set up your generator in the center of the valley?" suggested John.

Soon the frequency ran through the valley in search of the molecules of iron. The readings were not only there but they were under my feet, which necessitated a repositioning of the instrument to define the diameter and depth of the circles. They were some eight feet below, with more lines running off to a swampy area near the mouth of the valley and the top of the flow.

Another line was present that I could follow for some two hundred yards to the embankment of a hill, bearing 272°. It was this line the group chose to follow to its source.

It might do well at this point to explain the function of this instrument. An atom is the basic component of all matter. Atoms are made up of many different kinds of particles, each of different weights; some are positive and some are negative, but all are in constant motion within the nucleus. Atoms combine to form molecules, which consist of a complex arrangement of electrons revolving about a positively charged nucleus containing (except for hydrogen) protons and neutrons, as well as other particles. These types of particles that make up the nucleus are different for each kind of metal. Thus the wavelength of the radiation that is caused by this motion, which is dependent upon these factors, creates different frequencies.

Combining this knowledge with electronic technology, a small but powerful transmitter was developed utilizing the medium of soil or water to transmit and receive wavelengths for distances up to three-quarters of a mile, horizontally or vertically. It might be mentioned that the wavelength and signals are much stronger in salt water because of the presence of electrolytes and probably travel to infinity.

It was on the shores of Florida that I first met John Fales and his group of hopefuls who were searching out treasure wrecks along the Gold Coast between Sebastian Inlet and the Saint Lucie Inlet, near my home of Port Salerno. I had been hired to arrive off the beach with a team of divers and my salvage vessel on a certain date and anchor up.

Soon I was boarded by members of Fales' group from the beach who had left the shore in an expensive inflatable boat. Through the use of range markers they had set up by an instrument, they directed me to maneuver my little LCM (fifty-six-foot Landing Craft) over to a buoy that marked the spot where they wanted me to wash the sand away from the bottom.

"What are we looking for today, gold doubloons?" I asked, chuckling to myself. I'd had a lot of experience with treasure hunters in Key West, though they were mostly the coffee-house variety.

"No, brass and copper," came the serious reply. "Then we'll shift you over to some iron readings and you're free to go."

I shifted the vessel over to the buoy just outside the surf line some 250 feet offshore and dogged down the bow anchor winch. The inflatable boat ran out my stern anchors to the breakers, and after minor adjustments, I let the boat settle into the swell.

I pulled the pins on the deflector, which swung down into position to deflect the propeller wash to the bottom some fifteen feet below while my divers dressed in.

Soon nearly 500 H.P. gently scoured away the overburden of centuries down to the hardpan of fossiliferous peat. The one engine, ahead, raised the sand in suspension while the other, in reverse, swept it forward under the hull, where it billowed in clouds to the surface, turning the waters to orange hundreds of feet ahead.

We all went overboard for a look. There on the blackened bottom of peat among ancient conch shells lay hundreds of brass pins and fittings from an early wreck.

With several samples brought aboard, I was quickly shifted over to another area to repeat the procedure through the gadgetry of electronics ashore. This time there appeared iron and shards of olive jars. Although pleased, the shore crew retrieved only a breach block and retreated to the beach as soon as possible. Everything was quickly packed up ashore and I was directed to leave the area immediately. Fales and his team deflated the boat. With the motor and other gear shouldered by the beach crew, they silently slipped into the palmettos and disappeared.

I soon learned that this group was locating shipwrecks from the beach up and down the coast and securing admirality protection for their finds by bringing into the confines of federal courts a portion of the wreck in arrest and rem suits. This had been the purpose of our brief meeting and visit to the site.

When I next met Fales, I pressed him quite heavily for more information about his instruments. It took almost a year before I was able to secure a new prototype, actually the fourth one in existence, with the restriction that I would not use it nationally. It could be used only on my forthcoming project in Turkey.

I received one of Fales' finest units, which he jokingly dubbed his "Noah" model. After signing my name in blood that I wouldn't divulge the frequencies to anyone, I began my own tests.

The signal is omnidirectional, that is, the generator transmits the signal 360° out from the ground probes, which are sending the wavelength through the soil. The speed and distance of the signal depend upon the condition of the soil (working better in damp soil than dry sand), and to a certain extent, the length of time the target has been in the ground. The secret seems to lie in the analyzer that rejects frequency transmitted and cancels all those reflected back except the element (in this case iron) the analyzer is programmed to receive.

This process requires only several minutes to determine, as the radiations from the buried metal or mineral resulting from the phenomenon of nuclear resonance, which is the vibratory movement of electrically charged particles within the nucleus of each atom, form a line from the probes to the target. If the target is shallow, the line merely ceases to exist past the object. If the target is deep, then the line stops at the edge of a circle, the diameter of which is the depth as it cones on a 45° angle from the surface down to the target. It was accidently setting up the equipment on what proved to be this circle of iron below the instrument that necessitated moving the instrument and probes to a different location in the valley.

While in the valley, this line we had determined to follow brought forward one of the Kurds with interesting information. The head man told Ron that old structures were in that direction up on the hill, and we started off. This area to the west was safe to explore and was indeed under the watchful eye of a remote Turkish outpost. As we continued to move through the valley, some soldiers slowly descended to meet us. We spent a few minutes with the officer in charge, who spoke little English but was curious about our mission. Apparently the locals knew him and seemed rather relieved that he allowed us to continue. They were all very friendly and waved good-bye as we moved on.

We ascended to a plateau at 7,550 feet but located nothing. The iron line continued to lead up the hill, and a short hop up to 7,650 feet put us on the uppermost western plateau, where we were quite disappointed. We found the area previously described as containing low structures to be void of anything of interest. The only exception was an oval ring of stones laying on the surface of the ground. To me it looked as if it may have been a corral of sorts in which to keep animals, prior to falling into disrepair. Ron, however, saw this as a sign of the buried city he so vividly imagined. I wasn't doing well either, with my iron line now leading back downhill. I must have passed it on the way up after unplugging the probes from the ground, and this plateau yielded no readings for copper, brass, gold, or silver. I climbed to the uppermost peak at 7,750 feet for a panoramic view but spotted little of interest.

With such unimpressive remains I concluded that if pilgrims had visited this valley when the Ark was here, if it truly had landed this high, the pilgrims might have left the area at nightfall or simply used the Ark itself for shelter.

It also became obvious that the back door, so to speak, to these heights could more easily be reached in olden times by a ridge path from Doğubayazıt, or more properly the gates to the mountain pass at İşak Paşa! I decided to do more research before the next trip to study the possibilities that this might indeed be the case.

I again searched for graffiti and petroglyphs overlooking the early possible location of the Ark. I couldn't conceive of some traveler not scratching his mark, or the image of the great ship, to commemorate his visit to the site of the new beginnings of man. Although the iron readings in the valley below still stirred my interest, I concluded the area didn't warrant a second look based on the settlement's "structure," but the mysterious lack of any obvious evidence at all disturbed me greatly.

Now we trudged back down the western ridge of the valley, stopping to take panoramic photos of the area for enlargement and studies at home. Was the old settlement lost in the flow itself? Had it come down with the Ark? Was that where the clues would be recovered, or was it up on the eastern side and for now unaccessible?

We crossed streams and fields, and with the light beginning to fade and in a light drizzle, we finally reached the small village of Üzengili. Upon entering the mayor's house we were ushered into the coolness of the meeting room, where we were quickly served yogurt in cold water, followed by bread, cheese, and fruit. Our friends, still abstaining from all food and cigarettes, served us gladly and smiled in rest, relaxing against sumptuous pillows or, legs folded, on the carpeted ground.

Dilaver excused himself to go down to the foot of the hill for his taxi. He would drive the narrow road up to meet us when we were ready to leave. Ron went with him.

I finished off my second glass of tea and thought how much I would like to spend a summer in this village, exploring the area at leisure. Had I realized what the name of this village was in the past, and that what I was virtually sitting on was the key to the whole mystery of the site from Babylonian times, I would have been ecstatic. I calmly arranged neat little piles of lira for each of the adults, with small ones for the children. They came in one at a time and graciously accepted my gift.

Slowly opening my field book, I began drawing cuneiform characters on a block, politely asking "nerede?" and pointing to the page, then to the wall. They stared and gave the universal shrug of the shoulders. The taxi was outside and waiting. Dilaver was famished and the sun was setting. He hadn't eaten a thing all day and the women were preparing to feed their households. When a white thread and a black thread could be held to the darkening sky and the difference not be detected, then the meal would begin. Such was the fast of Ramadan.

One more shrug of the shoulder upon leaving, and with a finger pointing to the drawing, the mayor replied again, "Yok [there is not]."

And I departed unknowingly from the very subject and place of my search.

NISIR DISCOVERED

Where was the landing site of Noah's Ark according to the ancients? We have seen that the biblical text records it was upon the mountains of the land or kingdom of Urartu (Ararat or ancient Armenia), and from the Koran, Al-Judi. Berosus, in translating the Akkadian texts into Greek, reaffirms this and his comments are quoted by numerous historians:

> A portion of the ship which came to rest in Armenia still remains in the mountains of the Korduaians of Armenia, and some of the people, scraping off pieces of bitumen from the ship, bring them back and use them as talismans.

The most significant literary work to come out of ancient Mesopotamia is the text of Gilgamesh. The earliest copies of the story date back to Sumerian times and seven such texts in the Sumerian language have survived. The scribal schools have kept alive this great epic, down through the period of the ancient Babylonians, working and reworking the text to the time of the Assyrians, where it was found in the library of King Ashurbanipal (668–627).

The standard version, which has already been translated from the original Akkadian into a dozen languages, is the composition of the exorcist-priest Sîn-leqi-unninnī sometime between 1600 and 1000 B.C.E. The most recent translation is by John Gardner and John Maier, published by Alfred A. Knopf in 1984.

The landing site of the ship of Utnapishtim appears in tablet 11 in successive lines 140 through 144 five times. It is translated "Mount Nisir." In further explanation of this the authors include a rather dated footnote on page 238 that reads as follows: "The mountain Nisir is modern Pir Omar Gudrun, south of the lower Zab in Turkey; sometimes it is identified with the biblical Ararat."

I cannot agree with this interpretation, or with identifying it with Pir Omar Gudrun. Before I state my reasons for disagreement let me say that this in no way is meant to be demeaning to the authors or their fine work, and I highly recommend it to my readers.

To begin with, it is true that the *Zab* begins in Turkey, although in Turkish it is known as the *Zap*, becoming the Great Zab in Iraq until it pours into the mighty Tigris. Some seventy miles south another river, the Little Zab, coming down from the Zagros mountains, enters the Tigris north of Al Fatha. If this is what the authors call the Lower Zab, it hasn't been considered in Turkey since 1915.

Since these texts were available to Berosus, it is a mystery why scholars should suggest the landing site was in Iraq when Berosus seems to make it most clear it was further to the north in Armenia. Berosus, then, could not identify Nisir with Pir Omar Gudrun. In fact, this whole idea that Mount Nisir is in Iraq seems to have been an illusion of Komoroczy that due to the mention of bitumen he felt he must place the Ark's resting place close to where bitumen oozes out of the ground! Because Berosus says it is in the mountains of the Korduaians in Armenia does not automatically put Nisir in Iraq Kurdistan.

This idea was then picked up by E. A. Speiser in his "Southern Kurdistan in the Annals of Ashurnasirpal and Today" (*The Annual of the American Schools of Oriental Research,* No. 8 [1926–1927], pp. 17, 18).

Now bear in mind that at this point it is only a suggestion based on a false assumption by Komoroczy, and no discredit to Speiser for mentioning it. But by the time it is repeated in Speiser's Anchor Bible translation and picked up by Werner Keller's *The Bible as History,* it has become *fact!* Keller, then, is lambasting Ark hunters for not searching for the Ark in Iraq and making erroneous claims:

Despite the *precise* description in the Epic of Gilgamesh, Mt. Nisir has never tempted the curious to search for the remains of the giant ship.

Nothing could be further from the truth. Where is this "precise location" in the Akkadian text or even in the various translations, outside of erroneous footnotes?

By the time 1985 rolls around, a group from Japan is petitioning the Iraqi government for permission to scale the Zagros mountains in the middle of a war zone to make the great discovery of all times!

To put this in the proper perspective we must first try to determine what the word means. If it is a mountain, why is it called *Nisir?* Did Noah grab Shem by the scruff of the neck and shove his head out the window and ask, "Hey! Doesn't that look like Mount Nisir?" Of course not. I don't care what the mountain's name was before the Flood. If the Ark landed there it would be named after the event had occurred and in some way must be connected with the end period of the Flood.

The second question would be to check on the assumption of scholars that the name *Nisir* is in any way connected with a mountain at all!

The cuneiform signs appear below:

#366   #231   #374

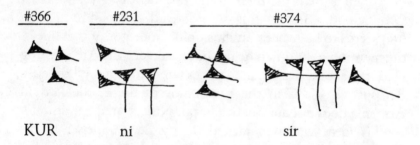

KUR   ni   sir

The basic tools of Akkadian vocabulary are always useful to consult, but since my active knowledge in neo-Assyrian sign values was limited to only a passive recognition, I needed help. It was at this point that John Maier, author of the translation, was an immense help in attempting to discover the meaning of the word.

The name is comprised of two signs listed by Borger as #231 and #374.[7] But the word is preceded by a silent determi-

[7]Rykle Borger's sign list, *Akkadische Zeichenliste* (Neukirchen-Vluyn: Verlag Butzon & Bercker, 1971).

native KUR which sometimes seems to be relatively imprecise in its meaning. It does not exactly mean "mountain" (šadû) or "land" (mātu) and perhaps is not far from the meaning of "place," but Mesopotamian tradition tends to use another sign, KI, pretty consistently for "place" both as a silent determinative and as a sign for the word place. However, in my opinion, since KUR does not specifically mean "mountain" (šadû), like all things in cuneiform, Nisir designated as such is worthy of rethinking.

The first sign after KUR is traditionally read as *ni* but could be read syllabically about seven different ways, none of which offered anything hopeful. We both agreed on the traditional rendering.

The third sign could be read syllabically as both *ṣir* or *muš* (š is to be pronounced as in the English "ship" or the Turkish ş). Here the reading *muš* appears to be rather late, that is neo-Babylonian, but still of interest. Wolfram von Soden's *Akkadische Handwörterbuch* (Wiesbaden: O. Harrassowitz, 1972) is very useful at this point in that von Soden likes to suggest interconnections among Semitic root languages, especially Arabic.

The interesting thing about working with three root consonants is that nṣr can be related to nšr, mṣr, mṣr and mzr. The most obvious would then be *naṣāru,* "to keep something under guard." The Arabic *nsr* is also the root that yields "Christian," but mainly its meaning is "helper and ally."

I felt we were now getting closer to the meaning of the word. What event could have taken place at this spot that could make a survivor of the Flood feel he was under protection of a helper and ally and that throughout the judgment on the rest of the world he and his family alone had been kept under guard?

I had whetted Maier's interest and we continued to correspond. He had just finished teaching an exhaustive semester and was now preparing to hold a summer seminar for secondary school teachers at SUNY College at Brockport, but despite his heavy schedule he responded. No one wants to tackle the meaning of Mount Nisir, he said, and we continued.

The *Chicago Assyrian Dictionary* is more detailed than von Soden's and not interested in the connections between Semitic languages, but its two volumes on *m* and two volumes on *n* gave a tremendous amount of information about the words Maier had checked up on in von Soden: *naṣāru, nazāru, našāru, nišru, nišertu, niṣirtu, nizirtu, mas/ṣ/zāum, maṣarru, maṣaru, maṣiru, maṣṣartu, maṣṣāru, mašāru, mašru, miṣru, mīšaru,* and a few others. Maier was hot on the trail.

Because the reed boat is called naṣirat napištum in one very broken version of the Atra-ḥasis, that is, the "life saver," and the god Ea is the one responsible for saving life [ú-uš-] ta-ṣi-ra na-pí-i[š-tum] in another part of the Atra-ḥasis, he thought it pleasant indeed to find *niṣir* meaning "guard" or "keep," a protector or some such. Another pleasant possibility, since it would pick up a minor but possibly significant motif in Gilgamesh, is that *niṣir* is connected to *niṣirtu,* "secret," as in the secrets of the gods held by Ea, passed along to Utnapishtim and thence to Gilgamesh.

Another secret passed along to Gilgamesh was of course the plant of life and longevity, The-Old-Man-Will-Be-Made-Young: "Let me uncover for you, Gilgamesh, a *secret* thing. A *secret* of the gods let me tell you" (XI, col. vi). I pulled out my chart and stared again at the words *Devşirme Menekşe,* "to gather or collect youth and flower," that was over the spot of the Ark in 1941. Could this be the secret the site was holding? I could see the village of Üzengili clearly marked as *Sar* in the old days – a Sumerian term for 3,600, the Saru of Berosus. *Not much to go on,* I thought. I reached for another chart that I'd been given by a friend several days before and rolled it out on the desk.

Then I saw it for the first time. I stared in disbelief! Neatly and clearly marked was the old village name. It was not Sar, it was . . . Nasar!

That evening I was driving on the freeway thinking of the three-root consonant nsr. *Nisir/Nasar,* I thought, *what could it mean?* Had we overlooked anything? Was the word still meaningful? I pulled off the road for a cup of coffee to keep awake and do more thinking on the subject when I happened to notice a handsome east Indian family settle down at the table next to me. I figured it was worth a try.

"Are you Pakistani?" I asked.

"Yes!" he replied.

I explained I was doing some research on a word, the meaning of which was uncertain, and perhaps he could be helpful. Did he speak Urdu? He smiled at his family. Everyone smiled back and seemed to be getting a laugh out of my query.

"Then perhaps you could tell me quite frankly what the word *Nasar,* or perhaps it is pronoucned *Nisir,* means?"

"That is quite easy," he responded. "It means two things. To make a presentation or a sacrifice!"

Could his answer be relied upon? He handed me his card. Aman Momin, it said, Program Officer, U.S. Information Agency, Professor of Urdu.

John Maier cautioned me about crossing from Arabic to Turkish to Persian, all of them from different families, and although finding my Urdu connection intriguing, he suggested a Semitic substrate for our word *Nisir.* However, let me propose the following:

The facts are that we have a boat-shaped object that appears to my untrained eye to not be a natural rock formation. With my maritime background I'd be hard-pressed to say it wasn't the remains of a shipwreck even if I didn't believe it was the Ark itself. The length is exactly three hundred cubits, and we are on the mountains of ancient Urartu, with the Kurds still living there. This would appear to be the mountains of the Korduaians of Armenia, according to Berosus.

And here, less than five hundred yards from "a portion of the ship," is a village called Nasar. Even the unconvinced spectator must recall that Noah built an altar of thanksgiving after disembarking from the ship and presented a sacrifice. This is Mesopotamian tradition as well as Hebrew. In fact, we must view the Genesis account prior to the call of Abram as nonethnic history and all of Noah's descendants as under the Noahic Covenant from this time and place on, until other special covenants were made with other groups in time.

This holy spot would then be long remembered as "The Place of the Presentation of the Sacrifice (Covenant)." The village name does not have to be Turkish, or an Arabic loan word; it only has to relay the meaning of God as our protector, helper, and ally.

According to the YENİ TÜRKÇE SÖZLÜK, REDHOUSE, ISTANBUL, page 884, we have the following meanings in Turkish, with the consonants *nzr* still effective.

Nezir: Vowing or devoting vow, a thing vowed.

> Ishtar drew nigh . . . . Oh these gods, I vow by the lapis lazuli gems upon my neck that I will never forget, I will remember these days for ever and ever. Let all the gods come hither to the offering.

Nezir: A prophet who calls men to virtue with warnings of God's wrath.

> And the Lord said, I will not again curse the ground anymore for man's sake.

NEZIRE: A thing done, given, or sacrificed in fulfillment of a vow.

> And Noah builded an altar unto the Lord; and took of every clean beast, and of every clean fowl, and offered burnt-offerings on the altar. . . . And I, behold, I establish my covenant with you, and with your seed after you.

I submit that Nisir has been found, as well as the meaning of the word, and that it is under the village of Üzengili.

5

Field Surveys

THE MEASUREMENTS

It was June 5, our second day at the site, and the sky again showed promise of rain in the distance as we ascended to the Ark in the early-morning hours. A cry was heard from a shepherd boy calling up to the village, heralding our early arrival. Sound travels great distances there, and anyone out of place moving into the area was no secret for long.

Soon the site was filled with curious children and mothers close behind, chasing them back home to their daily chores. Shortly after selecting an even number of adults and children as helpers and observers, we moved on to the Ark for what would prove to be the most decisive day of all.

I set the frequency generator up amidships and pushed the probes into the ground. With the frequency set on iron I gave the pulse some time to spread out through the structure. The response was strong. The object was so hot the frequency wave came up above the ground almost eighteen inches. Starting at the eastern wall or gunwale, the top of which I designated as zero, and walking west across the hull, I picked up the same longitudinal lines I had in March. At each line I set an aluminum rod into the ground. The spacing was 0, 8.7 feet, 21 feet, 33 feet, 38.5 feet, 46.4 feet, 55.3 feet, and 59.5 feet to the centerline of the hull. Although the line can be read this close, it should be pointed out that if I moved forward along this line the reading could go off center 6 to 8 inches either way.

Imagine a wide plank and the builder has pounded nails off center, first one side and then the other, staggering them down

115

the plank as he moves along. These readings really covered a width of approximately 1 foot. Therefore, the width from the side to the centerline at this point was approximately 60 feet, for a total width of the object amidship of 120 feet.

Around the rock impalement area on the west side, these lines are greatly distorted, showing the rock is definitely an intrusion that has damaged the object and is foreign to the symmetry of the whole. I had wondered in March if this rock was part of a man-made ramp leading into the Ark and would indicate an entryway or door at this location. The twisting of these lines around the rock looked like signs of damage. This means the vessel was pushed sideways by the flow into the rock outcropping.

Survey ribbons were attached to these stakes and some ten feet further uphill the process of walking across the hull was repeated, stopping at each signal long enough for Dilaver to direct the men to roll out the ribbons up to my position and the children, some fifteen in number, to lay rocks atop the ribbons to secure them in place. We proceeded uphill toward the sharply pointed southern end in the same manner. But at several points, something unusual occurred.

The thirteen lines doubled up into twenty-six! The answer to this would become clear later in the day.

As these longitudinals converged and the space between them became less, the closer I got to the pointed end; they finally came together and met in one final clump. "Here it is!" I exclaimed. "Here's the end of the ship."

You'd have thought it was a christening, and all the Turkish farmers became very excited. We were running short of survey ribbon so at Dilaver's direction they began removing every other line of tape while I carefully resumed the survey, walking slowly downhill between the lines. At forty-seven feet from where all the lines had converged the instrument showed the first bulkhead. "Okay!" the mayor sang out as he ran over and embraced me. "Nuh'un Gemisi, Nuh'un Gemisi," he kept repeating, and dancing up and down. The English "Okay!" was fast replacing the Turkish counterpart, and every step of the project was hereafter affirmed by the Kurds as "Okay!"

Ron and I started laughing hysterically in relief. "What do you think it is now, Ron? A natural object?"

"It might be a submarine," said John. "It's shaped like one. Maybe a secret site from World War II."

"Or a crashed wrought-iron dirigible," chimed in Ron with a smirk. The doublings of the lines from thirteen to twenty-six had occurred at the bulkhead or transverse positions of the iron lines, just as a builder today would lay a floor joist.

The next transverse line appeared 40.5 feet from the first. The beam width at #1 bulkhead was 35 feet. Now this second bulkhead's width was 63 feet.

Down the slope we went, measuring the spacing between these transverse lines and their widths from wall to wall, photographing and making notes in the log. Number 3 was 29.5 feet, and then twenty feet more to #4 bulkhead. At this point the ship was 86 feet wide, then on to #5, some 31 feet later. The last space measured was 46 feet to the amidships bulkhead, #6.

This #6 bulkhead was very thick and appeared to be made up of three transverse lines that ran from one side to the other of the ship, almost sandwiched together yet clearly distinguished as three separate lines parallel to one another.

From this point, removing all of the ribbon from the uphill end, we proceeded down toward the lower blunt end. It soon became apparent that this #6 wall had been a major division in the structure. For as I walked just outside of and parallel to the centerline, I encountered no transverse line across the width of the ship for just over 200 feet. I was locating the longitudinal lines. They ran parallel to the centerline, the first 4 feet out and the next 13 feet out from the centerline. What I was ending up with after carefully backtracking and double-checking was a large rectangular opening in the hull 201 feet by approximately 26 feet, maybe slightly more.

What was this open area? A ramp or a corridor? Certainly an enormous space to not contain transverse bracing!

I concentrated on the eastern wall, which seemed in perfect shape, because the western wall had been damaged and distorted by the rock intrusion. I discovered there were large room areas off to the side of this "center slot." Measuring along the east wall of this 201-foot slot from #6 bulkhead, I ran thirty feet to intercept and this wall ran fifty-four feet to the edge of the hull.

This wall I designated as bulkhead #7, but remember, it does not run from one side of the ship to the other, only to the center slot.

The next space was the largest. Walking the wall of the 26-by-201-foot center area for a distance of 128 feet, I encountered bulkhead number #8, which measured 56 feet to the gunwale. Although not immediately apparent while standing inside the structure, this bulkhead represents the widest overall breadth of the boat. The 56 feet plus the 13-foot distance to the keel line doubles to 138 feet total width. The last area continues for 43 feet again along the edge of this central area until encountering bulkhead #9. This last bulkhead is unique because it is the only bulkhead that is not at right angles to the keel or centerline of the structure. It runs from the corner of the 26-by-201-foot central area to the gunwale for an angled distance of 51 feet, while the distance at the gunwales between bulkheads #8 and #9 is 58 feet. The same areas appear on the west side of the structures, though not precisely measured due to distortion caused by the rock intrusion on that side. I believe this western wall is broken away from the main deck.

From the very end of this central area, which is an integral portion of bulkhead #9, and the only bulkhead since #6 to extend across the whole structure, it is only 89 feet until the walls or lines of metal converge into the 34-foot projection through the hull. Within this extension, all the longitudinal iron lines extend parallel spaced a foot apart, and abruptly end.

The overall length of the vessel involves some explaining due to the protrusion. The confusion is caused by the difference between where the inner longitudinal lines converge into straight lines running parallel to the end of the stem, as opposed to the point where the bows close off the inside of the structure.

The frequency generator gave very precise readings for this. Coming down the internal lengthwise bracing, whether they are actual walls (longitudinal bulkheads) or floor beaming, they *converge* inside the hulk at 504 feet. The length they run

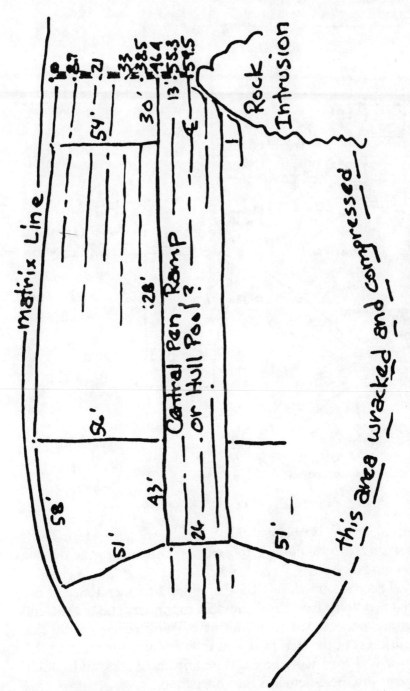

Field book sketch and notes on the central area.

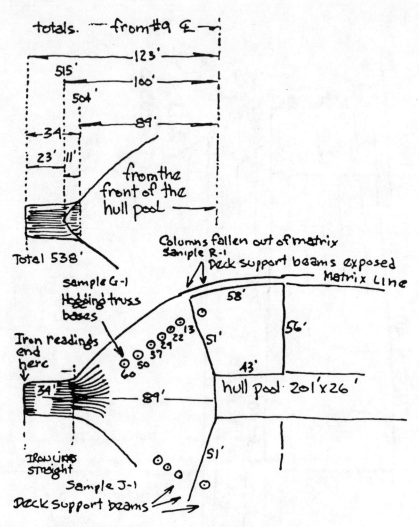

totals. — from #9 ℄ —

123'

515'

100'

504'

34'

89'

23' 111'

from the front of the hull pool →

Total 538'

Columns fallen out of matrix
Sample R-1
Deck support beams exposed
Matrix Line

sample G-1
Hogging truss bases

58'

56'

Iron readings end here

13
22
29
37
50
60

51'

43'

hull pool 201' x 26'

34'

89'

51'

IRON LINES STRAIGHT

Sample J-1
Deck support beams

Field book sketch of bow section.

parallel to the very end of the stem projection is 34 feet. They
are spaced here about 1 foot apart. This makes the overall
length 538 feet.

There is something else that should be mentioned. This
figure reflects the *inside* of the stern to the very end of the stem
projection. Thus, the overall length will be greater by the
thickness of the sternpost. I have every anticipation that the
boat will eventually be excavated by the Turks, and I don't
want my measurements misunderstood.

The iron lines show me that this is not some portion that
has toppled over and out of the boat, as expressed in my
March visit to the site. It is an integral part of the plan.

The bows, however, close 11 feet further, at exactly 515 feet. There is distortion for the width of the bows, then clarity again in the stem readings. The width of the bow walls would be a guess at best, and will say only that from this closing of the inner bows, it extends for another 23 feet. I feel it is a safe assumption the bows are over 6 feet thick, but in my estimation we are seeing the portion above the main deck and well above the waterline.

As a footnote to my measurements taken in early June of 1985, it should be noted that Maylon Wilson, a scientist from Los Alamos Laboratory, accompanied John Baumgardner and Ron Wyatt to the site prior to my arrival of August 17. They conducted a survey by transit and other sophisticated measuring devices establishing inside dimensions of 515.7 feet. Of further interest is Wilson's measurement of 123.6 feet from the end of the central area to the object's extremity. This figure I believe is more accurate than mine, confirming in my opinion that the curve of the north end is based on the logarithmic spiral of phi (.6180). The integers 123.6 is equal to the length of the angle's measuring reed if that reed is considered to represent pi (3.1416). Thus with the cubit in inches being 20.6, this cubit times the 6-cubit length of the reed equals 123.6 (Ezekiel 40:3, 5).

It should be stressed that this was an independent survey. Wilson, Baumgardner, and Wyatt did not have any of my measurements in their possession, nor was I present at the time. I have never met Mayon Wilson personally, nor have we discussed these figures prior to our communique of March 12, 1986. I would consider these two unrelated surveys to properly relate the measurements of the Ark's remains.

WHICH END IS THE BOW?

At this point in my investigations, I began having doubts as to whether we were using the correct terminology in describing the structure. When I first saw the Ark in the snows of March, Ron was referring to the uphill (south end) as the bows, and the lower end as the stern. Because it resembles a large covered canoe or perhaps a kayak, this didn't really present any problem. Ron's other fixation seemed to be that the stern had been dragged out, which accounted for the extension, and the vessel's being filled with earth had caused the lower end to spread. There is no fault in considering this proposal, but his motivations were in doubt. To Ron, this end greatly exceeded what he considered his biblical interpretations of the dimensions given in Genesis, thus a reason for this variance seemed most important. When I measured the structure in June, both ends were definitely *not* constructed the same, and indeed the internal layout either side of transverse bulkhead #6 seemed to act as a division in design.

It soon became apparent that Ron considered all ships' bows were the pointy end. They came aground headfirst and stayed that way. This has always been the point of one of our friendly disagreements. I find a diversity of opinion healthy ground for getting at the truth of the matter. It is not unusual for vessels to come aground stern first, or sideways. The deepest draft coming in contact with the bottom acts as a pivot point, and the wind and seas can turn the vessel at will.

If we consider the vessel's present position as its first point of contact, it then becomes difficult to explain how it became impaled through the side by the rock outcropping, almost to the centerline. It appears to me that this is a secondary position resulting from a slide with the alluvial flow at some later point in history, resulting in its being almost completely buried and hidden from view. The structure may have pivoted and turned during its descent. But the terms *bow* and *stern* can be misleading and must be determined by the structure itself, not which end came ashore first.

A vessel has a definite direction of travel and is usually designed as such. One must consider that a vessel's purpose is to go from point A to point B. Some Ark enthusiasts will quickly point out the Ark was not designed to go anyplace, just to stay afloat, but unless they consider the Ark was beamed to the sea and rolled along as a log, there must be a weather end and a lee end to the design.

Thus, being nonpropelled, or dead in the water, doesn't mean the vessel did not travel from point A to point B geographically at the mercy of wind and sea. The after end, or stern, followed the bow in its direction of travel.

In comparison to modern ships, designed to plow through

the seas, the reader may find it surprising that many vessels designed to travel with the wind and sea had blunt bows and sharp upswept sterns, for the stern was the weather end. To reverse these terms would be to say the vessel was designed to travel backward for the voyage. This is totally unacceptable in my view.

The lower north end is broader and might be termed *apple-cheeked* to become more buoyant by displacing more water. When the waves meet the lighter upswept end, and we can assume this is true as the compartments suggest smaller cargo areas, it is then likely to rise up with the waves. It is at the other end you need the buoyancy to accept the weight of the vessel now inclined by the front of the wave, which transfers the weight forward. This added buoyancy forward keeps the vessel from plunging.

It is difficult to imagine conditions during the Flood. At times it may have been worse than the storms I encountered in the Atlantic, where I experienced waves from hollow to crest of 43 feet, with a fetch of 560 feet. But there must have been quieter times as well, and I don't envision the Ark coming aground in a storm such as this.

Since the bulbous end has greater surface area below the waterline and would create drag, what then keeps the lighter end from pivoting around by the force of the wave?

Here I think we find the solution. It is not mentioned in the Genesis account but is mentioned in others. The answer is drogue stones. We will not go into a discussion of them here but in another chapter. Suffice it to say that these stones created a drag or resistance through the water that kept this end in tension, preventing the Ark from broaching by slowing its forward momentum. I believe they were trailing from the upswept sharp weather end or what should in this case be called the stern.

This method was employed by early vessels in the Mediterranean that were designed to run with the wind and the sea. Their hulls, too, were sharp at the stern and broad at the bow. When encountering bad weather they furled in their sails, shipped the steering oars, and cast anchor stones over the stern and rode out the weather. Such a story is related by Paul in Acts 27:17. The Greek reads, "And fearing that we might run on the rocks, they let out four anchors from the stern, and prayed for day to come."

The method of this "braking stone" as used in Egypt is also described by Herodotus:

> ... a pierced stone of about two talents [115 pounds] ... and the stone is made fast also by a rope to the *after part* of the boat. So, driven by the current ... the boat and the stone dragging behind on the river bottom keeps the boat's course straight.

The Ark's displacement was approximately 270 times larger than the small "baris" described by Herodotus. Thus the drogue stones needed for a ship the size of the Ark could total some 15 tons. They would not "brake" the vessel's movement by dragging on a river bottom but restrain the forward momentum by the flat surfaces of the drogues, offering resistance while being dragged through the water.

This is what I believe the statement in Genesis means when it says the Ark came to rest upon the mountains of Ararat. It does not say it *grounded* but came to rest as the drogues came in contact with the bottom. The Ark was at rest and anchored up, so to speak.

So in changing my opinion from Ron's that the lower, more bulbous end is the bow, a number of things must be borne in mind. Because we started at the upper end of the structure and worked more effortlessly backing downhill for the measurements, the result is contrary to maritime tradition. The transverse bulkheads are listed in reverse order. That is, #1 bulkhead is closest to the uphill stern. Those in disagreement with me will find them in order. I prefer to leave them as logged, and I hope the reader will bear with me. The next result of my survey that changed my opinion was I now didn't feel we were properly into the hull. Therefore, hull terminology such as *stringers* and *strongbacks*, *gunwales* and *ribs*, were meaningless jargon, and the lack of nautical terminology one might expect from my background I forced out of my vocabulary.

Just where the measurements of the Ark's three hundred cubits should be taken from is open to question. I consider it only a basis for Moses' giving a description of the space available for the carriage of cargo. The length overall then should be considerably greater. The practice of measuring a ship by the waterline, or the uppermost continuous deck, may also be out of place here in trying to conform to biblical interpretations.

Ron seemed distressed by the excess in width as described by Moses, and still continues to say the sides have fallen out. The widest point is at bulkhead #8. It is at this point 138 feet wide, when according to Scripture it should be only 85.8 feet. His continually mentioning this finally broke me down and was a turning point in our relationship. I absolutely refused to bend the measurements in accordance with his gut feelings, and I literally exploded.

"Ron! We're either here to discover how God designs a boat and Noah built it, or try and make it all comply with our ideas." I had committed myself to Noah's Ark before I met Ron, and we could do it together or apart, on separate expeditions.

"Look," I said, calming down, "these are upper deck support beams projecting out from inside the walls. They are in perfect alignment with those on the other side. They are perfectly horizontal, even with the western distortion further up the hull. If the walls were falling out, these support beams would be jutting up at an angle!"

"You're the expert," said Ron with a grin, leaving me and Dilaver alone to complete the measuring. Ron really knew how to hurt a guy. We both hated the word *expert*.

THE RATIO OF SHAPE

The problem appeared to be with the width of the object. Genesis gives the width of the Ark at 50 cubits. This would be a width of 85.83333 feet. The object was greater. Since I was sure the dimensions concerned volume, I used a quick salvor's method of squaring the hull for pumping to determine internal capacity. I enjoyed the idea of salvaging the Ark. I had gotten it this far off Ararat. Now it was only 750 kilometers to the Mediterranean! *If I could just break it loose,* I chuckled to myself.

A rectangle is envisioned, one half the beam and laid within the hull. The areas of this rectangle that fall outside the bow and stern are considered equal to the contours of the hull that fall outside the rectangle amidships. The length (515) is then divided by the width of the rectangle (60) for the ratio to be applied toward the hull material coefficients (like steel at 0.2) and mud break-loose factors (0.4), etc. I was surprised to find this as 8.583333. What was happening here? Even the ratio between the cubit (20.6) and two feet (24 inches) was .8583333.

Soon, everywhere I turned this strange number kept popping up. The 20.6-inch cubit times the 50-cubit width of the Ark was 1030 inches. If the angel's measuring reed was 6 cubits or 123.6 inches, this would be 10.3 feet! Yet the 123.6 inches of the reed was the 123.6 feet between bulkhead #9 and the very end of the Ark's bow extension. There must be a connection! The Ark seemed to be designed with some ratio in mind. This is apparent in the Holy Temple of Solomon as well, where the number 12 is important.

In 1 Kings 7:15 we are told that Hiram Abiff cast columns for King Solomon's Temple that were 18 cubits in height and 12 cubits in girth. To determine the cubit used, a simple method can be devised by dividing this circle of the column into twelve equal parts, each representing one-twelfth of the girth. The resultant 30° arc/portion of the whole is the cubit. Each cubit you move up the column toward its 18-cubit height, a corresponding value of 30° is removed from the 360° circle. At 12 cubits up the column the circumference is gone, leaving you with a line to the top of 6, the difference between 12 and 18. Isn't this then the length of the reed at pi/6 or .5236 when times 39.37 yields an inch measure of 20.6?

Besides a hint at pi, in meters (the width of the Ark in cubits, or fifty times pi giving the length of the Ark at 157.08), the length of 300 cubits gives another famous ratio in inches. Here, 20.6 times 300 results in phi, or 6180.

In Fibonacci's sequence of $1 + 2 = 3; 2 + 3 = 5; 3 + 5 = 8$; and so on, ad infinitum, after the fourteenth in the series, a strange ratio occurs. In the series 610, 987, 1597, 2584, 4181, each number can be increased by multiplying it by 1.6180 (the 1 is the number, plus .6180 of the number). Thus if this is applied to our 50 cubits for the width of the Ark (85.83333) then we could expect it to be as wide as 138.87832 feet. I measured the Ark at its widest bulkhead, #8, at 138 feet!

This ratio of .6180 is considered something that occurs in nature for the shape of everything from snails to the great spiral galaxies of outer space.

The golden rectangle formed by this ratio, commonly held to have been discovered by Pathagoras and Euclid, is called the "divine section." A composite of these rectangles can be connected to form the logarithmic spiral (equiangular) that forms the gap inside a breaking wave. This spiral formation is so closely allied to the relentless pounding of the sea that the Swedish treatise on shipbuilding, *Architectura Navalis Mercatoria,* even suggests it as the most effective curve for the arms of an anchor!

Why then are we surprised to find the bows of the Ark designed on the curve of the logarithmic spiral?

Carrying this discovery further, we see that the bulkheads are not randomly spaced, but we must approach this in turn.

First, consider that this ratio has increased the width of the Ark from 85.8 to 138.8 feet for a gain of 53 feet. This figure divided in half gives the center slot a width of 26.5 feet. I measured it at slightly over 26 feet, so we might assume this to be so. If we take 26.5 times 1.6180 we find it close to the distance measured between bulkheads #9 and #8. The correct figure should have been 42.877 feet. If we multiply this by three, we can calculate the next figure to be 128.631. I had measured it as 128 feet between bulkheads #8 and #7. Surely we are on to something here.

I would therefore suggest that the entire vessel is laid out by this ratio, that bulkhead #6 is indeed the dividing point of the entire design, and that the portion to the forward end, 318.27 feet, times the 1.6180, gives the vessel's inside measure as 514.96 feet, again almost exactly 300 cubits.

With my measure of 214 feet from the stern to the center of the triple bulkhead #6, the overall length of the vessel, including the bow extension, should be 532.27 feet. I measured 538 feet overall on 6/5/85 against the scientist from Los Alamos on 8/7/85, with his 531 feet. When the bulkhead at #6 can be excavated and the extremities of the Ark accurately determined, it will be interesting to see who is closest.

In closing, I should mention that the oldest structures of antiquity that contain these two ratios of both pi and phi are now seen to be Noah's Ark and the Great Pyramid. I believe that Imhotep, the Shepherd King, who was *not* Egyptian, and who was the designer and architect during the reign of Cheops, was Shem.

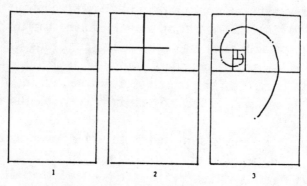

Above in fig. 1 is a square with .6180 of the square added to it, to form the golden rectangle. This upper portion also forms the same rectangle, now on its side. If .6180 of the whole of the upper rectangle is divided by a line, another square appears with the remaining portion, a golden rectangle as well (fig. 2). In continuum, fig. 3 shows what happens when a curved line is connected to the centers of the squares. This is called the logarithmic spiral, a portion of which forms each bow of the Ark.

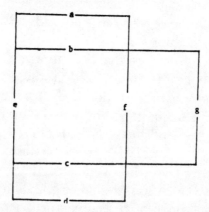

The square b f c e is Moses' 50 cubits or 85.8 feet. With the measured width of the Ark's bow at 138 feet, the 53 feet difference is the .6180 or 26.5 feet (a b and c d) on either side.

THE CUBE

It was the third day at the site, June 6. I had tackled the length and the width in the previous days. Now the height was all that remained.

If the cuneiform texts had said the Ark was as high as it was wide, or 120 cubits (Sumerian) or 121 feet, was this what they meant by *six stories*?

Josephus wrote in *Antiquities of the Jews* (Book 1, chapter 3):

> But Noah alone was saved; for God suggested to him the following contrivances and way of escape: that he should make an ark of *four stories* high.[1]

The KJV says in Genesis 6:16 (author's italics):

> . . . with lower, second, and *third stories* shalt thou make it.

This was going to be tough, proving everybody right! The Scofield Study Bible (Oxford NIV) says on page 11 in the footnotes:

> . . . these dimensions are in marked contrast with descriptions of the ark found in ancient mythology. Compare the cuneiform representation of it as shaped like a six storied cube of 262 feet with a mast and pilot on top.

The first figure that struck me was 262 feet. If Scofield's note was referring to the Babylonian texts, the revisionists have erred in the cubit. I decided to take the biblical scholar up on his suggestion to compare the cuneiform representation against the biblical description.

Now it has long been established that the Great Cubit of Babylon was 20.988458. I went to the text with the best translation available: *Gilgamesh*;[2] SÎN-LEQI-UNNINNĪ VERSION, Tablet XI, column ii.

Our purpose in studying this particular column of tablet

---

[1] *The Complete Works of Flavius Josephus* (Grand Rapids, Michigan: Kregel Publications, 1981).

[2] John Gardener and John Maier, *Gilgamesh* (New York: Alfred A. Knopf, Inc., ©1984).

eleven is to determine if the descriptions of Utnapishtim's Ark is in marked contrast to that described by Moses as suggested by the biblical scholar Dr. Scofield.

Line 56 On the fifth day I drew its plan.
    57 One IKU was its whole floor space; ten dozen cubits the height of each wall;
    58 ten dozen cubits its deck, square on each side.
    59 I laid out the contours, drew it all.
    60 I gave it six decks
    61 and divided it, thus, into seven parts.
    62 Its innards I divided into nine parts
    63 I struck water plugs into it.
    64 I checked the poles and laid in all that was necessary.
    65 [For the hull] I poured 24,000 gallons of bitumen into the kiln;
    66 The same amount I layed on the inside.
    67 The basket-bearers brought on three shars of oil
    68 in addition to the shars of oil consumed in the seed-meal
Line 69 and the two shars of oil stowed away by the boatman.

We should first note that this is not a story being told by Gilgamesh but a first-person narrative being told *to* Gilgamesh by Utnapishtim himself. In this tablet, where he states he drew its plan, it is in marked contrast to others that state "Ea" drew the plan upon the sand.

Described by some writers as the "word god" (who brought the word of the coming destruction) and as the "source of all things," Ea had a distinctive position and character during early Sumerian times. Although retaining a high position in the great triad, during later Babylonian periods Ea was described as the father of Merodach, and along with Anu and Bel shared the godhead. He became known by many names during these polytheistic times.

In these variant texts the ship itself was to be planned and built according to Ea's instructions, and to have a deck space consisting of one acre (line 57).

Notes to this column of the text by the authors, in referring to its enormous size, equate the Ark, or "elippu" to the great ziggurats of Babylon. The text appears to be describing a cube, but these are not the dimensions of the actual Ark. The writer is only trying to convey the volume or capacity. First it would be agreed that a ziggurat is not a cube. It may have levels of differing sizes, stacked one upon the other, but it is not a cube.

Professor Maspero recognized the ziggurats as representing the arrangement of the universe in 1901. Menon as well, in his work on early astronomy and cosmology, was of the same opinion. In fact, the Ziggurat of Nabu at Barsipki was known as the "House of the Seven Bands of Heaven and Earth," with each succeeding level painted in the planetary colors.

I feel the reason the ancients were so compelled to study the stars may have eluded many of these scholars and would appear to be a seeking after a sign of some eschatological event. The Temple of Jupiter at the top was dedicated to that planetary deity not so much because it was the subject of their concern but because Jupiter's movements seemed to bring about a cyclic event similar to what may have caused the Flood. It was certainly more serious than casting horoscopes for the masses. Berosus was still interpreting the omens in the second century B.C.E. during a period when the system seemed to have failed. He was quite emphatic that "the whole issue was brought about by the course of the planets," consigning the earth to flame or to Flood when a gathering takes place in Capricorn and Cancer.[3]

It is quite understandable that a connection with this structure might be made to the Ark and an understanding of its function is in order. The search is for the IKU of the ziggurat in the Ark. On the basis of a translation of a cuneiform text known as the Smith Tablet, some authors have mistakenly remarked that the third level represents one IKU. I perceive it as the fourth level, which was important to land surveying and can be explained briefly as follows:

The ziggurat, aside from fulfilling other functions, was a projection of the northern hemisphere. The base was one Sarus, the same as the earlier Sumerian Sar of 3,600, meaning "universe." The structure was used for finding the GP (Geographical Position) of stars under the rolling vault of heaven in sidereal time. Of course marks in the side could represent geographical points on the globe as well. We begin at the base (the equator), which is 300 feet square (3,600 inches). With 40 inches representing a degree of latitude, the base rises to a

---

[3]The Great Year, Babyloniaca of Berosus, 281 B.C.E.

height of 110 feet. This measure of 1,320 inches represents the latitude of Babylon at 33°.

Due to the curvature of the earth, the next level that rises above this *first* terrace is set in 360 inches from each side of the base, representing both the degrees of a circle and the days of a year during that era. The second stage rises 60 feet (720 inches) for 18°. The *second* terrace roughly represents the latitude of Calgary, Canada, and Southampton, England, or 51°.

Each side of this second level is 3,240 inches or 270 feet square. Again decreasing this square by 360 inches on all four sides, the third level rises 240 inches for a twenty-foot wall up the *third* terrace. This height represents 6° of latitude and at the third terrace we are now standing at 57° north just above Moscow.

It is the *fourth* level that is referred to in the cuneiform text, relating that the Ark's main deck area consisted of one IKU. This level has again been decreased by 360 inches. On this fourth terrace, which has again moved up 20 feet, we are standing at a latitude of 63° on a platform of 60 double cubits. Each side measures 2,520 inches, thus divided by the 120 cubits, we determine the Great Cubit of Babylon to be roughly 21 inches (20.988), slightly longer than the Ark's cubit and the cubit of the Great Pyramid.

This area is *exactly* the English acre of today, consisting of 44,100 square feet.

The levels continue in the same manner in rise of 6° until the *sixth* terrace, upon which sits the Temple of Belus. This structure was 1,440 inches (120 feet) square and 600 inches (50 feet) high, representing the last 15° of latitude.

The entire structure of the ziggurat rose from ground level at 40 inches to a degree, a total of 3,600 inches, the same as the square of the base, to represent the 90° of the northern hemisphere.

This IKU or acre we have found is comparable to other land measures in the ancient world as follows: The smaller Egyptian acre was the area a person could plow in a day. According to Herodotus, each face of the Pyramid consisted of eight Egyptian acres, which is a square of 100 cubits (20.6 inches) or 29,469 square feet. This is an area larger than the Roman acre (Jugerum) of 27,168 square feet, but still under the 43,560 square feet of today's American acre.

As we have seen, the IKU is the English acre and still not as large as the deck space of the Ark, for if we take the account of Moses, the Ark's deck space was 44,187 square feet (515 × 85.8).

The Bible's description is then slightly larger by a square of only 9.3 feet. This is almost insignificant to the whole and in my estimation cannot be in marked contrast to ancient mythology as the authority Scofield implies!

This accounts for the deck space of the main deck only, and if we used Moses' figures in describing the volume within the covering we could have the following possibilities:

One	Deck 51.1 in height	44,187 square feet
Two	Decks 25.75	88,374
Three	Decks 17.16	132,561 (Moses)
Four	Decks 12.87	176,748 (Josephus)
Five	Decks 10.3	220,935
Six	Decks 8.58	265,122 (Babylonian)

There is but one other dimension we should consider to see if the Babylonian description is at variance with the biblical account, and that is the height.

Let me make the suggestion that line 57 is not stating that each wall is 120 cubits high but that collectively the height of all four walls equals the same 120-cubit measure.

It must be realized that the speaker is trying to convey the size of the vessel, not the configuration! There never was a ziggurat built in the form of a cube, and there were never any of the seven stages of a ziggurat that were cubed or contoured (line 59). The text is simply giving the "basi" cube of 432,000 cubits, the same as giving the volume for a water jug. Each wall was then only 30 cubits in height and the difference between describing the net cargo capacity in Mesopotamic terms versus those of an Egyptian could be viewed as follows:

Babylonian (21.0″)	120 × 120 × 30 =	432,000 cubic cubits
	210 × 210 × 52.5 =	2,315,250 cubic feet
Biblical (20.6″)	300 × 50 × 30 =	450,000 cubic cubits
	515 × 85.8 × 51.5 =	2,275,630 cubic feet

That we shouldn't be searching for a rectangle any more

than a cube, "upon the mountains of Ararat" I think should be quite evident by line 59. I laid out *the contours,* drew it all!

We don't think of cubes as having contours but straight sides and corners. This term reflects curves, and the flowing lines of an "elippu" or "ma-gur," a reed boat the Babylonians were still familiar with. One text plainly describes it as such. The Atra-hasīs is an earlier text dealing strictly with the Flood story.

Thor Heyerdahl refers to these reed boats[4] quoting from a Finnish scholar who has amassed all the learned world has recorded of fragmentary references to them. Armas Salonen calls them in German "Papyrusboot," from the Babylonian term for reed ship, "elep urbati." This traditional vessel incised on the earliest seals was of the divine ancestor before Ur was settled. It was built from reeds, not from wood. It could refer only to the Ark.

That the Ark should be described as a cube is not surprising. Anything of volume was purposely described as such by the Sumerians, unless it was impossible to do so. In times when there was no recourse but to describe the volume outside of the square root number, they reverted to expressing two integers the same, then a third either increased or decreased by a unit. The Sumerians were so familiar with this they even supplied a term for it called "basi."

They were very adept at finding these solutions. When, for instance, a request for a jar for the stowage of grain or olives was given to the potter, it might be expressed in cubic volume such as 10. This would mean $10 \times 10 \times 10$, a cube. The customer of course was not wanting a cube but a jar consisting of the same volume, or 1,000 cubic finger widths (consider them as inches for our discussion). The potter would then go to his wheel and, applying the 10 to 11 rule, turn out a clay vessel of slightly larger capacity.

| Customer's order: 10 fingers cubed. | cubic capacity 1000 |
| Potter produced: | cubic capacity 1045 |

$$[r^2 \times pi \times 11]\ 5.5 \times 5.5 =$$
$$30.25 \times 3.1416 = 95.0334 \times 11 = 1045.3674$$

The added capacity posed no problem, as it is difficult to

---

[4]Thor Hyerdahl, *The Tigris Expedition* (New York: Doubleday & Co., 1981).

pour from a completely filled jar. The potter simply incised a full mark inside, and the remaining space provided room for the stopper or plug.

It should be noted that while it is tempting for me to suggest that the phrase in Genesis 6:15, "And this *is the fashion* which thou shalt make it of," actually *means volume,* there is no proof it does, for the phrase *is the fashion* appearing in the KJV does not appear in the original manuscript. The term supplied by the translators, *fashion,* is for the purpose of greater clearness. I am only putting forth the idea that it could refer to volume or storage capacity, as for many other objects made for containment.

VARUNA'S HOUSE OF CLAY

"I gave it six decks," the text continues in line 60, "and divided it thus into seven parts." In true maritime fashion, the lowest flooring was the bottom of the hold, and not considered a deck. The uppermost covering was termed *roof,*[5] and thus the structure consisted of seven spaces, yet only six floors are termed *decks.* This is a considerable departure from the other writers in the first part of this chapter. They used only the term *stories.* This term is ambiguous, as many people would consider a ground-level house as a one-story building, while others remark that a two-story building consists of the ground level and the first story above. Another problem in describing the structure from the outside is how high, or what is considered a story, especially by an eyewitness who dares not enter in.

In Persian traditions, the Ark is called Varuna's House of Clay. Thus the term *vara,* though meaning "an underground fortress or tomb," referred to the Ark, for when observers saw it, after the dust of time had almost buried it, they explained it was three stories *deep!* They described it as being *nearly* a horse run long (a stadia of 600 feet) with wide avenues inside. Apparently they entered it, explored the levels, and came away convinced Varuna had weathered the Flood by shutting

---

[5]The "overhead."

himself and survivors up inside, where they remained in safety until the waters receded. The Persian traditions will be found thus, not referring to it as a ship, due to their impressions of the site. They did not mention the levels of decks, just the stories as being three *deep,* or buried under the ground.

A very good example of a slipper coffin found in Anatolia is on display at the National Museum in Erzurum. My suggestion that it was in the form of Varuna's House of Clay was met with raised eyebrows, for they considered it Roman. It is true the coffin itself might be from Roman times, but this god was worshiped by the military aristrocracy of Mitanni, which held sway for a period over Assyria. In Roman times the worship of Mithra spread into Europe from Persia. The Assyrian word *metru* signifies rain. As a sky god, Mitra, like Varuna, was associated with the waters above the firmament. He was originally linked with the Deluge and "Ma-banda-anna," "the boat of the sky," as the Egyptian sun god Ra, whose barque sailed over the heavens and was originally the Uáa Nu, "the divine boat of Nu," or Noah.

In Persian mythology Mitra, as Mithra, is the patron of Truth, and the Mediator between heaven and earth. In later times he became regarded as the rain god. There are sublime Vedic hymns found in the Rigveda and striking passages in the Indian Mahabharata that associate this King Varuna with Noah, and worshipers of Varuna in the Punjab did not cremate their dead but placed them in a "house of clay" in the grave as in Babylonia.

Line 62 informs us that Utnapishtim's vessel had the innards divided into nine parts. Both the early slipper coffins, which this author recognizes as burial vessels depicting Varuna's House of Clay, have markings denoting nine divisions, as well as the remains of the Ark that show the structure divided by nine transverse bulkheads.

The coffin narrows and becomes slightly upswept at the foot, or stern, while the head of the coffin shows the strongly supportive bows.

The ancients have grasped the true concept of how the Ark was constructed. The Ark itself was only one component of a two-part system. The fortress, so to speak, built within the hogging truss support poles above the solid reed boat-shaped raft, nestled within the upswept stem and stern. This was then covered with reed matting and coated inside and out with what the Akkadians called "KPR," a bituminous mixture of feldspar and pumice that through a chemical reaction formed a zeolite that set up the mixture similar to portland cement.

Even the roof support beams displayed on the coffin suggest the fourteen described in other early accounts. The great amount of clay to be found within the confines of the boat shape is not due to a clay upswelling in a lava flow, as the experts suggest, but the remains of Varuna's House of Clay, and exactly what one should expect to find according to extrabiblical accounts.

"I struck water plugs into it" (line 63). These I would assume to be stoppers in the ports that would periodically be positioned along the main deck. Plugging the scuppers was something Utnapishtim might have wanted to do early on, so that no one could enter the Ark after he was sealed in. They could be knocked out after they were underway when no one was able to climb aboard, act as freeing ports, and be used for ventilation.

Line 64 continues with Utnapishtim saying, "I checked the poles." Here, I think, is our first clue as to what was the basis of the storied structure upon the reed boat-shaped raft. These would be hogging truss poles, which will be dealt with later, in the chapter explaining the Ark as I see it.

The subject of bitumen will be discussed in the chapter on the covering, so we will go on to the shars of oil.

Lines 66 through 69 refer to shars of oil being brought aboard. We have no idea of the total, as the amount of oil that was consumed in the seed meal (line 68) is not given. We have to assume also that it was either a fish oil or a vegetable oil fit for consumption, as it was apparently mixed into seed meal before being brought aboard. The other lines may then be referring to a petroleum product, not fit for consumption. The first mentioned, that brought aboard by the basket bearers, I would consider supplies, or simply lamp oil.

Line 69 also differentiates the purpose for these two shars brought aboard. Thus, I feel its separate mention for use by the boatman betrays its use.

The mystery as to why the boatman should stow away two shars of oil for his own use is quite natural.

Oil, from its inferior gravity, forms a floating film which

"defends" the surface of the water from contact with currents of air, and the friction between the wind and the waves is greatly reduced, in the same manner that friction between solids is diminished by the application of oil.

We continued to use oil for calming rough seas in the merchant marine, and one must really be on board to see the immediate and impressive results when applied. It was usually a linseed or fish oil, for best results. In most cases there were small cones in the sea anchors of lifeboats, with a petcock that allowed the oil to slowly leak out. This sea anchor, trailing astern the lifeboat as it is pushed ahead by the wind and the seas, then kept the waves from actually breaking upon you. As stated before, the action is quite impressive and I can envision the boatman on the Ark using it for the same purpose, trailing it down the anchor lines to the seas below and behind to ride as a film on the water.

The height of the Ark was still uncertain, and as for what was left, we would just have to see. We could assume it had three decks, but only within a structure that might be considered six stories high. The roof was most certainly gone, but there might be evidence of the roof beams I had discovered in another text as numbering fourteen.

We can see that historians disagree, but the description of the Babylonians didn't have to be considered that far off from the biblical one as some scholars suggested. The volume was almost the same.

In other words, let's forget for a moment that the Ark is a vessel according to our modern-day understanding. Let's look at it as a house or enclosed barnlike structure resting on a flotation device. If this entire utilized structure was six stories high overall, yet only the upper portion, *or the Ark* containing all the living creatures, consisted of the decks or the upper three stories, how do these various descriptions conflict with the Genesis account? If the upper portion, containing all the living, was above the hull and not within the hull, wouldn't this resolve the problem of the methane gas buildup and sanitation? All the waste would fall through the upper structure's floors to the main deck, to be washed overboard. It would be in a sense a free-bailing type of raft. It must be termed as such, since the lower portion could not become filled with water. In the Indian myths and legends, it was Manu, the Indian patriarch like the Babylonian Noah, who built a massive *raft* equipped with a long rope, and rode out the flood.

If this lower buoyant portion was 68.5 feet high, with the Ark and all the living space built within the hogging truss poles upon it containing the decks described, it truly would have been an imposing structure, easily described as six stories high.

THE UÁA NU OF CUBITS SEVEN

On June 6, 1985, I again stepped upon the threshold of the stem and, entering the Ark's interior from the bows, began walking uphill, looking at what lay before me in a different light. It was acceptable to have theories, but the concept would still have to be borne out by the evidence at hand.

On the starboard bow, near bulkhead #8, I looked again more closely at where two columns had fallen out of the matrix which seemingly held the structure together. I peered through the gap and saw them laying on the ground outside. They were badly broken, but from where they had fallen out they had left perfectly vertical slots. I could clearly see that the portion left standing contained two columns within. One projected upward through the matrix about a foot. It was not made of stone but seemed to be an agglomerated material. As crazy as it sounds, it looked like old portland cement and rough stone, or concrete. I motioned for Dilaver, and we measured them.

The columns had inward protruding extensions which appeared to me as upper-deck support beams that would run transversely across the span of the Ark to the matching projections on the other side. I had noted these before and mentioned them to Ron, but now I would measure them to be certain they just weren't an illusion. They were roughly two feet square and spaced on twelve-foot centers or spread seven cubits apart. That was a nice biblical number, I thought, and proceeded to the other side. Here were two projections wonderfully squared to the same dimensions, with a third faintly visible, and all seven cubits equidistant. I would love to have peeled back the matrix to find them connected with the

column, but we had no permit to excavate. That these projections were so evident at the bows, and not nearly as discernible
at the stern, was perhaps because they were more massive at
the bow end, or we were at a lower deck forward, while astern
they were intact and hidden under our feet.

The spacing of these upper-deck supports on seven-cubit
centers is interesting in light of the Egyptian concept of the
divine boat of Rā, for not only is the number seven divine in
biblical writings but in Egyptian writings as well. The Papyrus
of Ani; chapter 133, plate 22, line 19 and 20.

uáa   en   meḥ   seχef

The divine boat of cubits seven.

I propose the "divine boat of Rā" *is* the Ark of Noah, passing
over death's waters from one age to the next (or one life, or age,
into the other) and therefore the seven-cubit connection.

neter   ḥā   en   Rā   em   uáa   Nu

The divine body of Rā is in the divine boat of Nu.

I believe the divine boat of "Nu" was the original *Ark,* and
that Rā in a sense can refer to the first man. This will be
discussed in another chapter concerning the reliquary aboard
the Ark.

THE HULL POOL THEORY

These overhead support beam remnants indicated there was
once a deck that had spanned the mound over our heads and
that we were presently standing on a lower level, perhaps the
main deck itself. How then could this be a central ramp way?
It seemed logical that at this point, the widest beam of the
vessel, any deck feeling the age of collapse would fall here first,
since it was the widest span. Was the mound nothing but a
dunnage heap of above-deck material that had slid to the center
by the angle of the deck still attached at the walls? Or was it

God's mission completed, the members of George Vandeman's expedition returned home, accompanied by Turkish soldiers.

"It is not a stone formation. I know a ship when I see one." Words of a Turkish farmer named Reshit, 1948.

Panoramic view of the Ark's location.

I began the survey by locating the iron lines I had found in March of 1985. John Baumgardner looks on skeptically while an elder wishes Ron Wyatt good luck.

We attempted to locate transverse lines by walking between the longitudinal lines. The first one appeared at 47 feet down from the end.

Memet Erasalan holds tape at bulkhead #1. Width: 35 feet (10.66 m).

Down centerline to bulkhead #2. Distance: 40.5 (123.4m).

Centerline distance from bulkhead #3 to bulkhead #4: 20 feet (6.09 m). Width of #4 bulkhead: 86 feet (26.21 m).

Centerline distance from #4 to #5 bulkhead: 31 feet (9.44 m). No width recorded.

Centerline distance from bulkhead #5 to #6: 46 feet (14.02 m). Width: 120 feet (36.57 m).

Notice the starboard bow, at bulkhead #8. A column has fallen out. There is an upper deck support beam clearly exposed to the right.

Inside starboard bow, at transverse bulkhead #8. One column of side structure in situ. Column to right has fallen out.

Here, 2 columns are within the matrix, 1 with an upper deck support beam partially exposed. This and others are in perfect alignment with other remains, and equally spaced along the inner walls on the portside, showing the remains of a floor that had been above.

The upper deck support beams ran transversely from port to starboard, and at this point spanned a distance of 138 feet. Numerous vertical supports for these can be found running athwartship, and all give strong iron readings.

Dilaver Avci (right) and myself measuring the distance between each deck support. Cuneiform tablets state there are 14 roof support beams. If future surveys produce only this number, then these protrusions may indicate the upper deck. If more than 14 are found, I feel it suggests a lower deck.

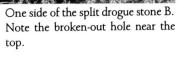

One side of the split drogue stone B. Note the broken-out hole near the top.

A field of sarcophagi and bones.

Rams and bulls appeared to be a favorite motif.

Mehmet Sali Gezen from Kazan and drogue stone G.

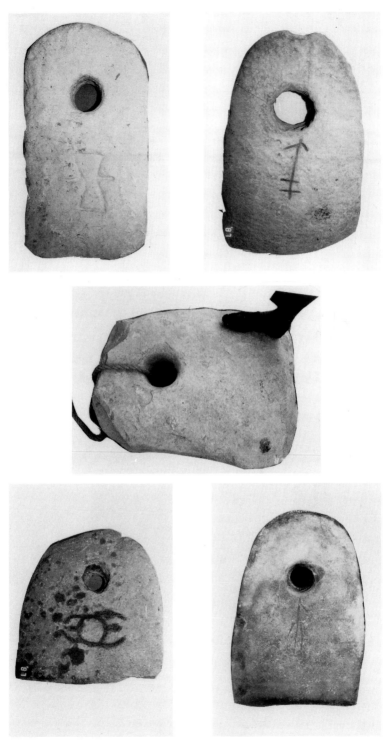

Examples of late-style anchor stones from the coast of Israel.

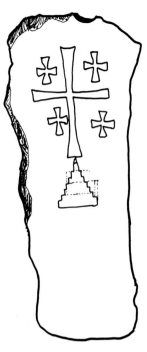

Anchor stone F field book sketch and notes.

Mehmet Sali Gezen shows hole remains.

Details of ziggurat.

"This is • ark mine • resurrection • son of • God † the boat • October 1245."

Ark symbol for "tomb" is considered by these early people as an enclosed structure mounted aboard another flotation device underneath, and slightly larger.

The hogging truss support poles showed clearly on the 69-foot scan, 75 feet down from the stern. The floors showed so clearly in this cross-cut view that the floorboards could be counted.

Two views of the Ark's innards taken in the positive mode.

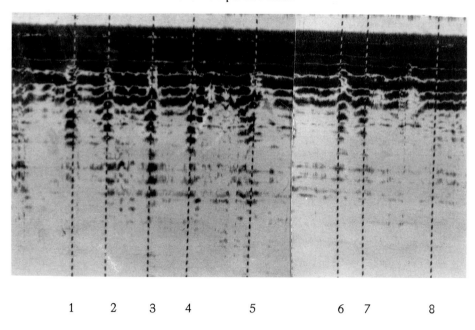

1   2   3   4   5   6   7   8

The event marker showing dotted lines on the paper printout of the radar scan was depressed as the transducer was pulled by the stakes showing subsurface walls by molecular frequency generation. One through 6 were dead-on, but walls 7 and 8 were missed. There are 13 walls running stem to stern. The photo below was the result of a scan running down the centerline. What appear to be walls may in reality be upright poles spaced closely together.

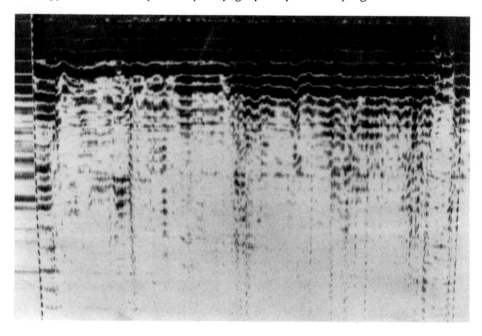

something else? What was suspicious was that there were no transverse bulkheads or walls to support it. What could it be, then?

There have been hull pools designed into ships for various reasons. I had two salvage vessels with them. The first use is as a handy way to dispose of something you weren't allowed to throw overboard. The second use is for belly lifts of heavy weights off the bottom, with no fear of capsizing. Drilling rigs have them, which enables the rigs to drill the ocean bottom through the center of the ship. It is in effect a bottomless pit through the hull of a boat, in most cases called a *hull pool*.

What reason should the Ark have for one?

A modern vessel cannot get under way with the hull pool open, as it normally creates too much drag. If it is of any size, it has hydraulic doors that close so the vessel can make some speed. But in this case, did the Ark desire any speed? It would appear that it should want to slow its forward momentum to let the sea go by her rather than be moved with it. In this case, then, the turbulence caused by a hull pool 26 feet by 201 feet would slow the momentum considerably. That could be one advantage, a hydraulic brake, in effect, to slow the Ark down. But there were more. If the Ark did carry drogue stones as the Koran seemed to be saying, then these trailing through the water in conjunction with the hull pool would be valuable storm gear indeed.

The water that extended up through the hull of the raft stabilized it. Since water cannot be sheared below the hull pool due to adhesion, any forceful action by a wave against the hull in any direction would cause an opposite reaction through turbulence created in the pool. It is then doubtful that any abrupt change in direction or momentum would occur in the Ark if it crested a wave, being taut on her sea anchor lines, or in the fetch (when the drogue lines might slack) because of the pool.

This is not to say the vessel couldn't be veered in direction or angle by a "liverpool sling" on her drogue lines if desired. These "brake" stones on an Egyptian vessel, as described by Herodotus, just kept the stern from breaking around. In the sea and on the Ark, in conjunction with the hull pool, it could keep it from broaching and coming beam to the sea!

It would also appear to be a keel in reverse. The water extends up into the hull instead of the hull keel extending down into the sea. Though I can't see this arrangement stabilizing the vessel to keep it from rolling in a following sea and yawing a bit, a normal keel wouldn't help much either in this situation. It did have the advantage of not striking bottom, and the vessel would remain upright on landing. Surely it couldn't be for a centerboard!

The main advantage I could see at this time was that it would relieve hogging stress loads on this portion of the hull due to its extreme beam width. It could keep the advantage of the width for stability and not suffer the stress caused by buoyancy with the hull open to the sea.

There could be an advantage for water runoff within the ship itself as the pool was a drain, in effect, a bottomless pit that would always remain at sea level regardless. I liked the idea. The Ark and my own vessels may have had something in common, and the more I enlarged on the idea, the thought of a hull pool advantage became almost limitless. Truly this was a survival vessel par excellence.

Why it could even breathe and ventilate itself with a system like this. The action of the sea within the pool acted like a large compressor piston moving up and down in a seaway! I was reeling with ideas as I approached the others at the stern who were waiting for me to begin scanning the walls.

The open pool relieved the hogging stresses on the hull. It had the seaworthy advantage of the wide beam without any negative effects, and it made the ship breathe!

THE IRON FITTINGS

At the stern I set up the frequency generator near the starboard quarter. This reading station would be set up differently. Instead of being within the Ark and setting up an intensely excited field through frequency generation of the molecules just below the frequency of iron, I would set up a field between the generator and the object's iron readings to the instrument's ground probes. John Baumgardner eyed me inquisitively. He had been impressed by the instrument's performance the day before and was startled by this different approach. "I would unhesitatingly say at this point that this instrument of yours seems to be working wonders," he commented. I set up the tripod and video equipment and we went to work.

Walking in front of the probes, the vector to the wall was like a pinwheel. I was in the flow some 50 feet away from the Ark with the instrument. I walked the outside line to the stern and then walked forward alongside the wall crossing line two. John marked the spot by driving an aluminum rod into the wall of dirt. We proceeded in this manner until we had exhausted our supply of rods. Then, laying the tape measure across the rods, we measured them: 3.4 feet, 7.2 feet, 13 feet, 18 feet, 21.6 feet, 24.5 feet, 27.8 feet, 31.6 feet, 36.9 feet. The distances between these iron readings then were 3.8 feet, 5.8 feet, 5 feet, 3.6 feet, 2.9 feet, 3.3 feet, 3.8 feet, and 5.3 feet. Not very encouraging! I figured the average spacing between the readings as 4.1 feet, and that converted to cubits showed me nothing of interest, just a random spacing of iron readings.

I walked behind the instrument and there were no lines other than those to the Ark. I shut the instrument down and assembled the pulse induction detector. John had set up Ron's deep probe detector and walked it up to the wall, tuned it between the rods, then swung it to a place he had marked. "When I tried to pound a rod in here," he commented, "I thought this looked like iron, and now I get a strong reading."

"Pull the aluminum rod out of the way and see if you still have it," I suggested.

"That won't make much difference," Ron responded. "It's a discriminator model." John yanked the stake and the reading was still there. He was getting excited now.

"What do you think, John?" I yelled. "Tell me this is natural. Look at these cracks. Don't these look like ribs with a crack on either side?" John hesitated. All scientists are slow to make a statement. He was certainly slow; he chose his words very carefully. He said something and hesitated again. *This is gonna be some statement,* I thought.

"I . . . would . . . say . . . that . . . the . . . cracks . . . are . . . a . . . consequence . . . of . . . the . . . rib . . . structure."

"We're here measuring pin spacing in the sides of the most significant boat in history, and you're playing semantics with me!" I exclaimed. "It's Noah's Ark!" I leaped into that state of mind Ron so often mentioned as being somewhere between tickled pink and pure hysteria. John's shoulders had dropped at the end of this grand statement. I put myself in his shoes for a moment. John was the guy who had to face all his colleagues at Los Alamos Labs. Would he lose all his credibility as a scientist? His eyes were sparkling now as he went slowly along the wall, removing the rods just to be certain.

There was iron above and below the spots I had marked with the rods. There was no doubt about it. John was going to be in trouble explaining this back home.

Wrapping up the gear on the outside, I followed the others back up through the dynamite hole blown out during Vandeman's visit, and into the stern area to the other side. John was on the port quarter about halfway between the stern and the rock intrusion area with Ron's metal detector bleeping away at regular intervals. "Well now, John, those are evenly spaced. Wouldn't you say these were vertical structural members and you're walking on top of them?"

"You mean I'm inside the boat and these protrusions are the tops of the ribs?"

"Yes," I answered. "Tops of columns or the sides of the structure, whatever you and Ron want to call them."

"Well no, I just seem to have iron readings from these stones."

"John, they appeared to you as ribs when you were below, outside on the ground. You can see they are part of the structure. You said so yourself."

"Whatever they are," he said, trying to resolve himself from the argument, "they appear to be just rocks that give signals. Look here," he continued, bending down to the source. He clasped his hands around the outside portion of one of the protrusions. He pulled hard and put all of his weight into it, his face turning red under the strain. It suddenly broke free. John stood and rolled it over in his hand. "Look at the color of this," he said in a muffled tone.

"John!" yelled Ron from a distance. "I'm surprised at you,"

he said half jokingly. "We're not supposed to be doing anything like that!"

John didn't hear the remark. I think he was off someplace in Tubal-cain's foundry five thousand years ago. He held in his hand a piece of wrought iron. The grain of the stretched and hammered angle bracket still clearly visible.

It was complete pandemonium after that. Once John knew what to look for, fittings were all over the place. He could walk down the top of the wall, with the detector going *beep . . . beep* every two or three steps. Now it was the trained eye of a scientist, looking for things out of place in the natural covering of the mud, followed by his "Look at this!" growing in excitement. I kept the video going as I ran around, stumbling behind him, then moved to the mound to record his discoveries from a distance to give perspective to the viewer. No sooner had I left him when he suddenly yelled, "Undecomposed iron!"

I ran down the mound again and crouched to my knees. I zoomed in on the mud wall. There, surrounded by the brown matrix of mud, was a perfectly rectangular beam end of a bluish-gray agglomeration of small rough stones. The upper and lower right corners were *absolutely* square, and projecting from within were what appeared to be iron flakes which had given the signals. "John," I said, "is this a ferrocement boat?"

I'll never forget the look on his face, though he never answered my question. His wide eyes and bright smile looked clear through me. He would say only, "I'd save those frames," and when I at last took my attention away from the beams, John was well on his way to the bow.

Ron, meanwhile, had positioned himself on the top of the mound near the bow. He wasn't going to miss getting this on film for the world. He was also restraining, with Dilaver's help, the farmers and children who wanted to rush to each new discovery. He was grinding away with his 16mm camera when I suggested to John that he try to get readings from what appeared to be piles of cementlike projections running along the inside curve of the walls. They were identical on each side, and I had measured them before. They were spaced in a gentle curve with the bow at 0 feet, 13 feet, 22 feet, 29 feet, 37 feet, 50 feet, and 60 feet.

John started by the base of the protrusion and walked slowly up the inside curve. Even areas that were under the earth before the obvious remains that were visible gave readings. John went beeping along. He got four readings before he got to those that were visible and those I had measured; ten, eleven, twelve, "You're on the supports for the hogging truss poles," I yelled. "Come on John, make a statement," I said while the video zoomed in on his face. He turned and continued up the hill, beeping at regular intervals, till he turned again and beamed a smile.

"Maybe I shouldn't make a statement quite yet," he said.

"Come on, John, what do you think this is you're walking on?" He fumbled again for the right words, started to speak, then hesitated. The video clicked off, out of film. "Good grief," I yelled, "you missed your chance! It's Noah's Ark!" "Ooookay," yelled the Kurds, having been held restrained out of camera range too long. They all ran down from the mound to our objects of interest.

It was about two o'clock and we had gotten the Turks as excited as we were. "Maybe we ought to break for a while," Ron suggested. "We don't want to encourage any digging on their part." It was a good idea.

I asked Memet and Ahmet to come back into town with us. We would leave the Ark, for now, to see some of the anchor stones Ron had discovered on a previous trip. First, though, we needed a little freshening up. We packed up our gear and with help from the villagers we proceeded to climb up the hill to the road and Dilaver's little Renault. Each child in attendance tugged at my pant leg as we climbed the hill. Would I take their picture before going? Musa extended more *dekan*, the magical Plant of Youth, and I tucked the stalks into my pocket. Each child was being shooed away by the elders as we continued our climb up the flow. I suddenly realized I might never return, and I turned to face them and waved good-bye. At the top of the hill we all shook hands and embraced in the Turkish custom of a touch of the cheek on both sides. I really loved these people! So close to the earth and so proud. They would always be close to my heart, and I'd miss them.

There wasn't any need for explanations to the Turkish peasants; they knew what it was. The world of the skeptic was ages from here, and I hated to leave. Our two friends climbed into the taxi and we crept slowly down the winding road, slipping back into our own place in time.

This book sucks total ass

6

Kazan*

THE GRAVE ROBBERS

We left Doğubayazıt late in the afternoon, which is not the wisest time of the day to set out on a project. In Florida, my home, the sun sets on the flatlands. Here, you can be halfway into a great adventure when the lights go out, blocked by the mountains to the west.

But we had time to show John Baumgardner the anchor stones Ron had discovered some years ago. That was the time Ron had gotten into trouble with the Kurds, and to hear him tell it, it had been a run for his life. Ron was still pretty shook up about it. He was tough and could handle himself, but because he was so big, they would go after him in numbers.

When we had visited this village last March, we became virtually surrounded while looking at the anchor stones. Of course we hadn't just barged in. We had entered by taxi and motioned that we would like to walk through the village to the other side to view the monuments. Women slammed doors and the children shrank back from sight as the dogs lunged in feigned attack on the strangers. The Elder would throw rocks at the dogs to drive them back and I had noticed before that Kurds seem pretty deft at throwing rocks. Many carried the scars to prove it.

I think our interest in the monuments as anchor stones was not understood by the younger men who formed a group around us. This village had been a Christian village at one time. That was quite evident from the graves that gaped open

---

*For those readers wishing to visit Kazan, see note on pages 156, 157.

148

in the abandoned cemetery surrounding the large, upright, flat stones, with their tops pierced by a hole.

Who were we, they wondered, and why our interest in Kazan, and its graveyard? It was not merely with natural curiosity and country hospitality that we were ushered into a meeting room to get out of the cold. Dilaver couldn't explain to them what we wanted, as this was his first trip with us, and perhaps he didn't know what we were looking for either. I wanted to explain to them by drawing pictures of the Ark and the stones, but Ron stopped me from doing so. Then they brought out the "goodies."

It was a bronze piece, probably Hittite or Scythian. We politely tried to show we weren't interested, but then with a figure of 300 lira (less than fifty cents) perhaps it was the way to go. Then we could leave, having conducted the "business." But the price then became 3,000 lira (almost five dollars), still worth it to complete the transaction. Ron asked if I could loan him the money, as he had only change showing in his hand. At first I thought, *What nerve! I'll buy it myself if you can't afford it.* Then I suddenly realized I couldn't pull out my wad of money in front of these guys. It didn't matter, for soon one leaned forward, smiled through his whiskers, and implied we had made a mistake again. The price was 30,000 lira. Dilaver could see they were baiting us as the figure scrawled in my field book by the man had clearly been 3,000. Ron stood up, towering over the men as they sat cross-legged on the cold carpeted dirt floor. Dilaver, too, showed that negotiations had reached an end.

One man stood up and headed to the door in response to a thump from the other side. It was only a woman, who handed him a tray of cups and a pot of hot tea. Everyone relaxed a bit. I enjoyed two cups and passed some cigarettes around, but Ron's anxiety showed. Now the villagers had really become suspicious as to what we were up to in Kazan; they still hadn't had that explained. Ron again rose, thanked his host with a big smile, and headed for the door. We all filed out in a bit of confusion, and the village men followed us to the car. Dilaver kept them busy in discussion about something, and finally, with the taxi as a means of escape, we pulled down the road out of town.

Ron's face was flushed. "I saw one of them," he said. "I'm sure that was him. If the guys who caused me trouble are from this town, we have to be careful.

"What do you think of them now, David?" he said after a brief sigh.

"Ron," I said, "I don't know how you find these things, but those sure look like anchor stones to me! That's really good scouting."

And now here we were, returning almost three months later. The area looked more inviting somehow in the greenery of early summer, as we turned off the main road toward Kazan.

Dilaver's little "taksi" accommodated the six of us snugly. Ahmet and Memet, our friends from Üzengili near the Ark site, rode in silence and doubt as to where we were heading as we bumped along the desolate back road. We skirted the village Ron felt was dangerous by heading down a track leading into a valley off to the side. Coming to a stream where the water literally gushed from the earth nearby, we all got out as Dilaver gently nursed his Renault through the shallows, while we skipped across stones to the other side. Reentering, we rode some three-quarter-mile distance, then stopped. Ahmet and Memet hoisted our gear to their shoulders and we began the walk to the ridge line that lay to the south. Dilaver would stay behind to guard his taxi.

We crested the top and walked east in the lee of the hills out of sight. It was getting to be quite a jaunt. "Is this how Ron finds things?" John remarked jokingly, remembering our circular trek looking for the anchor stone at the Ark. "They seemed friendly enough last March," I chided Ron.

"I'm trying to approach the area of the anchor stone so the villagers don't see us," Ron said, getting a little huffy. "I'm telling you, this village is dangerous."

The anchor stone overlooked the village of Kazan in a haze of smoke from kitchen fires in the valley below. At a time in the past, when the stone had been upright in the ground, it must have made a silhouette against the setting sun, for all to see.

For those who might want to dig underneath, it would be best to bring it down out of sight first, before beginning the job. There was an open pit, filled with shards, and the bottom of the anchor stone lay buried in the earth. "Look here," John said. "See these marks? Someone chiseled a dotted line across the monument and it broke when they hit it in unison. This couldn't have been the work of a loner but a group project to break a stone this size."

"Do you think it's a grave?" I asked.

"Yep!" John replied as he cautiously lowered himself down and tried to lift out the remaining piece to see what was underneath. "Ooooff!" he exclaimed. So we all lent a hand. Even all five of us couldn't budge it.

"Well, even if it was a grave, John, I'd feel very privileged to be buried in the shadow of an anchor stone from Noah's Ark," I said, climbing out of the hole. John wasn't convinced.

We looked at the stone itself laying broken in two pieces.

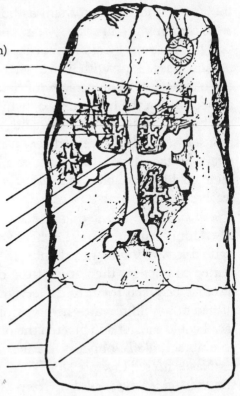

Diameter 7"-3½" (18cm-9cm)
9½" ×4" incised Teutonic

10" × 5" incised Maltese
7" × 4" incised Teutonic
11½" × 5½" relief Globed

8½" × 4" incised Maltese

11" × 5½" relief Globed

51" × 42" relief Eastern
   Orthodox (Greek,
   Russian, and Armenian)

16" × 8" relief Globed

Chisel marks
Portion still in ground

Division crack
Overall height 10 feet

Anchor Stone B Field Book Sketch and Notes 6/6/85

The hole was broken out but the pieces were there, so we assembled them all for a picture. The hole was off center, and I wondered if the makers had hung the stone for proper balance and thus determined where it should be, or purposely made it to the side so it would waggle or veer out like a trawl door on a shrimp rig. Whoever had carved the hole had done a beautiful and exacting job. At 3.5 inches in the center it widened out to 7 inches, accurate and smooth.

The stone's surface was gray, and spotted in orange and vermilion lichen growth from ages past. At the fresh break in the middle of the stone, where it had been split lengthwise upon hitting the ground, was a faint halo. It was 180° of a circle, like a rainbow of colors, a beautiful semicircle of multi-colored granules that would not have been visible had the stone not been broken.

There were eight crosses. Ron said they were iconographic representations of Noah, Ham, Shem, Japheth, his wife, and his three daughers-in-law. The Christians recognized what they were and regarded them as holy stones. "This type of cross certainly is Christian," John said, studying the composition of the stone. "Certainly clean, not fossiliferous."

John was talking with Ron about the stone being seemingly out of place with the geology of the immediate area, when I glanced down the hill and saw them coming.

There were seven of them, and only five of us. Memet's moustache suddenly seemed very dark as all the color drained out of his face. I told Ron not to turn around too fast and that there could be trouble. As I was speaking I saw one of them reach down and grab a rock. *This is all I need, getting into a rock fight at my age.* But one man looked familiar to me. I remembered him from the village, where we'd had tea last March. I figured it was worth the chance. If I approached first and it started to happen, then at least the others would have some distance between them to decide what they wanted to do. I rushed downhill toward them with the biggest smile on my face I could muster and greeted the one I had recognized with an embrace, like a long-lost relative.

"Nasılsınız? [How are you?]" My acquaintance appeared startled and let the rock drop from his hand. A faint smile of recognition crept over his face, but the others remained serious. There were some questions directed toward our porters, and a general milling about. A sort of jockeying for positions, it appeared to me, and no one wanted to be downhill of us.

The leader was as cold as ice, and his black eyes held our attention so we dared not turn away. I don't think he had ever smiled in his life. He held out his hand for my logbook and leafed through my field notes. He appeared satisfied and pointed in different directions. I pretended to understand but he wasn't persuaded. He then began to sketch things, and began describing a lineup of sorts. It was later recalled that the leader may have been trying to tell me that the holes lined up to show something, like a sight line to another grouping of objects, but I was just agreeing at the time.

Soon the leader beckoned us to follow him. We went off in the opposite direction he'd been pointing, and while trailing behind him I ventured a glance at Ahmet, who looked as if he were going to be sick. Memet, too, looked agitated and nervous, and I began wondering what we had gotten ourselves into. We trudged along the backside of the hills. I was sure we were walking past the taxi, out of sight, and Dilaver knew nothing of our plight. I didn't know how I was going to tell these guys, but I think I wanted to leave and go back into the safety of town.

The leader now descended to an area where the landscape was broken and jagged, a secluded corner in a hook of the turn of the hills. Suddenly it all became clear. The area was the size of a football field, and everywhere there were human bones. Coffins were uprooted and lay scattered about at oblique angles. There were monuments, too, of animals in stone. The men watched me closely and checked for my reaction.

I figured I had two choices. I could give them a stern look and say, "The minister of culture is going to hear about this," or give them something more laudatory, the equivalent to, "Hey, far out!" I chose the latter course. They grinned approvingly. I took some pictures and we all moved off again. Maybe they saw themselves as historians, too. At any rate, the situation was improving.

John was along for the walk but kept silent. He had given a disapproving glance at my reaction to the graveyard scene. We soon came to another anchor stone, which had only half the hole remaining. This stone anchor had earlier-type crosses, and it, too, had been rooted from its upright position. I was surprised to see by the lichen growth that it had been set upright with the hole down and buried. If the hole had been an important part to the meaning of the stone, why had it been stood upside down with the hole hidden? If this was the case, then many of the stones of the same size we had seen in the village in March may have had the holes buried, too. How many drogue stones had the Ark left here?

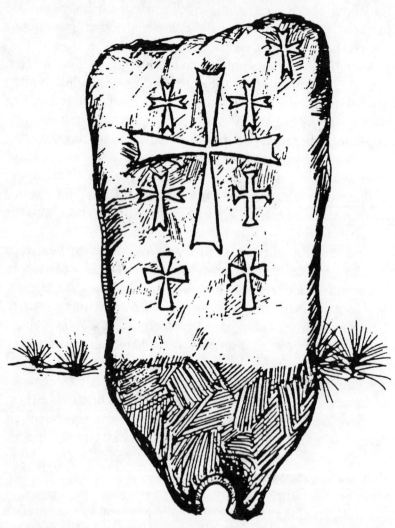

Anchor Stone C Field Book Sketch and Notes 6/6/85

These stones were recognized by Ron Wyatt in the late 1970s as drogues from the Ark. His discovery of this particular stone marks the first drogue, in my opinion, that brought the Ark to rest in the seventh month, seventeenth day, in the six hundred years of Noah's life.[1]

According to Ron's theory, the three Maltese (or eight-pointed crosses) above the central cross, representing Noah, are the daughters-in-law. The fourth, of similar design under Noah's right arm, is his wife. Under Noah's left arm, a wedged cross representing Shem, and below, two Teutonic crosses representing Ham and Japheth.

That this anchor stone had been mounted upright as a monument with the broken-out hole down made me suspicious that many more of what appeared to be tombstones in the graveyard at Kazan were in fact originally monuments and anchor stones as well. Had the crosses been placed on them by the early Christians, or had some been marked before? Did they simply take them over for their own use, and had they realized fully what they were?

This stone was in one piece and was slightly smaller. It measured 7 feet long but only 2 feet, 3 inches wide at the bottom. It was 10 inches thick and altogether a much lighter drogue, with the remainder of the hole showing it had a 4-inch diameter. I took bearings of the peak of Ararat at 70° and İsak Paşa bearing 122° standing out above Doğubayazıt in the setting sun. The elevation of this stone was 5500 feet, and before leaving, I started counting the crosses, slowly tracing them out in the failing light . . . five . . . six . . . seven . . . "heigşt,"[2] one of them growled, as the leader pointed out the eighth cross to me. Then rolling his hand over toward the heavens, he repeated several times, "Hazar, hazar, hazar!"[3]

We walked toward the road and taxi. What had he meant? Was he trying to tell me how old it was? And did he have any idea what it was?

Dilaver saw us coming, and acting nonchalant, began wiping the dirt from his windshield. He greeted the men respectfully with the Moslem Selâmaleyküm and they responded in return. Then with all of us anxious to leave,

---

[1]Genesis 8:4.
[2]"Eight," in the Kurdish dialect.
[3]Meaning "thousand."

Dilaver sat down. The villagers did the same. Dilaver leaned back, feigning he was perfectly at ease and had nothing to fear from his hosts. After some small talk we made ready to leave. I could gather that our purpose had been explained. I had watched Dilaver crossing his fingers in explanation of the use of my instrument, which drew approving glances from the others. As our team piled the gear in the car, the leader turned to me and, blocking the others from view, made that cracking sound with his tongue against his teeth. He held up three fingers, pointed to the heavens, to me, and to himself. A hand was raised in a gesture of leaving the others behind, then he placed his finger below his left eye. He had something he wanted to show me. "Ezzay baymay," I replied in a hushed tone, one of the few Kurdish expressions I knew. "I will come back."

They stood in the road watching our departure. The leader had not smiled once, and during the ride back I began to reflect on the encounter. "We invaded their territory unannounced," I said to Ron. "We broke a social code by doing so. Wouldn't it have been polite to have gone directly into Kazan, make our greetings as before, and make it known what we were after, more anchor stones? This guy could show us a lot if we could gain his trust!"

Ron turned to me in anger. "I'm telling you, David, these guys are killers. All sorts of people have disappeared around here."

Dilaver widened his eyes and, pulling his first cigarette of the day away from his mouth, sucked in a great draft of air through his teeth, shaking his wrist in the gesture of a close call. "Hayır güzel [no good]," he exclaimed. "Kazan, hayır güzel!"

I knew I would seek this man out again. There was no doubt he had something to show me. Dilaver had mentioned Noah's Ark in Turkish, and Memet had mentioned it, too. There was something he wanted me to see that, by his gestures, was known only to him and Allah.

And I began laying plans as we rode through the dark, back into town.

I cannot close this section without this important note. There seems to be confusion about the village being named

Kazan (meaning, "cauldron"). Although I have endeavored to solve this mystery, I have been unable to do so.

The villagers will tell you the village name is Kazan, yet it does not say that on the map! There is a large outcropping to the south of the anchor stones called Yalıntaşdağı. *Yalın* means "steep rocky slope," while *taş* means "stone." *Dağı*, of course, just means "mount." On the map, Kazan is plainly marked to the south of this mount, while it would appear it should be north of the mount. The village where the anchor stones can be found is marked Arzap, and a little farther west is a place called Sağlıksuyu, or "Healthwater," referring to springs in the area where carbonated water boils to the surface. There is no village there, only ruins. Nobody seems to know where Arzap is, yet if you say, "Take me to Kazan," they never go where Kazan should be (according to the map) but to the village we visited and I might add, appear reluctant to do so, if not just outright refuse to go.

It may have been wise for me to go to this place of Kazan, as marked on the map, to discover what *is* there, but time did not permit. It may be that the village no longer exists, and everyone just moved to Arzap, replacing it with the name of their old village, or those people we met wanted to remain anonymous enough to give us a false name to throw us off. This may be of little interest to the reader but could most certainly cause confusion for those who would like to see these anchor stones for themselves.

PUTTING TO REST THE ARK COMING TO REST

And the ark *rested* in the seventh month, on the seventeenth day of the month, upon the mountains of Ararat.

Genesis 8:4 author's italics
KING JAMES VERSION

And on the seventeenth day of the seventh month the ark *came to rest* on the mountains of Ararat.

Genesis 8:4 author's italics
NEW INTERNATIONAL VERSION

Although there is no real difference in terminology here, I want the reader to notice that these revisionists are still in the

habit of changing around the sentence structure of the statement. I cannot stress strongly enough that this will ultimately
lead them into serious difficulties. Their assumptions of the
Ark being built on the Hebrew cubit, and their misinformation
and interpretation of the meaning of gopher wood, has resulted in an erroneous assumption and should not have been
written into the text.

There are numerous cases where these biblical revisionists
have blatantly changed the meaning of the text by supplanting
a Hebrew word that can only be in the plural form, into the
singular form. As an example, in Genesis 3:5, the serpent
(Satan) said to Eve in her temptation, ". . . and ye shall be as
gods, knowing good and evil" (author's italics). In the New
International Version it has been changed to read, ". . . and
you will be like *God,* knowing good and evil" (author's italics).
Now I might not have any academic standing, but I'll be
toe-to-toe with any Christian revisionist who says that word
in Hebrew is in singular form!

The revisionists' reason for changing the original Hebrew
text would seem to stem from their dislike of the word in its
Hebrew plural form, suggesting that there are many gods,[4] or
at least more than one.

To the Christian mind (and Moslem as well) this is an
abhorrence, lending credence to the polytheists, necessitating
the change. But the reader will note that the statement is
Lucifer's (embodied in the serpent), and since Lucifer is the
"father of the lie," his statement should be taken as such. Satan
is suggesting, by stating "gods" in the plural, that he and
his friends are gods also, and possibly intimating at least that
Eve's Creator is nobody special, and at most, an outright fraud
in suggesting he was so.

The original lie, then, that is alive and well and living on the
earth today, is that through knowledge "ye shall be as gods,
knowing good *and* evil" (author's italics). You'll notice that
does not imply man shall be able to discern good *from* evil! This
direct expression of free will against the will of God was Eve's
free choice.

---

[4]The word is *el-o-heem,* and the plural of *el-o'-ah,* a deity or gods in the ordinary sense
as angels, and left in the plural sense in over two hundred other instances.

Lucifer had of course made this same decision himself, and learned that wisdom is knowledge rightly applied. Lucifer's motive of enticement toward Eve to make the same mistake in judgment might be viewed as an attempt to enlist her in his celestial revolution, or to cause the fall of mankind in envy of God's creation, or simply, "misery loves company."

The reader must forgive my digression in subject, but it is important to mention what can happen when a simple change from plural to singular occurs. In the context of our subject, the example was given to drive home the point that the revisionists of today have not changed the word mountains (plural) to mountain (singular), at least *not yet!* But will it stay that way for long? Here is a recent quote from an expert:

> If it can be verified beyond a shadow of a doubt that Noah's Ark is indeed still surviving *on Mount Ararat,* the significance of *such a verification* would be monumental. . . . *If this can be confirmed,* then it *indirectly demonstrates the existence of God.*
>
> Josh McDowell and Don Stewart
> Excerpt From *Reasons*

One might reason by McDowell's statement that if it could be verified the Ark did not exist on Mount Ararat but was somewhere else, it would be so unmonumental as to be almost insignificant to the point of not warranting a look, and if not on Mount Ararat, indirectly demonstrate that God does not exist!

The reader might now start to suspect that the real reason the boat-shaped object has been laying rejected by Christendom for so many years after the pseudotheologians blew the sides out of it with dynamite is not that they didn't see it had possibilities but that it might prove the Bible wrong, to their way of thinking.

This typical publication by Ark-hunting fundamentalists, in this case called the Omega Research Team, continues by adding another requirement to the search:

> To find such a vessel *at the 15,000 feet level* on a mountain in eastern Turkey would show that:
> 1. There was a flood and that it was global in nature.
> 2. The Bible is historically accurate and trustworthy.

3. There was a judgment which therefore implies the existence of
   God.[5]

The publication goes on with an appeal that they cannot
accomplish this mission without your help, but not before
giving a representative listing of the many reputable people
who have, over the last two thousand years, given testimony
to the Ark's existence "high atop Mount Ararat." The histo-
ricity of the Bible and trustworthiness of the Scriptures now
seemingly hinge on its not just being on Ararat. It must be at
15,000 feet. A vessel at 6,500 feet on another mountain isn't
even worthy of a second look.

When this difference of opinion is presented, the fundamentalists become very combative, which then causes me to
announce my conclusions in a forceful manner, and many
who find their pet theories challenged are antagonized.

It is true that a rack of carabiners, ascenders, and crampons
slung over a brightly colored nylon parka is more picturesque
than groveling through a mud flow at a lower elevation in
cottons, but I am more interested in finding the Ark than
adventure on Ararat!

The French archaeologist Andre Parrot has been quoted as
saying, ". . . the only appropriate attitude to be adopted by the
scientific community toward these periodically recurring attempts to discover remains of the biblical Ark high amid the
snows and ice is . . . silence." He sums up his position by
saying at the outset, "The search for the Ark on Mount Ararat
must be considered a failure," and as he so well expresses it,
"expeditions with Ararat as their goal have more to do with
mountain climbing than any search for the Ark or archaeology!"

Before the reader misunderstands my feelings about these
people, let me explain that they have caused me great consternation and heartache in their rejection, but the problem is
theirs, not mine. I love these people, I just dislike what they are
saying! Even a dear friend such as Colonel James Irwin,
though stating he was intrigued with my research, unjustifi-
ably commented that even if I could prove it was a man-made

---

[5] *Ark Expedition Circular* (Lake Arrowhead, California: CBC, 1986).

object or boat, he would not be convinced it was Noah's Ark. Because we are friends, he would joke that perhaps if I found Noah's logbook he might be swayed. I would unhesitatingly say that if I found a bronze maker's plaque on the main beam that said:

NOAH & SONS
CATTLE CARRIERS
SHURIPPAK
BUILT AT
TUBAL-CAIN
FOUNDRY

they would not be convinced, for even after Irwin saw the object and published a photo of it in his newsletter, he would say, "Could it be Noah's Ark? I doubt it. . . . If this is the Ark, then what about all the reports of sightings on Mount Ararat?" Irwin falls into the same trap as the others by stating:

> I think if the remains of the Ark are found high on Mt. Ararat, it will be additional verification of the truth of God's word.[6]

Yes indeed, what about all the reports of sightings on Mount Ararat? What is everyone really trying to verify – their own questionable research and these spurious eyewitness accounts, or the truth of God's Word?

Let me make it clear once again to the reader. The Bible does not state that the Ark is 450 feet long, built of cypress, or perfectly preserved under the snows at 15,000 feet high atop Mount Ararat. Only the revisionists do, and as to its material of construction and dimensions, this is not the Word of God, or even Moses, but an interpretive modern-day rendering by a panel of revisionists and published in New York City, not heaven.

These Ararat Ark hunters' motives are laudable, but unfortunately their impression that the world awaits their finding the Ark of Noah with bated breath to prove or disprove the existence of God is quite sad in light of their often-quoted statement from the late editor of *National Geographic:*

---

[6]James Irwin, *High Flight Foundation Newsletter,* September 1985.

> If the Ark of Noah is ever discovered, it will be the greatest archaeo-
> logical find in human history and the greatest event since the resur-
> rection of Christ; and it will alter all the currents of scientific thought.

National Geographic will tell you today what they told me last
year: "Noah's Ark is outside our readers' scope of interest."

Leaving behind the Noah's Ark of our Sunday-school days,
and going ahead with the creditable Ark of the historic event,
we will reason together the meaning of the term *rest,* or what
is really meant by the phrase *coming to rest.*

The Ark was not impaled by the peak of Ararat, nor was it
cast upon the shores of Ararat. The Bible says, "And the Ark
rested . . . upon the mountains of Ararat" (rendered as Armenia in the original KJV). At this very moment, there are ships
at rest all over the world, after their arduous journeys.

There are some phrases here that must be explained. They
are internationally acceptable the world over and have been
ever since men sailed ships. The term *at rest* can only mean
"not under way and not making way." It does not mean
beached, stranded, or aground! This is something quite different from the purpose for which a vessel is made, and that is
to *float!*

A vessel is not under way, then, when it is made fast to the
ground through an anchor or mooring. If a boat is tied to a
dock and the dock fastened to the shore or the bottom, then
the vessel is made fast to the bottom as well and is not under
way.

One might consider the captain of a vessel having success-
fully completed a trip from Japan across the Pacific without
incident, only to drive his vessel aground on the mud flats of
the south bay, as coming to rest!

I can assure you, this is termed *poor seamanship,* and I don't
hold such a low regard for Noah or his ability to command the
vessel of his own making!

Should he have allowed this to happen on an island in the
middle of nowhere, what would have been the result—the
replenishment of man on the Island of St. Helena in the middle
of the Atlantic?

If Noah had come to rest somewhere other than a continent,

without the means of escape, the preserver of the seed of mankind would have been in dire straits indeed!

The second phrase is *making way*. This can be a little more difficult for the uninitiated to grasp, but it must be fully understood for our future discussions. A vessel can be moving about even if loosely tied to a dock, or swinging at anchor. But technically, even if making way under power toward her anchor, the vessel is not under way until the anchor is clear of the bottom.

Then there can be cases where a vessel is under way yet is not making way through the water. A sailboat becalmed is an example of this. In my early career at sea, I many times shipped aboard foreign tramp steamers that broke down in the middle of the ocean. This needn't be a tense situation if you have plenty of sea room. However, in the straits of Singapore, at night, and in heavy traffic, it can be a pretty harrowing experience, for a vessel not making way has no forward motion through the water, and thus no steerage. With no steerage way and no control over a vessel's movements, being carried by wind and current and in general at the mercy of the elements at hand, you are out of command of your vessel!

THE LAUNCHING

Let's consider Noah's launching of the Ark in the following scenario. According to extrabiblical texts, it was not a steady lift-off in a heavy rain. These are childhood concepts that must be put to rest.

The Sanskrit text of the *Mahábhárata* (Vana Parva) states, "The earth, as if oppressed with an excessive burden, *sank down,* suffering pain in her limbs, and the earth in distress was deprived of her senses by excessive pressure" (author's italics). This certainly doesn't sound like a heavy rain that caused the Flood.

We must remember that the only description of this event was from the survivors, so on this point of the globe, those aboard the Ark felt this excessive pressure. On the other side of the earth, those doomed to destruction felt just the opposite.

As the celestial visitor, a heavenly body of great size, passed close to the earth, its gravitational effect could be sensed by humans as a growing feeling of weightlessness. During the planet's approach, the gravitational pull on the magma, the great deep beneath the crust, was beginning to heap, causing a bulge or oblation that moved with the force. This abnormal movement of magma created a void under the crust on one side of the earth, causing it to settle or sink, while on the other side of the earth, ocean plates were rising, dispelling the seas.

We all realize that the flattening of the polar crust is due to the magma beneath having moved through centrifical force to the equatorial zones, causing oblation of the crust in that area. As if the tidal influences on the magma were not enough, the earth, losing its equilibrium, now tilted in space in an axis shift and was *deprived of her senses!* This reminds us of Isaiah 24:1 KJV: "Behold, the Lord maketh the earth empty, and maketh it waste, and turneth it upside down, and scattereth abroad the inhabitants thereof."

Carcasses of mammoths and rhinoceroses in northern Siberia bear witness to this. The inhabitants need not have been all human! The Babylonians described the earth's crust sinking: "the god of the underworld tore out the posts of the dam." This speaks of movements under the earth's crust and a tidal surge of the magma. The Greeks describe it this way: "Zeus broke up the fountains of the deep." These fountains of magma shot through the crust at fissures, and the earth's atmosphere became darkened by worldwide volcanic activity. The Mesopotamian texts say that "a black cloud rose up from the horizon."

But still there was no rain.

With all this movement of the crust it can be seen that the Ark was definitely not held in her launching position by "stilts," as so often portrayed, but was protected by "earthworks."

The Babylonian accounts continue by saying that during this period, "All the earth spirits leaped up with flaming torches, and with the brightness thereof they lit up the earth." Only recently have scientists discovered through high-speed photography that in some cases, lightning does not come down to strike the earth, but the discharge is from the earth itself to the heavens. Such a display that could have occurred during this event may have been electrical discharges interacting between the earth and its "visitor" of enormous capacity, the Ann'-u-na-ki, the generic name for the gods of the earth as opposed to the Igigi spirits of heaven. Another text describes the Annunaki as departing the earth where they left it afire to cower in the heavens (an electrical display) like dogs fearful of what was to become of the earth.

These events prior to the Deluge itself are remembered in the Brazilian Flood legend, which tells us that Monan, the chief god, sent a great fire to burn up the world and its wicked inhabitants, and a magician caused so much rain to fall in extinguishing the flames that the earth became flooded.

The fact that the mammoth found at Beresovka during exhumation had undigested food in the stomach and buttercups in the mouth showed it had not died of drowning but had been quick-frozen with his last breath and suddenly covered by a layer of ice some four meters thick. This still remains a mystery today. Many scientists have tried to provide the answers, but as in the Book of Job (Chapter 38), the Lord answers, "Who is this that darkeneth counsel by words without knowledge?" (v.2). Where did this ice come from? The Lord asks man, if he has the understanding, to answer him. "Out of whose womb came the ice? and the hoary frost of heaven, who hath gendered it?" (v.29).

Who or what indeed! Did the waters come from the heavens as the waters that were above the firmament (Genesis 1:7) in this celestial canopy collapse?

The Deluge that resulted plus the incoming seas from the sinking plates and the onrushing tidal wave from the waters that were displaced from the ocean basins seem almost too severe to allow anything to survive, including the launching of the Ark.

What happens to all the well-laid plans for the preservation of life should the Ark be allowed to be swept at will across the antediluvian landscape, crashing into every obstruction in its path?

The biblical account gives only the faintest of clues concerning this most hazardous of operations in saving those aboard. In subtle terminology, easily discernible by those with a maritime background, it can be seen in Genesis 7:17 that as the waters were increased, the Ark was borne up and lifted from the earth. The Ark was not under way, however, but tethered to the landscape to prevent damage by being carried or borne upon the incoming seas. In the Sanskrit literature, Manu (Noah) had seen fit to furnish his *raft* with a long *rope!* It is mentioned in Mesopotamian accounts that there were several of these and that Noah (Utnapishtim) had appointed Buzur-Kurgala the sailor to be in charge.

When the waters were in sufficient abundance that Noah could safely pass over the submerged landscape, we read that "the cables of the ship were cast loose," and another named Uragal parted the anchor cable.

We read again in the next verse of Genesis (7:18) that the waters prevailed (continued) and were increased greatly upon the earth, where it was now safe and advisable to cast loose. The Ark was now *under way:* "The ark *went* upon the face of the waters" and made geographical movement over the earth.

Noah was not at the mercy of the elements. The Lord was master of his destiny, Noah captain of his ship, but it was *not* "out of command."

The biblical account declares that the waters covered the tops of the mountains by fifteen cubits, but the precise rendering implies something else: "Fifteen cubits *upward* did the waters prevail; and the mountains were covered" (Genesis 7:20 KJV).

Of course the waters were moving upward, but the account is not suggesting the height to which the waters rose should then be calculated against the elevations of the mountains on the earth today! It is speaking about the *draft* of the vessel. The Ark, laden with the tonnage of supplies and all aboard, drew fifteen cubits of water. Because Noah passed safely over and above all the obstructions of the landscape, he never scraped bottom.

The Editorial Revision Committee of the New International Version of the Bible has rendered this: "The waters rose and covered the mountains to a depth of more *than twenty feet"* (author's italics). Back in 6:15, this same committee was so sure the cubit was the Hebrew (18 inches) that they saw fit to print the Ark was 450 feet in length. Now they seem not too sure of their position, for 15 cubits would be *22.5 feet*. True, more than 20 feet could be 22½ feet, but they are missing the point. The loaded draft of the Ark was more like *26 feet,* and should any of the committee members have been aboard the Ark they undoubtedly would have been keelhauled for their mistake.

It should be a rule that revision committees be made up of people with maritime backgrounds when they choose to tamper with a text to make some "revised edition" a little bit different from that already in print. Their text is followed by a footnote stating, "The dimensions of the Ark are themselves an evidence of the accuracy of the Scriptures."

With that interpretation, the Ark may have run aground early on in the voyage!

THE DROGUE STONES

If the early accounts say that Buzur-Kurgala cast loose the cables and Uragal parted the remaining lines tethering the Ark to the landscape, what then would they use to bring the vessel to a halt?

In the Koran in the Sura of the Houd, we find the answer: "In the name of Allah it will cast anchor." This is N. J. Dawood's translation (Penguin Books Ltd., 1974), which I feel is quite good. It certainly is better than Arthur Arberry's translation (Macmillan Publishing, 1955), in which he cites, "be its course and its berthing." I cannot conceive of anybody thinking the Ark was on a set course and berthed at a dock after the Flood! Such are the various interpretations one can get from the scholars at large on Sura 11:44. There are other indications of anchors in the Babylonian text that will be touched upon later on. Perhaps Mohammed Marmaduke's interpretation of the Koran into English is the tiebreaker: " . . . be its course and its mooring." A ship "at rest" on its mooring is still afloat and not under way, which for all practical pur-poses could be considered anchored and made fast to the bottom.

A well-known media personality and producer of an ABC "20/20" segment on the discovery, in referring to these stones, laughed and said, "These are only Armenian tombstones!

They cut holes in the top to drag them over here. I have it from
a good source that Soviet Armenia is loaded with iconographic
stones exactly like this." I would suggest her source was
another expert from the Ararat group who most assuredly had
never visited the Soviet Union to see the stone *Khatchkars* of
which Levon Azarian has made a lifetime study. Not *one* has
ever been found with a hole pierced through its top.

These experts should enlighten ill-informed marine archaeologists, plucking the same stones from harbors and shipwrecks on the Mediterranean coasts, that what they are recovering are only small Armenian tombstones!

It should be pointed out, using anchor stone D as an exam-

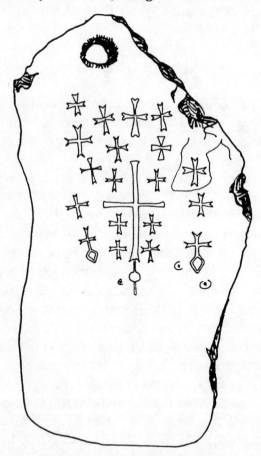

Anchor stone D field book sketch and notes. This anchor is one of the
largest at 11' 5 " (7'8 " above ground), and 4'11 " at its widest point, yet it is
only 13" thick. Hole has a 6" diameter. There are 6 type crosses represented, totaling 20, plus bullet hits.

ple, that the placement (location) of the hole in the drogue stone appears to be too high to effectively support the weight of the stone itself. It must be remembered that the stone was never intended to be suspended freely in the air. Only placing the hole at the utmost forward portion of the drogue ensured its maximum effectiveness. Note also that the thickest portion of the stone is at its head near the hole. This is why I feel on many occasions the stones were erected as monuments with the *hole down,* as it appeared to be more stable in an upright position with the heaviest end in the ground, thus leaving the broad, smooth, and flat area a good surface for inscription.

The weight of this stone is considerably reduced when immersed in salt water, and it was never intended for it to be brought aboard. I believe the stones were lifted up as the Ark was lifted up. Should a spare stone be lowered through the hull pool to replace those lost, cutting it loose from its bindings near the hull pool, allowing it to plunge into the water below and surging the line to a halt would certainly not break the hole out of the stone. This is another indication that these are *not* gravestones or that the holes were put into the stones to facilitate moving them around, as the woman media personality suggested. If they were intended for anything else, the hole would have been more toward the center. Thus by the very location of the hole it can be seen that the purpose of the stone was to be supported by a medium heavier than air!

Perhaps the correct term for these should really be *drogue stones* since they weren't made to hook in or catch the bottom. A drogue is used on a ship quite differently in purpose, and there was a need for just this equipment aboard the Ark.

Their purpose was to create a drag causing tension to the stern of the Ark, to restrain it from being cast sideways in a following sea. This was of course the Ark's situation, under way in a following sea. It could be cast sideways and broach if it didn't maintain a position keeping the sharp upswept stern into the waves.

It is important to remember, too, that it was not the weight of the stones that accomplished this but the surface area of the stone. That's why they are long and flat and need not be thicker than what is needed for strength, not weight.

The stones vary slightly in size but average 10 feet in length and 5 feet in width, with the thickest portion near the top by the hole. If we figured the largest at 100 cubic feet, and a specific gravity of 1.2 (cement, 87 pounds per cubic foot), the weight would be 8,700 pounds or nearly 3.9 long tons. While underwater, however, the stones' volume would displace 100 cubic feet of salt water at 64.3 pounds, or 6,430 pounds, so the in-water weight of the stone was 2,270 pounds. I realize the stone might have a higher specific gravity, but this was a large stone, so I feel it is a good average to work with.

The weight was then sufficient to keep it from rising to the surface and skipping, and a sea that fast is hard to imagine.

The size line one might expect to be used is really an unanswerable question. We could compare it with hemp lines of today, and if others care to work it out, the holes in the stones in the centers ran no less than $3\frac{1}{2}$ inches (9cm), sometimes 4 inches, and tapered out to the surface to 7 inches (18cm). The use of heavy lines of course goes back into early history, and I was amazed at the examples I saw in Egypt. They were a nine-string, three-strand, right-hand lay, almost identical as to what we have today. I also found reference to a "three-stranded towrope" on line 24, column ii of tablet V, in a Babylonian text.[7]

As mentioned before, the Ark obviously wasn't making way on its own but was constantly being overtaken by the waves. So we can assume that through this action and the force of the wind and sea, it was being carried across the globe.

Several of these stones may have trailed on longer lines far astern of the others. This usage was discussed by Herodotus. In Egypt, the vessels sailing the Nile upstream are assisted in overcoming the current by a steady northerly wind. Sailing down the Nile would seemingly present no problem, but it did for the larger vessels with a lot of windage for the following reason. When rounding a bend in the river, the current continues to push against the stern that is now sideways to the current, and the high sides of the vessel are "stalled" by the northerly wind. The vessel goes ashore on the bank.

---

[7]John Gardner and John Maier, *Gilgamesh* (New York: Alfred A. Knopf, Inc., © 1984).

To prevent this, the Egyptians came up with an amazingly clever contraption that consisted of a low-lying raft which presented no surface area to the contrary wind. It was equipped with a sail under the raft, which caught the currents full force. This was made fast to the cargo ship's bow by a towrope. Men on the raft then shot off downriver with the vessel trailing behind.

The raft, of course, was equipped with sweep oars and darted around the curve in the river with the vessel's bow "in irons." The vessel's stern tended to "whiplash" around but was made to "track" through the use of a "braking stone," as Herodotus called it. The weight of the stone was about two talents (120 pounds), which was just enough tension on the stern as it dragged through the mud of the river bottom to make the tow follow correctly.

The Ark, of course, did not intend to drag these stones. Striking a hard bottom could break them. In a forceful sea, they trailed far astern, but as the sea moderated, they hung lower in the water until finally in light airs and a tranquil sea (if there ever was such a thing), they would hang directly down. Those on the longest lines (probably the lightest stones) would act as sounding weights checking the depth. I believe this is what happened as the Ark drifted onto the Anatolian Plateau.

A note on the labeling of these stones before we go further. They are labeled in the order of their being found. Anchor stone A was the one we had searched for near the Ark's landing site and may or may not be the figment of someone's imagination. I will take Wyatt's word on having seen it there previously.

The first stone that touched bottom, giving warning that the Ark was coming into shallow water, would be the westernmost stone we have located and which was the second one found, so it is labeled drogue stone C. It is found at the elevation of 5,500 feet and is the smallest, at only 7 feet long and 2 feet, 3 inches wide at the bottom. The thickness is greatest at the upper portion at 10 inches near the 4-inch diameter hole, a portion of which is broken out and missing. Judging by the lichen growth and its position to the hole where it was found uprooted, it had been buried hole down.

This was the "signal stone" that caught, probably breaking out the hole as designed, for it was only a signal stone and easily replaced. It was the line they would want to save, not the stone. They did not want the vessel to halt on these occasions; just a surge of warning was sufficient. It may have caused the Ark to veer slightly to the south, for the second stone is found farther to the east in the Ark's direction of travel and 500 feet south.

Another possibility, and perhaps the correct one, was that these stones were "lost" on purpose, leaving more stones on the port side of the vessel to cause the Ark's bow to pull to the left or north to avoid coming too close or striking Yalıntaşdağı, quite a large upthrust of rock that may have been visible or at least showed as a boil under the surface of the waters.

This is drogue stone B at an elevation of 5,350 feet. It is 10 feet long, 4 feet, 6 inches wide, and 14 inches thick. The upper end increases in thickness to 18 inches, where the hole is offset with a diameter of 3.5 inches. The hole was found broken but the pieces were there and reassembled for a photo. We might safely assume the hole had not broken on contact, for the uprooting of this monument has been recent and it has suffered vandalism.

The main grouping of the anchor stones is, of course, where the Ark finally came to rest, north of Yalıtaşdağı and on a magnetic bearing of 69° straight toward the peak of Ararat from drogue stone B. It is the village of Kazan.

Eight of these are easily discernible as drogue stones with either holes intact or portions remaining. Others could well be the same. Further excavations by the Ministry of Culture of Turkey should be encouraged, but I would like to point out again to the reader that to do so on his own would be in direct violation of the law and the preservation of these artifacts. The area has become somewhat of a graveyard over the years, and even obtaining permission from the local villagers to see if other monuments have their holes buried down would be construed as grave robbing—a serious offense in any country.

The village of Kazan is located in a bowl depression and the stones are situated in disarray at the eastern side of the village on the western slope of a hill at 5,200 feet elevation.

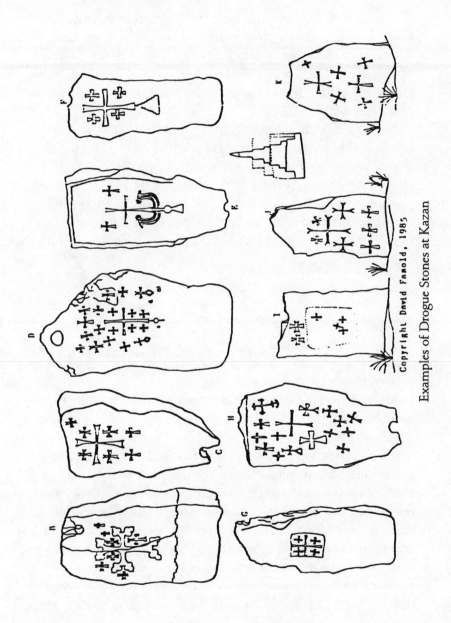

Copyright David Fanold, 1985

Examples of Drogue Stones at Kazan

WAS THE ARK'S VOYAGE EASTWARD?

To answer this question, we can determine that the Ark's entry into this area is clearly defined by the drogues being to the west of the actual grounding site of the Ark on the slopes of Mahşer. The drogue stones that would first catch the landscape at the higher elevations are also to the west of the main grouping.

I believe this shows conclusively that the Ark's direction of travel had been eastward, where it came to rest. It stayed in this position, by my interpretation of the Genesis account, for exactly seventy-four days. It then slipped its anchor lines and traveled eastward in a slow and gentle arc to the south, sliding onto the soft slopes on the very birthday of the patriarch, or the 601st year, first month, first day of the month, of the life of Noah (Genesis 8:13 KJV).

> ... and Noah removed the covering of the ark, and looked, and, behold, the face of the ground was dry.

Noah was aground, as opposed to being at rest. Why had he waited this period of time before landing?

In the period of time that passed between the coming to rest and the slipping of the lines, Noah needed time to make a commitment.

If I had been in Noah's sandals, I would have waited to see what kind of landmass I was over. As mentioned earlier, if I made a hasty commitment to stay where I was, I may have found out too late that it was an island not large enough to sustain life. However, if I found I was on the edge of a continent, I might want to hang on. If I continued it could be madness. Suppose I went drifting onward, only to see I had left the land behind and was now over an ocean with no means of turning the Ark around? I would then be helplessly adrift with no means of returning.

I would have hung on, sending all the stones to the bottom with as much scope as I could spare. I would then take soundings, easy enough through the hull pool, searching for obstructions below. I would carefully search the coastlines of the mountain ranges within my view for boils in the waters over new obstructions not yet uncovered.

From this point, Noah could watch the comings and goings of the waters in their tidal bulges. Psalms 104:9 seems to imply that the waters turned again and again in tides, scouring the bottom during the Flood. At times these tides may have scared him that the scope in the lines had become such that he might drag a bit, but the lowering of the waters continued, exposing more shoreline by the day. The best course of action would of course be to search the hillsides for a soft landing site, but the rocky shore looked pretty desolate, just as it does today.

I don't know if Noah could see his landing site from this position. I might actually have to get up in an airplane to determine this, but let's assume he could. If he could see the soft landing, or at least that the slopes below Cudi showed promise at low water, his attempt should then be at high-water slack, with just the beginning of the flood (current) to give him steerageway toward his mark, and let the Ark settle to the earth at low water. If the waters were decreasing daily, the next high water would not touch him.

But Noah knew he could not hang there forever. A decision must be made soon, for as the waters were decreasing, the current was becoming stronger. Soon the waters would become a raging torrent—no longer a sea but a river of great waters returning from off the earth, rushing by mountains that were now providing brief shelter, and through the highlands toward their gathering together unto the new place God had founded for them. Then across a bound that they may not pass over, so that they turn not again to cover the earth. For a landlubber, King David certainly had grasped the true circumstance of the Flood.

Noah must act quickly while the tidal bulges were still in effect, or be dragged over the landscape to the sea and almost certain destruction.

First he must unship the large steering oar that was lashed to the overhead above the hull pool. This would be lowered so the blade extended below the bottom of the hull of the boat-shaped raft, and aft of #6 bulkhead (this may be a clue as to why this is a triple strength sandwiched structure).

The blade then would extend like the feet of a duck under

the almost bird-shaped hull floating upon the water. It could be twisted by the line that was rolled in coils around the heavy shaft of the sweep oar, perhaps tied to a domestic beast of burden for ease in turning the great vessel.

A team of oxen were hooked to the line, and through the working parts of a block Noah pulled one drogue, in successive overhauls of the purchase and use of rope stoppers, to within two hundred feet from the side of the Ark, near its pivot point. He did the same to the other side, so that once under way, these drogues could be slacked on the side he wanted to veer toward, like a modern-day tugboat pulling a barge on a Liverpool bridle, should the steering oar give way. A drogue was also taken in aft to act as a braking stone should the current prove too strong.

Noah sent off a piece of wood and watched it go out of sight, riding the current toward the slopes, watching for boils in the waters at low tide that would be indications of snags.

All looked well. Tomorrow, at high-water slack, Noah would commit himself to driving the Ark aground into the new world. It would be a day to remember. Why not make this auspicious occasion coincide with the celebration of his birthday!

In the 601st year of Noah's life, the first day of his first month, the sun rose slowly in the eastern sky, dawning on a memorable day in the history of man. The sun's rays brightened the weathered face of the old patriarch as he again gave the order to cut the lines. The drogue stones, having held the Ark at her place of rest, were now left behind on the submerged landscape, where they can still be found today. The Ark moved forward in the rising sun, gliding gently eastward upon the slackening tide. There was enough current in the receding water covering the earth to give him steerageway. The Ark was under way and in command. It was heading toward the slopes of Mount Mahşer. Noah called below, and in the chain of command, the shaft of the sweep oar was rotated slowly. The Ark veered in a semicircle to the south, where the "High Place of Cudi" (Al Judi) acted as a marker to check against sideways drift.

The drogue stone aft touched bottom, now acting as a braking stone surging the line taut, holding back the great Ark, now catching and falling and catching on obstructions below, slowing its foward momentum. The starboard drogue was slackened to decrease the angular track, and the Ark came back down to earth, stranding in some fifteen cubits of water at the bow. It was here the soft slopes of Al Judi caught the Ark like the palm of an open hand in the New Age.

The crew labored in rejoicing and thanksgiving while removing the covering. The large steering oar was now buckling under the strain of weight as the hulk of the Ark settled to the shore in the receding waters. The sea was actually draining from the hull pool and little sea creatures, along for the ride, were now scurrying after the sea, abandoning the wreck that would soon be left high and dry on the landscape.

The broken sections of the oar were swung on tethers from the overhead bracing like battering rams against the reed covering, knocking off the coating of cementlike KPR on the outside. In the time required, the tide had fallen considerably and the vessel took on the angle of the slope. Items that were loose while at the anchorage now slid precariously down the deck as the survivors worked their way to the opening.

Noah looked out, " . . . and behold, the face of the ground was dry!"

I stated earlier that my belief was the Ark carried at least fifteen tons of drogue stones trailing astern. They were never brought aboard, but there may have been spares aboard that could have replenished a percentage of those lost. These should be looked for in the remains of the Ark upon excavation. Since ten have been located to date, I anticipate at least three more will be found. These could be at or near the wreck site, but there could have been more.

Early on, during the worst part of the Deluge, Noah may have required all he could trail astern. As the sea conditions moderated, he may have released some to fall on the landscape below. These could be traced back to the land they had left.

I had long been fascinated by two Flood myths that involved a man and his family who had escaped the destruction. He had repopulated the world by throwing stones over his shoulders. What was really intriguing was that one myth was Greek and the other was South American. Could these tales be referring to lost drogue stones?

Suppose when these were found by the descendants of the survivors and recognized as anchor stones from the Ark, to the west of its landing site, they settled there until news reached them that another had been found farther westward. Obviously it must have occurred to them that in following the stones, hence the track of the Ark, it might be possible to relocate the lost civilization of their ancestors. The drowned cities would have left their riches to the first finder to come upon them. Certainly the dream of being the first to discover the wealth of Atlantis can still be found among us today.

Fodor's *Travel Guide to Turkey* gives an interesting account of the city of Ankara that can be traced back through history for thousands of years. Legend attributes its foundation to the redoubtable Amazons, but archaeologists through recent excavations have brought to light even earlier Hittite traces. The derivation of the name is as problematic as the rendering, Ancyra, Enguriye, Ankara, Phyrygian for "ravine," or Greek for "anchor." Fodor's goes on to say, "An Egyptian anchor captured in battle was featured for some time on the city's coins."[8]

Ankara is some five hundred kilometers from the sea and nine hundred kilometers from Egypt. Could the anchor referred to be another similar to the stones found near the Ark site? Is it another Ark anchor stone, lost as it passed over the area that was to become Ankara? The phonetic name not only denotes what is pictured on the coins but also implies that the founders knew they were in the cradle of civilization. Perhaps one day this stone will be recognized for what it is in the area of Ankara. And I doubt if it will be found to be Egyptian in origin.

Since Bjorn Landstrom is an expert on Egyptian vessels and states that no Egyptian anchor from Egypt has ever been found,[9] I can't accept that the Hittites got the only one and dragged it back to Ankara. Anchor stones that are assumed to be Phoenician have been discovered in the harbor of Byblos.

---

[8]*Fodor's Travel Guide to Turkey* (New York: Fodors, 1985), p. 276.
[9]Bjorn Landstrom, *Ships of the Pharaohs* (New York: Doubleday & Co., 1971).

These are very much like the anchor pictured on one of Una's ships.

My problem is I have the drogue stones located 750 kilometers from the Mediterranean, at fifty-two hundred feet elevation, and on the same latitude as the city of Ankara.

However, we may now be on to something that could serve as a solution to another biblical dilemma, that being the complicated directions found in Genesis 11:2. By looking at a map it can easily be seen that to enter the plain of Shinar from the landing site of the Ark, one must travel south. Following rivers is normal procedure for anyone lost, and I'm sure that Noah and his numerous descendants, finally moving out of the area of grounding after many years, and having no knowledge of the shape of the new world, would find it natural to follow the rivers down from the higher elevations to where the rivers meet the sea.

In the King James Version of the Bible we read, "And it came to pass [after the population increased], as they journeyed *from the east,* that they found a plain in the land of Shinar; and they dwelt there" (Genesis 11:2 author's italics). In the New International Version, it is stated *exactly the opposite!* "As men moved *eastward,* they found a plain in Shinar . . ." (author's italics).

Leaving those who want to take *both* these renderings as the literal truth, and heading in opposite directions, I propose the following solution, based on the fact that the Ark's movement over the globe had been from west to east. We can see, both from the anchor stones themselves and the anchor stones in relation to the Ark site, with possible additional confirmation from Ankara (when that stone is found), that their movement from the Old Age to the New Age had been eastward, passing

Anchor stone on one of Una's ships in Sahure's temple.

over central Anatolia, following closely a track of forty degrees latitude. I would expect this track to be a portion of a *poleward curve* from the place of the Ark's origins.[10] In the overview of Noah leaving the land of his origins for the new place where civilization was reestablished in the plains of Shinar, the journey of the Ark had been *eastward*.

THE MYSTERIOUS STONE THINGS EXPLAINED

The SÎN-LEQUI-UNNINNÎ version of the Epic of Gilgamesh has mentioned the nautical nicety of a three-stranded towrope in Tablet V, column ii, and in Tablet X, column ii, I may have found mention of drogue stones.

Urshanabi is the boatman who will take Gilgamesh across the waters of death to the dwelling place of Utnapishtim, our Babylonian Noah. There has been some sort of fight, and Urshanabi reprimands Gilgamesh for the damage he's done.

> Line 37 Your own hands, Gilgamesh, have hindered the crossing.
>   40 the stone things are broken.

Perhaps in an argument the drogue stones were struck, breaking the holes out, and their attaching lines. Was Gilgamesh attempting to take the boat by force, or simply breaking up the boat's equipment as Urshanabi refused to take him across the waters? Apparently feelings were patched up, as well as the equipment:

> Line 41 and the stone things [he loaded] in the boat,
>   42 [the stone things] without which [there is no crossing deaths waters].

Urshanabi felt the drogues were most important to his safety in the crossing. It was as though one might be afraid to drive a car without brakes.

---

[10]When the earth's rotation was disturbed, waves of translation *moved eastward* because of inertia, and poleward because of the recession of the waters from the equatorial bulge where they were held by the rotation of the earth. Immanuel Velikovsky, *Worlds in Collision* (New York: Pocket Books, 1977), p. 332.

The author of this translation suggests an interesting parallel. Another Babylonian text has the boatman explaining that the stone things he carried across the waters were so that the waters of death would not touch him (Tigay, 114).

Naturally anchors aboard boats are very important, even small mushhufs like Urshanabi's. If, as I believe, he was crossing a salt inland sea and a squall occurred, he would need an anchor or a "dragging stone" to keep his boat from broaching and throwing him into the waters of death. Fresh waters give life, bitter seas bring death. I feel I have located this inland sea and it is discussed in a later chapter.

I believe the mysterious "stone things" of the Ark were already set up as monuments during the time the Epic of Gilgamesh was first composed. People knew the relationship of them to the Ark and that they were very important to the Ark's crossing the waters of death into the new age.

The magical properties attributed to Urshanabi's drogue stones in calling them simply the "stone things" find their counterpart in the drogues at the site near the Ark. These monuments, set up thousands of years before the first Christian of the area ever considered them his, had been covered with representations of people and esoteric meanings over the ages. Amid the signets of Tammuz[11] and the Egyptian cross, the early Christians found little space to add their pectoral and eight-pointed Maltese symbol among the Nem Ankh of life. That these crosses were in use some fifteen hundred and more years before the Christian era is no longer considered scholarly debate. One should not be surprised to find that an expert identifies these cross types of early origin.[12]

There is one fine example of an Eastern Orthodox cross in relief on one single stone, but to pass them all off as late Armenian is to give them a cursory glance.

Here you will find Babylonian symbols of great importance in connection with the Flood story and the Chaldean representation of the tree of life, and for good reason. This is the ancient

---

[11]The cross was the symbol of Tammuz, identified by some historians as Nimrod.

[12]Colonel Alexander A. Koor (1890–1971), Russian researcher in antiquities, deciphered cuneiform inscriptions near the site relating to the Flood. *Bible Archaeologist,* Fourth Quarter, 1946.

The sign of Tammuz, the god of fire.

land of the Ram people of the Caucasus and their god (K)Haldi, for the Urartians were the Chaldeans! It is a mistake to assume the Chaldeans were from lower Mesopotamia. I believe they migrated from here, and the people from this area called themselves the Chaldini. They migrated from nowhere, they began here. The Chaldeans are credited with being the first astronomers.

Bailly and others assert that astronomy "must have been established when the summer solstice was in the first degree of Virgo, and that the solar and lunar zodiacs were of similar antiquity, which would be about four thousand years before the Christian era. They suppose the originators to have lived in *about the fortieth degree of north latitude,* and to have been a highly civilized people."

The drogue stones are at *latitude 39° 39.2'N*. Based on this thought, Layard should not have been surprised to find a lens of considerable power in the ruins of Babylon. It was an inch and a half in diameter and nine-tenths of an inch thick.

Leonard Woolley, when excavating the Royal tombs at Ur, made one of his greatest finds. The famous "goat in a thicket" is actually a tree of life, an ancient symbol to be found on the west face of a drogue stone mounted upright in the grouping and standing today.

Like the Tree of Life, the cross many times stands for the world axis.[13] The Chaldeans' Tree of Life had eight branches and eight petaled flowers extending from an axis pole rather than a trunk.

On the anchor stone, it extends from a circle or globe. This would normally suggest infinity or the universe[14] if it were not for the geometric image of the ternary. According to Nicholas of Cusa, the truncated ternary (triangle without an apex) symbolizes the earth.[15] The vertical arm of the added cross, which in iconography is identified with the tree, further implies the symbolic central point of the cosmos.

THE CHALDEAN/HEBREW CONNECTION

The Chaldean Tree of Life found carved on drogue stone E reminds us of Abraham when he lifted his eyes, "And behold behind him a ram caught in a thicket by his horns." As it

---

[13]J. E. Citolot, *Symbols* (New York, Philosophical Library, Inc., 1962).

[14]Ibid., p. 118.

[15]Ibid., p. 332.

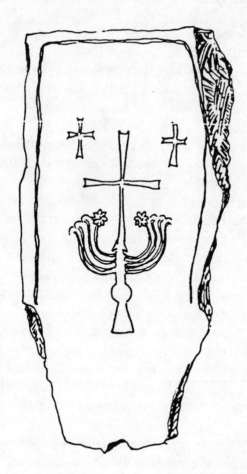

Anchor Stone E Field Book Notes and Sketch

closely resembles the "goat in a thicket" found at Ur in the
Royal Cemetery (2500 B.C.E.), there is not wanting a Chaldean
connection. Most people think of Abraham as the patriarch
and father of the Jews and Arabs. Of course this might be an
oversimplification, but it is a good place to start getting into
detail. However, where I want this discussion to lead us is back
in time from Abraham, or Abram, at this point, before God
said, "I will make thee . . . after I have created thee as a new
creation."

Was Abraham a Chaldean? And did he live at Ur of the
Chaldees, and was this the Ur of Sumer as suggested by some
of the most eminent archaeologists of our times?

To begin back at the anchor stone grouping, why should we find the Chaldean Tree of Life carved on these monuments so far north if we are led to believe that the Ur of Sumer was home of the Chaldeans and Abram?

To get back to where Abram's ancestors really came from, an observation was made by Moses Khorenatsi, the Herodotus of the Armenians, that while everyone persists in calling them Armenians, they call themselves *Hai*. This is most noticeable from the people of the Lake Van region, who pronounce it *Kh(o)ai*. This word *Kh(o)ai* of course means "Ram" in Armenian, thus they identify themselves as the "People of the Ram" who worshiped the god (K)Hal-di. They are, then, the original Khaldini, better known since Achaemenian times by the unfortunate Greek spelling, *Chaldeans*.

Anthropologists in general hedge against identifying this area of the Khaldini as Urartu before the thirteenth century B.C.E., but I see no reason for not doing so. The Khaldini are considered by Josephus (Book I, chapter VI) as the descendants of Arphaxad, the son of Shem born two years after the Flood, or at least an offshoot of Kesed, whom they claim was a son of Nahor. Since this is the name of both Abram's grandfather and his brother, I think we can safely say that Abram was one of the people of the Ram. The House of Terah, Abram's father, was at Haran (sometimes spelled *Harran* to differentiate between the place name and that of Haran, Terah's son, father of Lot).

Harran, then, is only some 530 kilometers due southeast of the anchor stone grouping, called Altınbaşak today, which in the archaic can mean "gold arrowhead," but today it most likely means "a golden ear of grain" or those grains left by reapers. The site of Haran (or Harran) is a typical tell and I have often wondered why archaeologists have not taken more interest in it. It perhaps could tell us just when Abram left the city with his formidable army and indicate a period for the Flood, as it was probably settled soon after. Nicolaus of Damascus, in the fourth book of his history, says, "Abram reigned at Damascus, being a foreigner who came with an army out of the *land above Babylon called the land of the Chaldeans*. But after a long time he got up, and removed from the country also with his people, and went into the land then called the land of Canaan but now the land of Judea" (author's italics).

With the above information available for over 1,900 years, why do we keep reading in slick coffee table publications that Abram came from Ur in southern Mesopotamia, just because Sir Leonard Woolley thought so? The Ur of Abram was north of Babylon, and further still, above Mari and Ashur. In Daniel 2:4 KJV it says, "Then spake the Chaldeans to the king in Syriack."

Interestingly, today Harran is still only eighteen kilometers from the Syrian border. Syriack in the King James is of course Aramaic, the ancient language of Syria, and substantially identical to Chaldaic. Yet Woolley would have Abram speaking Sumerian in the Ur of Sumer. Deuteronomy 26 says the father of the Israelites was a wandering Aramean. And the Kabbalist recites Abram's surprise in learning from the Lord that Sarah will have a son: "No! Not Sarah! As a child, my Lord, I spent much time jesting with the young men of the mountains of Urartu. Yes, played I satire with the men of Ur. . . ."

Ezekiel maintains as well that the land of the Chaldeans is by the river Kebar (Ezekiel 1:3 KJV, Greek spelling). Thus the Ur of Abraham is most probably Ur Kasdim in upper Mesopotamia near the Khabor River of today. Abraham's servant set out for Aram Naharaim, the city of Nahor. In Genesis 24:5 it is said this was the land from whence Abram came!

We should not then be surprised to see this Tree of Life symbol carved on the anchor stone alongside another with a Babylonian ziggurat. And if anyone wants to say that the symbol is Armenian. . . I agree.

THE BABYLONIAN CONNECTION

"Compare the cuneiform representation of it [the Ark] as shaped like a six storied cube . . . with a mast and a pilot on top," suggests biblical scholar Scofield.[16]

---

[16]Oxford New International Version Scofield Study Bible (New York: Oxford University Press, 1984), footnote p. 11.

Let's do just that. Again on the western face of a drogue positioned upright with the remains of the lower portion of the hole for the anchor line, and incised deep into the surface of the stone, is what might be considered a proper Babylonian ziggurat, if it were not for the fact that it doesn't have seven levels.

What is pictured here is exactly what I was looking for – the Ark connection engraved on the stones themselves. It is a six-storied ziggurat with a cylindric mast and a lookout atop the structure. It is the Babylonian symbol of Utnapishtim's Life Saver, Noah's Ark.

There are faint lines, lightly incised, that appear to be the work of another who didn't agree with the first stonecutter's impression of what the Ark looked like. This unknown revisionist attempted to bring the rendition into a more favorably acceptable assumption of what his contemporary Christian Armenians thought the Ark *should* look like. Had he completed the job, we would have had a three-storied box, one smaller box atop a larger one, and completely lost the Babylonian connection.

7

The Ark's Reliquary

THE BONES OF ADAM

In the times of the Assyrians, we read of a king who recorded that he loved to read from the writings of the age before the Flood. Assurbanipal, who founded the great library of Nineveh, referred to these records from the time before the Great Deluge and implies that with great difficulty he learned to master the inscriptions and held them most treasured among his collection.

In one early text we read that Noah was to bury the beginnings and the middles and the ends of all writings in the City of the Sun and recover them after the Flood.[1] Seemingly these writings would be of great importance. Why weren't they brought aboard the Ark? Did the survivors and early descendants recover a hoard of tablets from the ruins after the Flood? In the early literature of the Sumerians we learn from the Epic of Gilgamesh that our hero may have recovered some himself.[2] We read that the walls of the city of Uruk, one of the four cities mentioned as built by Nimrod,[3] were actually rebuilt upon the foundations and remains of a pre-Flood city, and a threshold that was ancient. Gilgamesh claimed they were originally laid down by the seven sages (or the Cainite civilization) long before the destruction of the waters, and it was now his proud city and possession.

---

[1] In Sippar. According to the Poem of Erra (Tablet 4, line 50) this Sipparian city was not completely destroyed by the Flood.

[2] Tablet I, lines 22–25.

[3] Genesis 10:10, the city of Er'ech.

Find the copper tablet box,
slip loose the ring-bolt made of bronze,
Open the mouth to its secrets,
Draw out the tablet of lapis lazuli
and read it aloud.[4]

These early finds from the remains of the cities destroyed in the Flood may have been the source for the writings mentioned by Assurbanipal and the king lists that were finally recorded in Greek by Berosus millennia later.

Even in the Bible there are many books referred to that are nonexistent today. The Book of the Wars of Jehovah may have been written in part by Abraham (Numbers 21:14), and the Book of Jasher (cited in Joshua 10:13) and numerous others of which there is no trace. Jude quotes the judgment of Enoch (Jude 14, 15), but his source is neither identified nor included in the authorized versions.[5]

There are many translations of works today claiming to be these lost books of the Bible. Many of the originals were in circulation during the early Church period and may have been composed contemporaneous with those times. They are called "pseudepigrapha," that is, works considered erroneous and unhistorical, and with this I am in partial agreement. We must remind ourselves that the Bible is a collection of books composed from different time periods and people. Upon what principle were books accepted and rejected? We are free to examine the books of the Scriptures which have been canonized into the Authorized Version, but what of those books that have been eliminated by various councils in order to make up our standard Bible of today? Of course we may take people's word for the reason certain books were eliminated but it is always satisfactory to come to our own conclusions by examining the evidence ourselves.

In one document, of which numerous portions exist in Greek, Syrian, and Hebrew, I made a study of the Ethiopic and Egyptian (which is claimed to be the original). I found many

---

[4]John Gardner and John Maier, *Gilgamesh* (New York: Alfred A. Knopf, Inc., © 1984). Note: Gilgamesh describes himself in the first person when he says "[I] Gilgamesh, who saw things secret, opened the place hidden, and carried back word of the time before the flood" (Tablet I, lines 4–6).

[5]Jude is quoting directly from the Book of Enoch 1:9, 5:4, and 27:2.

inconsistencies, including Enos dying at the age of 985. His father, Seth is in attendance. Seth's life span, we are told here, was 912, which leaves a difference of 73 years. This document states that Seth begets Enos at 20! Now if your son, 20 years your junior, lives 73 years longer than you do, how do you attend his funeral? Close examination proves they attended each other's!

So, it is safe to say that a comparison of the accepted books with those rejected may be relied upon! However, this particular document was of interest to me because it may have carried a theme set down from oral traditions, that Shem had carried aboard the Ark the bones of Adam in a reliquary, to be reinterred in the new world.

> And thou shalt take the body of our father Adam, and place it with thee in the Ark when the Flood comes.[6]

For those who might consider this strange, we are reminded that the bones of Joseph were brought out of Egypt and carried through the wilderness forty years until being interred inside the cave in the field of Machpelah. According to Jewish, Christian, and Moslem legends, this is the resting place of the patriarchs and their wives, Esau and the twelve sons of Jacob, among others. It is also considered the final place of interment for the bones of Adam. For this to have been possible, the bones of Adam would have to have been carried aboard the Ark, as claimed by tradition. The Papyrus of Ani alludes to this idea, as shown in the hieroglyphics below:

neter	ḥā	en	Rā	em	uda	Nu
THE DIVINE BODY	, OF	KA	(IS) IN (THE) SACRED BOAT (OF) NOAH

The Ethiopic document continues this thought: "And thy son Shem, he it is who shall lay the body of our father Adam in the middle of the earth."[7]

---

[6] *The Forgotten Books of Eden,* chapter 21:10, "Adam and Eve" (Iowa Falls: World Bible Publishers, Inc., 1926).

[7] Ibid., 21:11.

The middle of the earth to the ancient world, and only true geodetic central point, would have been the apex of the pyramid in the land of Miz'raim. It is interesting to note that this structure, the Great Pyramid, was designed by someone who knew the cubit of .5236 (20.6 inches), the same as that employed in building the Ark of Noah.

Could it be possible that the architect and designer of the Great Pyramid, the mysterious Imhotep, who came into the land under the reign of Cheops, fulfilled his purpose, and then just as mysteriously disappeared from the land, was none other than Shem himself?

The Egyptians describe Imhotep as a sort of Leonardo da Vinci of his time, and many years after his demise he was elevated to a position of demigod for craftsmen and technicians. Until recently there were many Egyptologists who insisted that Imhotep was a legendary figure. Their argument was that there is no evidence in Egyptian history of an ordinary person ever being divinized. This is a peculiar notion contrary to the researches of Herodotus in the fifth century B.C.E. Only recently has Imhotep been accepted as a real person, and it has even been possible to gather information about his physical appearance.

Scholars are now willing to grant that a man named Imhotep walked in the land of Egypt, but they are not yet ready to admit that Egypt could have produced a mind such as his. There are numerous indicators that he was not Egyptian. Although held in awe by the reigning Pharaoh, he was held in contempt by the workmen employed in the building of the Pyramid. He was considered an outsider, a foreigner, and a shepherd king quite unlike themselves. He was of ruddy complexion with red or auburn hair. As a result of their dislike for him, the Egyptian commoners carried an unreasonable contempt for persons of the same physical appearance for centuries thereafter, representing them in hieroglyphic forms as grotesque beings in humiliating positions. They also expressed their hatred for shepherds.

It is interesting to note that the same hatred and depiction is associated with Typhon, whom I have identified with Shem. Within the labyrinth of the Great Pyramid itself, the workers left their expression of contempt for their employer in red paint. The man responsible for the workers' plight was in their eyes a "red braying ass."

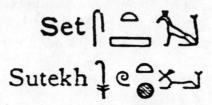

This would explain Plutarch's remark:

> Hence their ignominious treatment of those persons whom from the redness of their complexions they imagined to bear a resemblance to him; and hence likewise is derived the custom of throwing a [red] ass down a precipice merely on account of the resemblance which they conceive it bears to Typho.

It was during the reign of Cheops that the Great Pyramid was constructed. Herodotus reveals that during construction, Cheops closed the temples and forbade the Egyptians to offer sacrifice. This is something Shem, if he was indeed Imhotep, would have required them to do. The labor force required for construction was, according to the priest whom Herodotus was interviewing, a gang of one hundred thousand workmen, laboring continuously and being relieved every three months with a fresh lot. While the blocks were being quarried and brought to the site, the ramp was under construction. It took ten years to complete the causeway itself, which Herodotus claims was as great a feat as the pyramid. It was some five furlongs in length (about three thousand feet), ten fathoms wide (sixty feet), and eight fathoms high, at the highest part. It was built of polished stone and covered with carvings of animals. Herodotus continues:

> To make it took ten years, or as I said, to make the causeway, the works on the mound where the pyramid stands, and the underground chambers, which Cheops intended as vaults for his own use: These last were built elsewhere on a sort of island, surrounded by water introduced from the Nile by a canal. The pyramid itself was twenty years in building.

It has always been clear to the Egyptians that the edifice was not built as the burial chambers for the Pharaoh. These vaults or chambers may yet be found, but despite this priestly knowledge recorded by the father of history, the Great Pyramid is commonly thought of today as being the tomb of the Pharaoh Cheops. If it is in fact recorded by Herodotus that it is not Cheops' tomb, whose is it?

Consider again that Shem was instructed to carefully remove the bones of our father Adam from the cave of treasures and place them in a reliquary aboard the Ark. After the Deluge, he was to reinter Adam's remains in the middle of the earth.

The pyramid was designed to incorporate all of the earth's measure and was placed in the geographical location of the earth's landmass as well.

Tompkins would concur that this structure is a carefully located geodetic marker or fixed landmark upon which the sides represent the four quadrants of the northern hemisphere in a sophisticated map projection of the ancient world. It is so brilliantly constructed in the ratios of pi and phi that it correctly incorporates the elliptic oblation of the equator and the flattening of the poles long before the discoveries of Newton, the projection of Mercator, and the Pythagorean ratios of the Greeks. Who was Imhotep and from what age of genius did he obtain this knowledge? The clue is to be found in the design of the Ark.

Even skeptical cartographers have to admit the Great Pyramid's location could not be coincidence. It stands in the center of the landmass from the North Cape of Norway to the Cape of Good Hope of Africa, and from the east coast of China to the west coast of Mexico.

Could the purpose of Imhotep have been to place the bones of Adam in the middle of the earth and centrally within an enormous sepulcher of stone to stand forever as a monument to the father of the human race? And what would be the status afforded a nation possessing the final resting place of the first man? History records the fury that resulted over the theft of the funerary cart of Alexander the Great when it was spirited off to Egypt, and the battle for his bones that followed. One can then imagine the intrigue that resulted when Nimrod discovered the true purpose for the edifice being built in the land of Miz'raim. It was to this awakening that Nimrod entered Egypt.

The Ethiopic text continues with a prophecy that the sepulcher would be plundered:

> The city in which the gold, the incense, and the myrrh are found with the body, shall be plundered. But when [the tomb] is spoiled, the treasure shall be taken care of with the spoil that is kept; and naught of them shall perish, until the word of God made man [the seed of the woman] shall come; when the kings will take them, and offer them to him.

Here I believe we find the suggestion for both the source and purpose of the Magi's gift laid before the feet of the second Adam as the infant Jesus. It is not expected that the function of the Magi should be to travel at great lengths to lay gold, frankincense, and myrrh at the feet of nurslings. But here, perhaps, a remnant of the treasure that had been brought back to Babylon by Nimrod was now kept and preserved by the Chaldeans for this very moment in history. We find in the genealogy provided by Luke (Luke 3:23–38) the preservation of these gifts through Shem from Adam to Christ. The very name *Shem* alludes to this purpose. Shem (Strong's #8034) is from *Sîym* (Strong's #7760), meaning "to convey something, place, or preserve something for a purpose."

The similar-sounding name, *Set, Sut,* and *Sutekh* means the same in Egyptian and for the hieroglyphic, it portrays the red braying ass painted by the workers within the pyramid itself. I think we may have identified here the true personage of the mysterious Imhotep.

Professor E. A. Wallis Budge, late keeper of Egyptian Antiquities at the British Museum, informs us in his work *The Egyptian Book of the Dead* that Set was the eighth member of the company of the gods of Annu, in the boat of millions of years. When the sun rose at creation out of the primeval waters (the dawning of the first day of the new age, by my interpretation), Set occupied a place in his boat with the other deities and was a son of Nut. Thus it is not surprising to find in Hebrew that *Shem'i-nith* literally means "the eighth." It would appear that the professors of uniformitarinism really must have struggled to condemn the notion that the Flood was unknown to the Egyptians, and the occurrence was not an historical event, to not have made this connection.

Rather than note numerous other examples, belaboring my

point that Shem was known to the Egyptians as one of the
eight survivors and godlike antediluvians from the divine boat
of Nu, we might again note what Herodotus has to say about
the builder of the pyramid and the period in time that the
ruling Pharaoh became the common man's taskmaster:

> The Egyptians so detest the memory of these kings that they do not
> much like even to mention their names. Hence they commonly call
> the pyramids after "Philition," a shephered who at that time fed his
> flocks about the place.[8]

Obviously the name *Philition* could not refer to both Cheops
and Chephren but only to the name of the builder of the first
true pyramid, the Great Pyramid, for this Greco-Egyptian
word means "lover of righteousness," another name not for a
shepherd but a shepherd king, known by the Jews as Melchizedek, "King of Righteousness." From the words *meh'-lek* and
tseh'-dek in Hebrew, we arrive at the same name and meaning
the Egyptians used for the designer and builder of the pyramid.

Could this be true, that Shem and Melchizedek are one and
the same person? If the Masoretic text is upheld, this could be
possible, and Jewish tradition suggests this is so. According to
the Midrash, the bones of Adam again came into the hands of
Shem and were last seen by Jacob in the cave where Shem was
dwelling called "The Place of the Skull." It was in this cave
that Jacob saw the bones of Adam and received the oral
traditions of the Torah.

Accepting the chronology of the Masoretic as correct, we
would list the passing of the early patriarchs within the life-
span of Shem as follows:

SHEM'S AGE	WHEN DIED	WHOM SHEM OUTLIVED BY NUMBER OF YEARS
440	Peleg	162
441	Nahor	161
470	Reu	132
493	Serug	109
527	Terah	75
540	Arphaxad	62
567	Abraham	35
570	Salah	32

---

[8]George Rawlinson, trans., *The History of Herodotus* (New York: Tudor Publishing,
1928).

The list may differ from other interpretations by two years due to my dating of Shem's age at 102 rather than 100 at Arphaxad's birth.

Accordingly, then, we have Shem outliving all the early post-Flood generations with the exception of Eber. But the possibility of Shem's being alive during the time of Jacob is questionable if one accepts the death of Terah, the same year that Abraham left his father's house in Harran.

Basically, some scholars' arguments are as follows: Most assume that the death of Terah occurred when Abraham was 75 years old (he was known then as Abram). In the Book of Acts, Luke says in 7:4 KJV, "Then came he [Abram] out of the land of the Chaldeans [Ur], and dwelt in Charran [Harran]: and from thence, when his father was dead, he [God] removed him [Abram] into this land, wherein ye now dwell." Luke is interpreted by the scholars as stating that Abram didn't depart from Harran until his father was dead at the age of 205, or the year 427. It should be mentioned here, too, that Luke is most likely taking this from the Septuagint rather than the Hebrew. It was the Septuagint that was read by the early Church, not the Masoretic text that we have in our Bibles of today. There are even quotes from the earlier books by Jesus and Paul that do not appear in the Masoretic, or our Old Testament.

In Genesis 12:4 we read that "Abram departed, as the Lord had spoken unto him, and Abram was seventy and five years old when he departed out of Harran. Thus the scholars' solution: 427 less 75 means Abram was born in the year 352.[9]

I will now show that if the Christian scholars are correct in this assumption, then the Midrash is wrong. My disagreement with the scholars begins with the Hebrew text discussing the event (Genesis 11:31–12:4), where I find nothing to suggest Abram didn't leave until his father died but in fact says Abram was to leave his father and relatives behind. "Get thee out of thy country, and from thy kindred, and from thy father's house" (KJV), indicates that his father was still alive! Verse

---

[9]*Aid to Bible Understanding* (New York: International Bible Students Association, 1971), p. 334.

11:32 is only making a statement of fact on the age of Terah at his passing.

The following will emphasize the problem: These scholars in question have as a starting point a Flood date of 2369, which I find totally unrealistic and unacceptable. For the purpose of discussion we will use their date because we are using their figures.[10]

Scholars' Interpretation of Dates	B.C.E.		My Interpretation of Dates
Terah died in 427 (post-Flood)	(1942)	(1942)	Terah died at 427
Terah had begat Abram at age 130	(2017)	(2077)	Terah begat Abram at 70
Abram begat Isaac at age 100	(1917)	(1977)	Abram begat Isaac at 100
Abraham died at age 175	(1842)	(1902)	Abraham died at 175
When Jacob was 15			When Jacob was 15
Therefore, Jacob's birth was	(1857)	(1917)	Date of Jacob's birth
Shem died 500 years after Flood	(1869)	(1867)	Shem died 502 post-Flood

The results of the scholars' interpretation show the event in the Midrash was impossible, for Shem was dead twelve years before Jacob was even born. However, my interpretation of the dates based on Terah's death after Abram's departure show Jacob and Shem contemporaries for some fifty years. At least the meeting of Shem and Jacob was possible with my dates, but generally speaking, Christian scholars don't bother themselves with reading the Midrash or learning Hebrew. This story relates to that of Joseph telling his father, Jacob, his dream. Then Jacob remembers an incident when Shem was speaking to him concerning the beheaded ox or heifer. The Agala Arafa is paramount to understanding the importance attached to the ashes of the Red Heifer, the discovery of which will ultimately come to pass as the most significant discovery in the end times of this age.

But the Masoretic text and its *Midrash Rabbah* traditions are not without their problems. There is a growing feeling among many students of chronology today that perhaps the period of time from the Flood to the year Abram left Harran is too short. The Samaritan text gives 1077 years and the Septuagint gives 1377 years for this same period, thus pushing the time of the Flood further back into history. Both these dates would rule

---

[10]Ibid., pp. 860–864.

out the Shem-Melchizedek connection but enhance the Imhotep-Shem possibility. The Masoretic date of the Flood is suspect, with the Sumerians already recording the event some 600 years earlier. The dating of the pyramid falls nicely in line with the other texts within the life span after the Flood of Shem's 502 years.

The most ancient traditions of this structure, and the Great Pyramid alone, is that it was erected to memorialize a tremendous cataclysm in the planetary system which turned the world upside down, affecting the world with fire and flooding. Referring to the phenomenal accuracy of the work embodied in the Great Pyramid, Petrie was moved to say that "it was limited to the skill of one man."

I am convinced that this man was Shem and that it was the first edifice erected. Those that followed were futile attempts by vainglorious kings to match the wonder of the original and were for their own interment next to the sepulcher of the first man.

Is this structure the center of the world which Shem sought out? In pursuing this theory, it is only fair to say that early Jews, Christians, and Moslems venerated Jerusalem as the heart of the universe and foundation of the world. It is called Even ha-Shetiyah, bringing to mind again the idea that it is Shem, Shet, or Set who placed the mark as the center. It is on the summit of Mount Moriah, upon which stood the Holy Temple.

The sages of Israel in the third century interpreted Ezekiel's words "that dwell in the middle of the earth" to also mean Jerusalem. Certainly the Crusaders did, marking it on medieval maps as Umbilicus Mundi, the navel of the world. But to the Moslem, it was Nafs ed-Dunya, located over the Place of the Skull. This is the Golgotha of Christendom, or Calvary in Latin. Beneath this hill is a great cave, that of Shem from Jewish tradition. It is owned by a Palestinian family who graciously allowed me to explore it. It is presently being used to store bananas but is large enough inside to turn around a tractor trailer.

Was this the halfway point from moving the bones of Adam from the original sepulcher to the cave of Machpelah?

An imposing structure called Haram el-Khalil, or "the sacred precinct of the friend of the Merciful One," stands upon the field of Machpelah, which in Hebrew means "doubling." My feeling is that its place was known by Abraham as the final hiding place of the bones of Adam, placed there by Shem, and this accounts for the high price of four hundred silver shekels he was willing to pay for the property to Ephron the Hittite. The story is recorded in Genesis 23 and stands as the oldest legal document of purchased real estate in Hebrew writings.

Perhaps deep within this cave lie the bones of created man, secreted away by Shem who escaped the ravages of the Flood, to be preserved until discovery and scientific examination at some future time.

THE MIDDLE OF THE EARTH

The Bible records that the sons of Ham were Cush, Miz'raim, Put, and Canaan (Genesis 10:6). The biblical Miz'raim is actually the Akkadian Miṣraîm. This name is derived from the Semitic root which in Akkadian gives the verb aṣaru, "to cut, to delimit, or to delineate." Egypt is called today in Arabic al Miṣri, and denotes a country built according to a geometric plan.

Miz'raim was the founder of Egypt, and cut the earth with the equivalent of today's prime meridian of Greenwich. This line split the sinuoisities of the Nile River and was called the Sokar, or main axis, of Egypt and the world. Today it is represented by the meridian of 31°14′E.

The earth thus divided between east and west, with the Great Pyramid located at 30°00′N, established a firm geographical position for the center the ancient world that enabled survey parties through astronomical observations of sidereal time, or the apparent steady roll of the great vault of heaven,[11]

---

[11]Sidereal or stellar time is the method employed by the ancients in observing the apparent rotation of the celestial vault of heaven, which flows evenly through one full revolution more than the number of circles made by the sun in a year. Today we measure by solar time, an artificial concept employing the chronometer.

to establish other fixed geographical points in measuring the earth. Surveys by the Egyptians left their mark not only on the land of the Nile but throughout the ancient world as well. Noorbergen,[12] following in the tracks of these ancient explorers, suggests the name *Almodad,* fourth generation after Noah and first of Joktan's thirteen sons,[13] means "measurer." His source is the Chaldean Paraphrase of Jonathan, which observes that Almodad, "qui mensurbat terran finibus" (who measured the earth to its extremities) is also the progenitor of the southern Arabians.

Actually my research discloses Almodad as chief of the tribe of Jurham, and father of a wife of Ishmael. Noorbergen credits this as the reason many Renaissance maps revealed peculiarities of Arabian influence with the ancient source never fully identified. Even the Piri Reis chart and the Reinal chart (1510) are based on a circular projection with the focal point in Egypt.

Another enlightening discovery is presented by Livio Stecchini in the appendix notes of Peter Tompkins' work,[14] where Stecchini describes a map being used in Russia that was based on information gleaned from cartographic sources from the sixth century B.C., relying upon still more ancient geodetic points. It was based upon a system of Egyptian origin, revealing that Russia had been surveyed in earliest times. A base line of 45° 12' was revealed along this parallel beginning at the Danube, cutting east across the northern side of the Black Sea, through the Crimea, ending at the Caucasus range. Beginning with this base northern latitude the ancients then surveyed three hundred miles north and south of this line for 10° along the meridians that formed the three axes of Egypt. It would appear that the ancients considered the river Dnieper a symmetric counterpart of the Nile River, running between the same meridians, so much so that points along the Dnieper corresponding to key positions along the Nile were given Egyptian names in Russia.

I found it incredible that the ancients could give geograph-

---

[12]Rene Noorbergen, *Secrets of the Lost Races* (New York: Barnes & Noble, 1977).

[13]Joktan was Peleg's brother. Peleg lived 101 to 340 years after the Flood.

[14]Peter Tompkins, *Secrets of the Great Pyramid* (New York: Harper & Row, 1971).

ical positions at roughly the latitude of Moscow and probably beyond, while no one had bothered to record the exact coordinates of the position for the Ark!

8

The Riddle of Five by Two

DID BEROSUS GIVE THE ARK'S LOCATION?

It appeared to me, and perhaps to me alone, that the oldest geodetic marker on the surface of the globe should be the final resting point of the remains of the escape vessel of the antediluvian age, or the very door through which passed the seed of mankind into the new world. The silence on the subject spoke rather loudly. If anyone knew the exact location, were they keeping it a secret?

I was struck by Berosus' often-quoted and familiar statement that the Ark was five stades in length and two stades in breadth. Some authors gave three dimensions, while others used stadi or stadia. Where had they gotten these variant descriptive terms? Some said the Ark was "five by two." In my estimation these could all pose different meanings. If Berosus had all the ancient knowledge at his disposal, including the historical texts of Babylon, why had he not described it as those before him? If he claimed to know the exact date of the Flood and its cause, was he leaving a cryptic message of its location?

Today, one doesn't usually measure anything in stadia but stadiums. In the ancient world, however, it was a common unit of geographical measure.[1] It was assumed that a man marching or a ship under oars could cover a distance of thirty stadia in an hour. A ship under sail could cover nine hundred stadia, or one and a half degrees in a twenty-four hour period.

Since a stadia was, give or take, some six hundred feet,

---

[1] I would assume it to be one-tenth of a minute of the sun's arc.

scholars were quoting Berosus as stating the Ark was three thousand feet long and twelve hundred feet wide. This of course would be unacceptable. Since I had seen in my own time the interpretive wanderings of well-meaning Bible scholars and revisionists who changed the long-standing biblical text from cubits into their concept or equivalent of feet, I could only assume the early copyists had misquoted Berosus as well.

Attempting to gain an understanding of just what Berosus might really have said involves consulting a modern Latin translation of an Armenian translation of the lost Greek original of the Chronicle of Eusebius, who borrowed from Alexander Polyhistor, who recorded what Berosus had written in extremely poor Greek. I decided to skip over to where I thought the problem should lie, and went directly to the Armenian.

The Armenian word *vtawank* corresponded to a measure of 606.75 feet, and was therefore the Greek stadia, but there was a similar word, *vtawan,* that was a shorter distance. This term, sometimes identified as an *asparez,* was an arrow's throw and a distance given as 150 paces.[2] My pace of approximately 2.2 feet times the multiple of five[3] given by Berosus would make the Ark's length 1,650 feet. Impossible! What was the unit of measure Berosus may have used that could have been misinterpreted as stadia?

Had the original works of Berosus used a Chaldean symbol that had been erroneously translated as a Greek fret meaning stadia? The Egyptians referred to their land as To-Mera, or the land of "mr." The "mr" is essentially a right triangle comprised of 36° with the other by necessity 54° to total 90°. This was used in land surveying in a similar manner as the basic surveying square of the Babylonian cuneiform texts, and called an IKU, a unit of land surface of 44,100 square feet. This idea of "mr" is symbolized by a peculiarly shaped geometric figure which in principle represents two triangles shaping the Egyp-

---

[2]Zaven Arzoumanian, *History of Lewond, the Eminent Vardapet of the Armenians* (Wynnewood, Pennsylvania: St. Sahag and St. Mesrob Armenian Church, 1982), p. 153.

[3]The Armenian version contains a scribal error that gives the length as fifteen stadia.

tian delta. Could a similar "fret" have been used in Berosus' original work, meaning it was the *geographical location* of the Ark rather than the Ark's exaggerated dimensions?

I began by plotting squares from the geodetic center of the ancient world east of the "Sokar," or prime meridian, of Egypt. When this failed to provide anything resembling a ratio of five by two into the area of Urartu, I next tried the geodetic centers of Greek times. Delphi was also considered as such. But was Berosus writing from an Egyptian or Greek perspective? No! Wasn't Berosus, after all, giving the Babylonian or *Chaldean* perspective on world history?

Even though Berosus lived during the era of the Seleucid calendar,[4] he had still used the Babylonian word *Aiaru,* or May. This was clarified at a later date by Greek scholars copying Berosus' text as being "Daesius" (Daisios) from the Macedonian era. The perspective of Berosus for the center of the world would be the Persian *world navel* in Persepolis.

During the reign of the Chaldean King Nabonasser (747–734 B.C.E.), the Persians overran Egypt, supplanting the Egyptian lunar calendar with their solar calendar, and moving the prime meridian of Egypt to their empire. One can understand why the prime meridian of Greenwich runs through England today, for in her day, Britannia ruled the waves. During the time of Berosus the Chaldeans would still consider the world divided by their prime meridian, even though they had been conquered by Alexander.

Actually it was King Darius the Great who ultimately had the Sokar moved from Egypt and established it just to the west of his new capital. The exact center of this world navel was to become his tomb. This is why the Greeks refer to the tomb of Darius as an "Amphalos," which today is located at 30°00'N and 52°50'E.

This was done very precisely as follows: The old geodetic center as mentioned earlier was the Cheops Pyramid, located on latitude 30°00'N. The Sokar is today represented by 31°14'E of Greenwich and is a meridian indicating the main line of the course of the Nile that divides the delta into two equal parts or right triangles.

---

[4]The Era of Antioch in the early years of the fourth century (312 B.C.E.).

When the Persians drew a series of geodetic squares out in all directions, they were aware that the earth's surface was not flat, and they had to lay these squares on a midlatitude, for example. When squaring off an area from 30°N to 36°N, the width of this square was considered 7°12' of longitude. This occurs because 7°12' of longitude is equivalent in actual length to 6° of latitude at the midpoint between 30° and 36°N. These surveying plots are thus true squares.

The moving of the old prime meridian was accomplished by three units or squares of 7°12' of longitude east along the parallel of 30°N for a distance of 21°36'. This, added to the old Sokar of 31°14', equaled 52°50'E.

The new geodetic center of the world thus became 30°00'N and 52°50'E on our maps of today. The location of the Ark would thus be *two by five* from Berosus' understanding, and pivoting on this newly established world navel. If one imagines moving northward along the prime meridian to the latitude where the Ark is to be found, this angle becomes *five* times 18, or 90°. From the geodetic center another line forming an angle of *two* times 18, or 36°, will intersect at the Ark's latitude. What determines this interesection point is the length of the Ark itself converted to minutes of arc. This would be a clever cryptic message one could expect from someone who represents himself as interpreter of Bel, steeped in the mysteries of the Chaldeans, and guardian of secrets from antiquity.

In the works of Flavius Josephus, *The Antiquities of the Jews,*[5] he states that "Arphaxad named the Arphaxadites, who are now called Chaldeans." Surely Arphaxad, born two years after the Flood, knew the exact location of the Ark, and it was held as a sacred place in the annals of Chaldean knowledge.

Another way to reach the Ark's location would be to convert the cubits to geodetic feet of 515. This converted to minutes of arc (divided by 60) equals 8°35'. This subtracted from the prime meridian of 52°5' leaves the line of Berosus as 44°15' for a present-day longitude for the remains of the Ark.

It was on this faint whim and speculative hope that I

---

[5]Chapter VI:4.

perceived the Ark might be found on a line running east of Doğubayazıt, where it converged with a line running north-west from the tomb of Darius. I had mentioned to Irwin that I wanted to search the foothills to the south of Ararat, and he suggested I talk it over with Wyatt, who felt he was on the site at Tendürek. Wyatt, however, clarified his position as not being on Tendürek at all (which is west of Bayazit) but to the east, and very close to my position. This meeting was the catalyst in bringing our two goals together, for the boat-shaped object and the line of Berosus were literally side by side.

DILMUN OR DILMAN

While working on these possibilities with Berosus I began reading a book entitled *Looking for Dilmun,*[6] in which the author states, "Nothing is gained by pretending a certainty that does not exist." In light of my line of Berosus, I certainly wasn't sold on the idea that it existed anywhere but in my head, but I found something along this line of mine that seemed to contradict the accepted view, which again lends credence to the possibility I was headed in the right direction.

Geoffrey Bibby's work is titled *Looking for Dilmun* rather than *The Discovery of Dilmun* for the reason put forth in the first paragraph. He is a true scholar and his work leaves no doubt among his readers that he has indeed located the ancient land of Dilmun, which is the present-day island of Bahrain in the Arabian Gulf.[7] However, my research has led me to suggest the following: There are two Dilmuns. One is the *Dilmun* of Commerce spoken of by Saragon and in so many of the records of commodity transactions in the ancient world, and the other is the *Dilman* which appears in the Sumerian Flood story and is the abode of Ziusudra, the Sumerian Noah.

Dilmun was thought to be nothing more than a little kingdom somewhere on the periphery of the Assyrian empire, until Captain Durand published his survey of the antiquities of

---

[6]Geoffrey Bibby, *Looking for Dilmun* (New York: Alfred A. Knopf, Inc., 1969).

[7]If you are in Iran, you call it the Iranian or Persian Gulf. When in Arabia it is wise to call it the Arabian Gulf.

Bahrain in 1880. The Royal Asiatic Society asked the great Sir Henry Rawlinson to comment on Durand's report and in his extensive reply Rawlinson claimed that Bahrain was identical with Dilmun.

Before this becomes fact and appears in everyone's foot-notes in the future, as with Nisir being the modern Pir Omar Gudrun, a few inconsistencies to this assumption should be pointed out.

In a translation of a tablet from Nippur, published in 1914, the last part of the text reads as follows:

> Anu and Enlil cherished Ziusudra.
> life like a god they gave him.
> breath eternal like a god,
> they bring down for him.
> Then Ziusudra the king,
> the preserver of the name of vegetation,
> and of the seed of mankind,
> in the land of the crossing,
> the land of Dilmun,
> the place where the sun rises,
> they cause to dwell.
>
> Translated by Professor Kramer of Philadelphia

First, it should be pointed out that this is the Sumerian Flood story and not the Epic of Gilgamesh. Bibby states, "the Babylonian version tells us, as we have seen, that Utu-nipishtim was to be granted immortality and to dwell in the distance, at the *mouth* of the rivers." This would indeed suit his Bahrain setting, but the latest translation of the Babylonian text reads, "at the *source* of the rivers."

From the Sîn-leqi-unninnī version translated by John Gardner and John Maier (lines 195 and 196):

> Let Utnapishtim live far off,
> at the *source* of all rivers.
> They took me far away,
> to live at the *source* of the rivers.

Since we can assume that water runs downhill in Mesopo-tamia, the place far off where Utnapishtim dwelt was in the highlands, the source of all the waters, not down in the lowlands at the *mouth* of the rivers, in the delta of the gulf region.

Bibby admits that some eminent authorities have later disagreed with this identification. Since Dilmun seemed to have been a bustling seaport engaged in brisk trade, it hardly seems to be the dwelling place of Rūqi, the reclusive "Utnapishtim, the remote"!

Other problems arise when following the trek of Gilgamesh in seeking Utnapishtim out. We know that our hero began his journey from his city of Uruk. According to Bibby he would journey south to Arabia, a distance of some 200 miles into present-day Kuwait, then another 242 miles to the point where he made the crossing to the island of Bahrain, or Dilmun.

Now admittedly, if Noah lived 350 years after the Flood, he may have lived and traveled in many places. He may have in fact lived in Dilmun, the Bahrain of today, but in the Gilgamesh epic we find our hero, the "joy-woe man," seeking the meaning of life from Utnapishtim, "he who has found life," and hopefully, immortality as well in the upper steppes of Mesopotamia (Tablet IX, column v): "At nine double hours . . . *the north wind bit into his face"* (lines 38 and 39). For the north wind to bite into your face you must be heading north. To consider Bibby's Dilmun, then, we must assume Gilgamesh was walking backwards into Arabia!

Another striking departure from the Sumerian original is Gilgamesh praying to the moon god Sîn (Sumerian Nanna) before his departure from his city of Uruk. This should not be surprising if one considers him heading north rather than south to Bibby's Dilmun, for in the north country they worshiped the moon.

Harran was the home of Terah, Abraham's father, and was one of the centers for the worship of Sîn. It lay between Nineveh and the fords of the Euphrates River at Carchemish. Harran eventually became the site of perhaps the greatest temple ever built for this deity.

The path Gilgamesh takes to the *source* of the rivers is called *"harran* (ilu) samas" (Tablet IX, column iv, line 46).

In my opinion, Gilgamesh is now entering the "Land of the Crossings," or the area where the early survivors crossed from the Ark, the last vestige of the antediluvian world, over into the new world to Shinar.

It is from here that the "gods," or those antediluvian survivors still retaining their unseemly longevity of life, came— from the mountains of the north, a mysterious place, a land of darkness. Thus Gilgamesh prayed for guidance from the moon; it was a place unknown and fearful, the abode of the gods: "Gilgamesh came to the mountains whose name is *Mashu"* (Tablet IX, column ii, line 1).

Here we have the name *Mashu,* which is very close in pronunciation to Mahshur (Maḥṣur), the mount of the Ark. "I will sit also upon the mount of the congregation, in the sides of the north" (Isaiah 14:13 KJV).

This passage of Scripture goes well beyond the kings of Tyre and Babylon, and I suggest the concept of these days of pagan deities was that the assembly of the gods was considered in the north. The Hebrew "Jehovah-shammah" ("the Lord is present") does not comfort Gilgamesh, for though he travels the road of Shamash, there is no light (Tablet IX, column iv, lines 46–48), and he travels in darkness (column v, lines 1–44). It is in this remote area, not Bahrain, that we find Dilmun, and the abode of the reclusive Utnapishtim (Noah).

In walking this line of Berosus we come first upon the mountains of the Kurds that are mentioned by numerous historians as the land of the Ark. It is still considered such today and noted on maps in the extreme southeastern corner of present-day Turkey. The mountain is spelled "Curid," but it is the land of the Cordene, or Curid, from the root word *krd.* Its peak is an imposing 11,000 feet (3331 meters). It is here that one finds the source of the Greater Zab River (Büyük Zap) that feeds the Tigris, and nine miles from its *source* we find Yiğit Dağı (Hero's Mount).

Gilgamesh states, "On a long journey I wander the steppes" (Tablet X, column ii, line 9). Where, I ask, are the steppes of Bahrain? Where is the source of the rivers of Mesopotamia in Bahrain? Surely Gilgamesh is referring to the Tigris and Euphrates, and Mr. Bibby is wrong!

The Bitter Sea crossed by Gilgamesh cannot be the Persian Gulf but only a shallow body of water, for Urshanabi, the boatman, directs Gilgamesh to go *down* to the forest to cut

GUIDE TO THE SOLUTION OF THE PUZZLE OF BEROSUS' "FIVE BY TWO" LOCATION.
THE SITE OF NOAH'S ARK AFTER 2,276 YEARS.

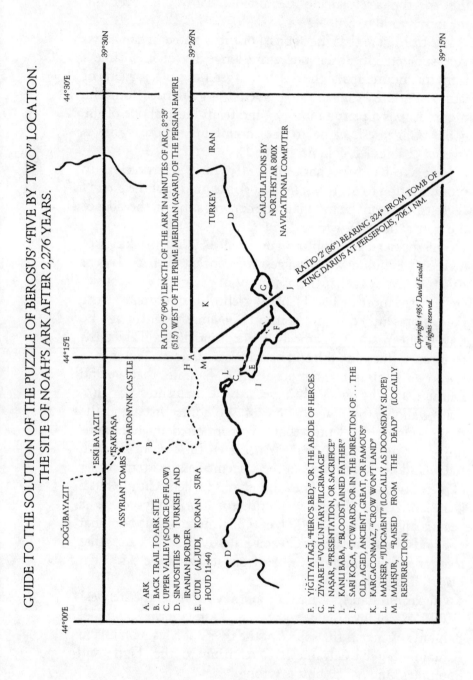

A. ARK
B. BACK TRAIL TO ARK SITE
C. UPPER VALLEY (SOURCE OF FLOW)
D. SINUOSITIES OF TURKISH AND IRANIAN BORDER
E. CUDI (AL-JUDI, KORAN SURA HOUD 11:44)

F. YİĞİTYATAĞI, "HERO'S BED," OR THE ABODE OF HEROES
G. ZİYARET "VOLUNTARY PILGRIMAGE"
H. NAŞAR, "PRESENTATION, OR SACRIFICE"
I. KANLI BABA, "BLOODSTAINED FATHER"
J. SARİ KOCA, "TOWARDS, OR IN THE DIRECTION OF . . . THE OLD, AGED, ANCIENT, GREAT, OR FAMOUS"
K. KARGACONMAZ, "CROW WON'T LAND"
L. MAHŞER, "JUDGMENT" (LOCALLY AS DOOMSDAY SLOPE)
M. MAHŞUR, "RAISED FROM THE DEAD" (LOCALLY RESURRECTION)

RATIO '5' (90°) LENGTH OF THE ARK IN MINUTES OF ARC, 8°35'
(515') WEST OF THE PRIME MERIDIAN (ASARU) OF THE PERSIAN EMPIRE

RATIO '2' (36°) BEARING, 324° FROM TOMB OF
KING DARIUS AT PERSEPOLIS, 706.1 NM.

CALCULATIONS BY
NORTHSTAR 800X
NAVIGATIONAL COMPUTER

poles of sixty cubits to use in making their way across death's waters. At sea level, you cannot go *down!* But at Lake Urmia, now officially called Razaieh, the elevation is 4022 feet above sea level. This area is in fact the Land of Bitter Seas, for the Caspian, Urmia, and Van Lake are some of the largest bitter seas in the world.

It is here you will find Dilman, the abode of Utnapishtim, not Bibby's port city of Saragon's commerce in Bahrain spelled Dilmun. The Dilman of Noah is buried beneath the modern city of Shapur. It is only fifty-eight miles east by north to Marand, where by tradition lay the remains of Noah's mother. Some authors insist this is his wife, as the biblical account states only eight were aboard. In considering these variations, it might perhaps mean that Noah's wife was the mother of all living.

9

The Lost Expedition

TERRORISTS OF AUGUST

The interim between our returning from Turkey in mid-June until our next trip in August 1985 was one of preparation and worry for my plans of scanning the site with the radar equipment. The search had now depleted my savings and was causing a real financial crisis at home. I had become obsessed with the Ark. I began by selling my salvage equipment, and the June trip had eaten up the proceeds of that sale. I had stopped working. I couldn't keep my mind on anything but the buried Ark. I put my salvage boat on the market but didn't hold much hope of selling it before it would be time to leave again. The date was set for August 15.

I hated the idea of trying to promote the next venture as so many others had in their expeditions to Mount Ararat, yet Christendom should take an interest in what we were doing. When I heard that a well-known nationwide Christian network had plans to televise another group's *search* for the Ark, I called to see if they would be interested in having the exclusive and being on hand when we proved that we were *on* the Ark. Naturally I was met with skepticism, as all searches were *always* on Ararat itself. I offered to show some evidence I hoped would support our claim. They said to fly up and we'd have a meeting on Saturday morning. Due to flight schedules, that necessitated flying up Friday night, which I did, and I was kindly met at the Norfolk Airport by a driver. When I had entered the facilities, I was told our meeting the next day had to be canceled. The staff representative apologized and said he'd forgotten that Saturday was the network's barbeque, or something.

The camera team was leaving to set up for the activities, but they had about fifteen minutes for an immediate videotape interview. I cordially refused and explained that it would be detrimental to our forthcoming trip to have anything aired until after we had left the site, and besides, I had not discussed this with the other members of the group. Preannouncing our intentions could lead to problems. There was much unrest in the Middle East, and we didn't want any attention focused on us while we had the expensive equipment on the site. We had all agreed there should be *no* advance publicity. The staff rep did, however, spend a few hours with me while I attempted to lay out the evidence to establish our site as the Ark. "Isn't the Ark, according to the Bible, supposed to be on Ararat? Aren't all the other Christian church groups going to Ararat? Isn't Irwin, the astronaut, going to Ararat?"

I could see it was no use. In his eyes we were obviously way out in left field, almost twenty miles south, and hadn't all the experts debunked this site years ago? "There is absolutely no doubt that this is the remains of a shipwreck," I said. "It meets the requirements of Noah's Ark too perfectly to be anything else."

"It's not rectangular," he said dryly.

I tried an hour more but he never was convinced enough for me to even mention our financial plight. I had foolishly presumed that Christian television could help support us in giving the evolutionists the biggest stumbling block they had ever come up against.

Apparently the only one I convinced was the driver who had picked me up at the airport. I left him with two photographs of the Ark (stamped David Fasold, All Rights Reserved) and headed back home. The cost of my airfare could have been put to better use on the underfinanced trip in August.

Returning to Florida, I again contacted Geophysical Survey Systems in New Hampshire about the proposed rental of the subsurface interface radar unit they manufactured. At this point, I should explain how it works and the purpose for which I intended to use it.

   This is the high-tech, state-of-the-art development of GSSI for peering down into the ground. Many times the shutter imagery camera systems in NASA's satellites detect unknown geological features that are then "ground truthed," so to speak, by the radar unit at a later date. An example of this would be the apparent suggestion of a dried riverbed under the sands of the Sahara desert. The radar unit is brought to the site and pulled over the area. The underground feature, which is unseen from the surface, is printed out on the graphic recorder. It is virtually the only solution to problems of strata profiling, rock fracture, and fault mapping. It is used in various industrial applications for pavement thickness (runway integrity testing), reinforcing-bar location, and sinkhole prediction. I felt that since it profiles everything from boreholes to peat to permafrost, why not profile the mound to reveal the Ark?

   Since the unit is the electromagnetic equivalent of the single-trace acoustic profiling systems used in marine subbottom profiling,[1] it would be conceivable to make up a third-dimensional display through a computer. If in conjunction with a data recorder, these data bits of the entire site could be softwared into projecting the image of the infrastructure on a cathode ray tube and commanded to rotate, it would be possible to view the Ark under the earth from various angles.

   My first idea was to make up a simple graphic account of what was there before getting into the programming. This would be done as follows: Establishing a bench mark on the limestone outcropping the Ark was impaled upon, I would then establish 686 altitudes at the grid line intersections, and draw the transducer over the surface, hitting the event marker at these points. I had designed a simple electric reel that would ensure the rate of speed over the surface would remain constant. The graphic recorder's printout would then be transferred onto clear plastic and positioned onto thin glass. These thin plates would then be positioned in a case, each plate representing a scan line down the object with the event markers aligned and light projected through the ends of the

---

[1]It should be pointed out that this is an oversimplification of how the unit operates, since the dielectric constant of seawater remains the same, while earth materials can vary from 1 (air) to 81.

glass, highlighting the features of the infrastructure. Each event marker at the grid points would determine the depth below the surface to the interface.

The company would provide all needed equipment and an operator (technician) for a price far less than alternate services, as the project intrigued them. Their schedule was heavily booked, however, and in order to reserve the radar equipment needed, I would have to pay them fully in advance. It was nonrefundable, so if plans were changed, and I did not go exactly on those dates, the money was forfeited. It was worth the price, as this was the best model of their equipment available and would most certainly solve the riddle of the mound for good. If the results showed the structure of a boat within this mound, the company would stand on the evidence as an impartial and unbiased source. On top of that, the technician, Thomas Fenner, was a respected member of the exploratory geologists' group and rather skeptical of the existence of Noah's Ark in the first place. I had every hope of blowing his mind with the results.

I had corresponded with this company since February of 1984, and it had become by now a "do it or quit talking about it" situation, so I began the necessary paperwork to mortgage my house.

Then John Baumgardner called. He had been in touch with a group in Texas that was very interested in what John had told them of our discoveries. John of course had scientific credentials. I didn't. Therefore he was more acceptable than Ron or me to be head of the group. Ron and I were flown out in late July 1985, at the group's expense (which was a switch) for an early-morning meeting.

When we arrived, I met with a California attorney who listened carefully to what John had to say. He asked me how much we needed to get the equipment to Turkey. What I needed from him, I explained, was to cover the cost of the radar rental and the technician. I had enough money for the portage of equipment, airfares, and ground transportation. "You've got it!" he said, and I went to bed that night sure that this man's generosity would change history.

The next day at the meeting with the Texas group, the situation broke down. It was difficult for me to discover just what was wrong here. They had promised beforehand to match funds. Now they balked, and the attorney said he would provide the total funds himself. It was an uncomfortable time. All parties involved were gentlemen and I had hoped that no friendships would be lost over this. I had the impression that what I was seeing was an interdenominational squabble building up. Ron was a Seventh-Day Adventist, and I was a renegade ex-fundamentalist from the Plymouth Brethren. We were odd running mates, to be sure.

It began to appear that this Texas group was in the publishing business and in some way connected with trying to get creationist textbooks into the public school system. Perhaps they just wanted Ron and I out of the picture. The Ark then could become the "Treasure of the Sierra Madre" of academic prestige and fundamentalist exploitation. I wanted no part of this.

The attorney made good his commitment to provide all the funds on his own. Behind the scenes, however, strange things were happening. Although having nothing to do with financing the expedition, the Texas group was sending along a published writer to take notes on our results, and the attorney was bringing a film crew to make a documentary. It was difficult to fault him. He certainly deserved something for his time and money, but the Texas group was getting a lot for bed and breakfast. Worst of all, they were all arriving at the site ahead of me and the radar equipment.

Antiquities officials were beginning to turn their backs on high-profile foreign archaeological expeditions. I felt it was imperative that we leave without fanfare and just get the job done. Perhaps the best idea would be to let the Turkish press make the announcement on the results. After all, it was they who granted permission to allow the investigation.

But Ron would hear none of it. I felt that what had started out as a team effort was now quickly dissolving. Everything was under control, he said. He and the attorney were anxious to depart. For various reasons, the expedition was on without me. I was locked into my original departure dates, awaiting insurance and an International Carnet to enter the equipment into Turkey.

Five days before leaving, I was stunned to see my photographs held to the screen on a Christian network with the announcement that "they are racing toward scientific confirmation of the Ark . . . news is preparing an exclusive report to air in the next few days!"

Well, I thought, *they sure got their free ride after all!*

The staff representative called from the network for an interview, and I got pretty mad. "What's the big change? I thought you weren't interested. I didn't have the proper credentials! I'd like to know how you got the exclusive without putting a nickel in on the cost," I said.

"Well, we have to be careful with the Lord's money," he responded. "It might not be the Ark!"

"Well look, it cost me round-trip airfare and three days of my time to hear you say you weren't interested. Please don't use my photographs over the air. You are hurting what we're trying to accomplish here. All this sensationalism will result in delays to get the evidence."

"Well, we met with Mr. Baumgardner at the airport in Atlanta and set everything up from there."

Soon there followed daily broadcasts: ". . . has this report on what the scientists have found so far . . . . could this be the final resting place of Noah's Ark? . . . Dr. John Baumgardner, a geophysicist at the Los Alamos Research Lab in New Mexico . . . using a metal detector, Baumgardner has been able to confirm the existence of metal at regular intervals. Baumgardner says he believes that metal is at the points where these lines intersect, giving rise to speculation metal was used in the infrastructure of the craft." The viewer was then shown exclusive pictures by a Turkish camera crew accompanied by a television producer. It was a reproduction of all my survey tapelines laid out on the site of the Ark that I had done last June.

"It is still not clear if the formation is petrified wood," said the commentator. Then Ron came on. "We have found the remains of deck timbers, we have found the remains of rib timbers, we have found the remains of a keel timber." All of which was news to me. *Well!* I thought. *So much for sensationalism.*

Soon after, I was not surprised to hear, "Research in the field has been temporarily suspended because of military tensions in the area. But other searchers remain skeptical," the news coverage continued. "Among the skeptics is former astronaut James Irwin . . . who has been trekking up Mount Ararat, looking for Noah's Ark. Ararat is fifteen to twenty miles from where this expedition is conducting its probe. Irwin believes that if the Ark is to be found at all, it would be high on the mountain, encased and preserved in ice. Irwin has visited the site with Wyatt but is not yet convinced.

"Irwin is recorded as saying, 'I'm fascinated by it, maybe not as fascinated as they are, because I think that it ought to be examined *by experts.* So I'm waiting for experts' opinions, confirmation that it could be, really, a man-made object. If it's a man-made object, it's probably a man-made boat, and perhaps, ah, perhaps it is Noah's Ark.' "

Great, I thought. *I wonder who's watching all this?* With bombing and hostage crises going on all over the Middle East, here they were on national and worldwide television. Just what we had all agreed not to do. No coverage until after the scan.

News traveled fast. Soon the radar people called to say the *Boston Globe* had printed that an American team headed by Ron Wyatt had been captured by terrorists. It was misinformation, I said. I had just talked to Ron by phone that morning. The technician slated to operate the radar believed me but was now not too anxious to go to Turkey.

Jim Burroughs, well-known documentary filmmaker, called from New York. "Get up here fast; we have to do a story on this." I figured the story was out, and if everyone was looking for sensationalism, what the heck!

I called the company back and said, "Here's your chance to show the world what the equipment can do. ABC is covering it, and it may be the last time anyone gets on the site. Let's go for it!"

We arrived in Doğubayazıt to find the entire operation shut down. John said that in the last week they were able to get out to the site for a total of five or six hours. There had been a group of terrorists who had crossed the border of Iran into Turkey and caused havoc with the climbers in that area. The military had imposed martial law. The financier and all but the last cameraman had left before my arrival. Gone, too, was

Maylon Wilson, Ph.D., also of Los Alamos, whom I had hoped to meet. The writer from the Texas group had also departed.

All I had needed was two hours on the site to prove it was a man-made object. Two days would have done the entire scan, hopefully showing the entire boat to a depth of fifty feet and the voids and decks intact. It was a big show from a false start, and it got us nowhere.

The other teams were frustrated, too. Up on Ararat, some of my friends had been held at gunpoint by the terrorists, their equipment burned and broken up. They had been forced to descend from camp in their nightclothes. We waited for days, rental time on the radar ticking away. The radar technician, Tom Fenner, and I sat around looking at the transfer cases containing the instruments, while back home in the States his wife delivered their first child. I decided on a little side trip. I'd slip off to Kazan for another look around. I needed transportation out to the site. Mustafa, our minibus driver, was on standby for the ABC camera crews, and Jim Burroughs was using Dilaver's "taksi" for his group.

There was a guide in town who was well known for taking tourists into the foothills of Ararat and safely back out. I decided to sleep on it and maybe I'd see him the next day.

I'll call him "Achmed."

ACHMED

The waiter set the tray of tea on the low table before me, and I plopped sugar cubes into the little glass of hot Çay that would start my morning. *Well,* I thought, *here's to the beginning of another do-nothing, get-nowhere day in Doğubayazıt.* The hope of getting on the site with martial law in force was pretty dim. If I couldn't come up with a constructive idea today, I might just succumb to the mounting pressure of buying a regional rug from the shop across the street out of sheer boredom.

I was thinking of breakfast when I saw Achmed come in. Well, he didn't actually come in, but sort of hung around the outer lobby, drifting around the doorway of the hotel, shooting side glances inside to see who was there. He was no doubt checking out the new arrivals to ply his trade while keeping a wary eye out for unhappy tourists he may have met last year. His line of work required him to have a good memory. I watched him pass cautiously through the doorway and relax when no one seemed to take special notice of him. Soon a smile of confidence spread across his face, the type of smile that indicated he was available for conversation and ready to discuss business with anyone in need of his services.

Achmed was neat in attire, as is customary in Turkey. He was rather short and paunchy, and did not give the impression he was into physical pursuits. He looked as if he'd slept in his clothes, which was acceptable in Doğubayazıt, but sported a clean new shirt.

His eye caught mine and he beamed me a smile. I guess he smiled, as you couldn't really see his lower face. His enormous mustache seemed to spread out as he walked toward me and held out his hand. "Mr. David, are you not?"

"Yes," I replied.

"Achmed bey, it is a pleasure to meet you. I was just thinking of having breakfast. Will you join me in the dining room?" His head tipped to the side and he smiled again. His day was starting out with promise.

Martial law was hurting his business, too. I knew he had been wanting to talk with me. We walked through the lobby into the dining area, past tables loaded with fresh-baked bread, hard-boiled eggs, and every kind of fruit imaginable. The Turks ate well, and it was a land of plenty. No one need go hungry in this country, it seemed. We loaded our plates and headed for a secluded corner. Ron and I had the potential for hurting Achmed's business. If we were on the Ark site just outside of town, for whom would he now hire horses and guides to take the seeker of truth up the holy mountain in search of the legend of the lost Ark? His services would be much curtailed, for without the Ark on Mount Ararat, the mystery was gone.

I had arrived with a crew of seven from ABC's "20/20." The lobby was jammed with camera gear and over seventy-four thousand dollars' worth of sophisticated archaeological survey equipment to peer down into the mound to look at the remains of the Ark. The rental on the radar unit with Tom

Fenner the technician was costing a thousand dollars a day, and I purposely chose a corner table where I didn't have to look at it. The thought of all the plans and expense we'd gone through to prove the Ark just sitting there idle was enough to make me lose my appetite. The only persons asking direct questions in Turkey for which you'd better have an immediate response are the police and the military "JANDARMA," both as tough as nails.

But to the average Turk, everything is rather laid back. The subject of the business at hand is never brought up until after tea, and we were well into the middle of breakfast when Achmed turned pleasantries around to his services. He told me he was the Chief Muhtar (Elder) of all the villagers. He was well respected by all the local people, and any area was open to him.

"Do you have a car?" I asked.

"Yes, I have transportation. Where would you be wanting to go today?"

"Kazan," I replied.

The yogurt spewed out of his mouth as he tried to recover his composure.

"Oh, there is nothing of interest in Kazan," he said in a muffled tone, moving closer and wiping the front of his shirt. He looked around, and when he was sure we were not being watched, leaned across the table and stared me right in the eye. "Kazan is a very dangerous place, Mr. David," he said.

Achmed was either genuinely concerned or he was playing his game well. Obviously, wherever one wanted to go would be stretching his ability and under the circumstances would require an additional charge. To be sure, no one should consider going it alone without Achmed's protection and expertise with the locals. I tried hard to keep from laughing.

"Kazan," he hummed, nodding his head. His lower jaw disappeared under his mustache again. "We would need more men!"

"Why?" I responded.

"An interpreter," he replied.

I assumed Achmed knew English well enough but concluded he needed someone fluent in the local dialect.

"Okay," I agreed. "How much for, say, half a day? I want to do right by you, but as you can see I'm working on a low budget."

"It will be an honest and agreeable fee," Achmed replied, "because I will leave that up to you."

This time I could see his teeth. It was the best smile he had. I always hated it when they said that. Even being overgenerous was never enough for people like my friend Achmed.

We drove through the dusty streets of Doğubayazıt as if looking for someone. Finally Achmed spotted a "Taksi" and motioned for it to stop. I think Achmed was in several businesses and the taxi driver worked for him. There was a quick conversation, and the man loaded a spare tire from his trunk into ours. Then we started off again down the side streets and soon came to a storefront. Achmed left briefly and brought out a man of enormous stature, pushed him into the car, and introduced him as Kuni. If this was Achmed's interpreter, his size conveyed volumes. He didn't look very scholarly, either. This was certainly starting out to be some trip, I thought, until at our next stop Achmed introduced me to our final fellow traveler. He was a thin old man, rather studious looking. Achmed proudly introduced him as an historian.

The old man settled into the backseat, nearly disappearing into Kuni's bulk, and we rambled out of town. As we approached the turnoff it was suggested we take a different route to where I had wanted to go. It was a detour miles out of our way to bypass the village, and I tried to urge the more direct route.

"Hayır!" Achmed said firmly. "No, we stay clear of Kazan."

Miles and almost an hour later we arrived at the spot I had pointed at in the hills where I wanted to go. It was a small clump of trees nestled in a crack in the side of a mount called Yalıntaşdağı, where I had spotted some ruins. It required a long walk to the site. As we grew closer I could see it had been a church with a graveyard. Now it was all overturned. The floor stones of the church were in disarray. The heavy stones had been uprooted and someone, possibly animals, had enlarged excavations everywhere under the walls. There was not a stone too heavy to move that hadn't been excavated under-

neath. I focused my attention to one stone on the ground
bearing two lines of inscriptions translatable as:

AIS•DABANS•HAROUTENI
VORTE•DER•+•NAVIN• TIVIN****
                                            HOGDEMPER

Between Achmed's and the old man's English, we worked
it out. "The name here is family name, but can also be
mahşur."

"Resurrection," I said.

"Yes!" Achmed looked at me strangely. *I'm sure getting a lot of
mileage out of these words,* I thought, as the old man went on,
"Yes, to be alive again, on the last day."

"Yes, on Mahşer Günü!" I shouted excitedly. The Judgment
Day. Now the old man was peering at me over his glasses. I
didn't bother to explain. "It doesn't say anything about Noah's
Ark, 'Nuh'un Gemisi,' does it?" I asked.

"Navin is the same like Gemi, yes," the old man said, "and
so is Dabans, but more like a *sanduka* [sarcophagus] or a *kutu*
[coffin]."

"Well, the Egyptian word for Ark is the same as a coffin, I
read somewhere. Could he be saying Ark?" I suggested.

"The first word, *aise* means, 'this is,' and *dabanes* means, 'it
belongs to the owner and is his coffin.' *Harouteni* can be the last
name, is what the old man is saying," Achmed spoke up.

The old man continued studying the inscription. "The *deri*
means, 'maker or owner,' but if the full word is not here then
it just means, 'God, Allah,' not really the same but for the same
meaning. Then *vorte* means, 'it is his son,' or 'somebody's son.'
But *navin* is a gemi, the boat," said the old man standing up.
"The date I must try later, it is very difficult."

Kuni was slowly searching the landscape, never taking his
eyes off the surrounding hills. "Let's go," urged Achmed
nervously.

I was taking a few more pictures when something caught
my eye. I recognized it immediately. It was a streamlined
object laying next to the inscribed rectangular stone. It was
similar in design to what I was beginning to think the Ark

looked like. Was this monument carved in the shape of Noah's Ark? I snapped several more pictures of it, then raced down the hill where the others were waiting for me and anxious to leave.

We crept carefully down the road so as not to raise even a whisper of dust to signal our approach. "With the reference to a boat, *navin,* couldn't the inscription be saying, 'AIS [this is] DABANS [Ark mine] HAROUTENI [resurrection] VORTE [son of] DER [God] NAVIN [the boat]'?" I asked.

"I suppose you could take it that way for one interpretation," said the old man.

" 'The man Harouteni made the coffin for his son,' would be another," replied Achmed, dryly.

"But the reference to a boat is the Ark, and VORTE DER you said means, 'son of God,' didn't you?" I interjected. The old man kept silent.

"As you know, Mr. David, we are Moslems here, and we believe Allah begets not, nor is he begotten," said Achmed.

"Well," I replied, "the stone was part of the remains of a Christian church, and I think it's wonderful he can read it. He doesn't have to agree with what it says." Again I saw something familiar. "Over here," I said, and we pulled off the road. I had spotted two sarcophagi sticking out of the ground, and excavations I had sighted before, too. What I wanted to photograph was directly up the hill from here. We were soon walking past the graves and I started the climb. Achmed paused at the opened graves, then reluctantly followed us up. The rock jutted out from the side of the hill that leveled off onto a plain to the north. On the west face of this large boulder were carved crosses and interspersed among them was more of the strange writing. The old man traced out the letters again. "I only know this one," he said. "Saint Thaddaeus."

I photographed all eight crosses with a rather uneasy feeling. If one of the eight crosses stood for Saint Thaddaeus, could I still cling to Ron's idea they represented the eight survivors of the Ark? To associate crosses with Christian times was only a natural reaction, yet Colonel Koor on Karada Mountain had identified the same type crosses as being of early Sumerian origin.

One could easily assume them to be older since the cross was originally not a Christian symbol at all but was the mystic "Tau" of the Chaldeans, the true original form of the letter *T*. The initial of the name of Tammuz was used in a variety of ways as a most sacred symbol, especially the cross, as Layard had found them used as a sacred symbol in Nineveh. Had these early Christians simply appropriated these earlier symbols to their own meaning? Why hadn't they used twelve crosses for the disciples if they had indeed carved them in the first place? Or why not eleven for the remaining faithful disciples? Why was Thaddaeus (Judas, the son of James) singled out? Eight. Always eight.

We descended to the road and pressed on. The old man was figuring now with pencil and papers.

"I did not know of these inscriptions before." He shared with me how he was deciphering the date. He laid out four rows of nine letters each. Each letter stood for a number. The first row was one through nine; the next row in tens, ten through ninety, and so on. The date on the grave inscription came out 1245 A.D. That late! And still referring to the Ark!

Suddenly, without warning, BLAM! Everybody automatically ducked, but it was only a blowout. The road at this point was really just a goat trail that would eventually lead us to the next site. We all piled out and Achmed got the spare out of the trunk while Kuni kept a sharp eye to the hills. Apparently even Achmed's hurried repair wasn't fast enough for Kuni. He pushed Achmed aside and finished the job. He was frantic to get us moving again. These guys were beginning to make even me nervous. We all leaped into the little Datsun and sped away.

"Are you guys kidding or did you see someone?" I asked. Kuni was serious when he said, in his best American television English, "Apache territory." His message was loud and clear.

We returned to town with my companions in deep conversation. The historian was doing all the talking, with Kuni and Achmed doing all the listening, throwing in an "Evet! [yes]" confirming their agreement.

We arrived back at the Ararat Hotel, sank into the lounge chairs exhausted, and ordered tea all around. "Thank you for a very interesting day," I said. "You've all been most helpful." After the customary interval of more tea, I dealt with the business at hand.

"What would be a fair price to be divided among you for the four-hour trip?" I asked.

"About one hundred and fifty dollars," ventured Achmed, with the look of a saint. Our eyes locked. He was holding his breath and I waited him out. His throat wanted to swallow but wouldn't.

"Achmed, my friend, that's round-trip airfare from Erzurum to Ankara, twice. We just took a little ride in the country before lunch, on me."

"All right," he said, his mustache lifting slightly in a faint smile as he took his much-needed swallow. "Whatever you think is fair."

I pushed the lira equivalent to seventy-five dollars across the table discreetly, yet for Kuni and the old historian to see there was enough for everybody. The old man and Kuni gestured approvingly. They smiled again as we rose to walk under the cool of the revolving fans and relax within the shaded confines of the hotel.

DOĞUBAYAZIT

I want the reader to imagine that he is sitting in the lobby of the Ararat Hotel, which is something like "Rick's Bar" in *Casablanca*, consuming some ten glasses of tea interspersed with an occasional warm Coke (it's never good to drink the water). Wyatt has already consumed every Pepsi in town and I've been waiting fifteen days for a permit to visit an area where the terrorists are waiting to take potshots at us.

Outside, the heat and dust of the street is unbearable. Tom Jarriel of ABC stopped by a few minutes ago. He said the place reminds him of Dodge City before Wyatt Earp arrived. All the Ark hunters know this place, and if the reader has gotten this far, he's one of us, or at least he should know how to pronounce the name of the place. If you ever saunter in here, I don't want you to say "Dog bites it," as all the newcomers do. It has to be pronounced right to really show you've been to the place where it all began. The big stumbling block to outsiders is of course the ğ. Surprise! It doesn't have much of a sound and is pronounced lightly. It should be seen as a code letter that tells you to elongate the vowel that precedes it, thus: *Dough-u-bye-a-zit* will get you in.

I made the mistake of asking what the word means. Nobody seemed to know. I had recorded official spellings as *Eski* (old) *Bayazıt, Bayazidi, Bayzid, Beyazit, and Baitzit.* The place name is preceded by the word *Doğu,* meaning "east," thus, East Bayazit with or without the dot over the *i,* east of somewhere.

The elder scholar who was with Achmed strolled by. I hailed him and asked him what it meant. He wasn't sure. It had always been East Bayazit, even in antiquity. Of course it seems the place has always been here, so some call it Old Bayazit. The town seems to be slowly moving downhill. It was much higher in antiquity, kind of a tell in reverse. The town that exists here now is the new town, built to the west of the original site. *Great!* I thought, as the old gentleman went on his way. Why didn't they call this West Bayazit, then?

I began to realize that this place was exactly halfway between the Ark site and the anchor stone grouping, at the base of the long highland valley, nearly at the midpoint of the strategic road that links Tabriz in Iran and the lower Araxes valley, to Erzurum, Turkey. This trade route, which is one of the oldest and most active in Anatolia, pivots in a westerly direction at Doğubayazıt. The topography of this region explains the importance of the site. Since the road is confined to the intervening valley-corridor, caravans were forced to pass by Eski Bayazit. The eighteenth-century governor's palace, or İşakpaşa Saray (Eshakpasha), is to be found on the slopes of Kızıl Dağ, at 9,583 feet. This is a very prominent mount of the same range the Ark landed on called the Akyayla, which most probably means, the "white high plateau." A little higher up the slope, with a commanding view of the entire region, is the castle of Daroynk, which has many alternate spellings as well, and held the distinction of never being captured.

This fortress is built upon a Bronze Age site containing Assyrian or Urarturian tombs, which Dilaver and I explored at our leisure. Undoubtedly, this early site is here for similar reasons, but it may also have served another purpose as well. Could it have guarded the trail to the Ark? Could the clue be found in the word *Bayazit?*

Robert Edwards[2] suggests the name *Bayazit may have been* derived from the Ottoman Sultan Bayazit I, 1389–1403 A.D., or the brother of Sultan Ahmed, 1382–1410 A.D., the Celayir prince Bayazit.[3] It appears logical that a sultan or prince of a place name like Bayazit or Beyazit might just take on the name of the place he ruled and henceforth become known simply as Sultan of Bayazit.

Long before Sultan Bayazit, the son of Abd al-Malik,[4] ruled this very place from 720 to 724 A.D. He was known as simply Yazid II. He is remembered for his order to remove all the icons from the Christian churches in his realm in 723, including the famous Icon of Dariwnk. It is tempting to suggest that the respected term *bey* (sir) could precede his name, thus Bey-Yazid comes close to Beyazid, but this is always used as a suffix.

I propose the place name is much older than all its rulers and is in fact a Khald-ini word for *house,* referring to the surviving house of Noah. In considering this possibility we must remember that written history began here with records from Assyrian traders about 1900 B.C.E., and one of the clues in establishing interrelations is the point that Hebrew, Arabic, Akkadian, Phoenician, Aramaic, and Chaldaic all use the same system of a three-letter root that is then modified with varying vowels, prefixes, and suffixes. As an example, the *grm* of the Bible is Togarman, but in Assyrian texts, it is Tilgarimu.

Judging from tombs above the town, it is not surprising to note that the Assyrian King Ashurnasirpal II, 883–859 B.C.E., claimed to know the resting place of the Ark. He said it was Nisir.

One could suggest Nasirpal is actually preceded by the name of Asshur, who was one of the five sons of Shem, and the ancestor from whom the Assyrians were reputed to have

---

[2]"Revue des Etudes Armeniennes" (Dunbarton Oaks Papers, Harvard University, December 1984).

[3]V. Parry, *The Encyclopedia of Islam,* 2nd ed., 1960.

[4]Zaven Arzoumanian, *History of Lewond, the Eminent Vardapet of the Armenians* (Wynnewood, Pennsylvania: St. Sahag and St. Mesrob Armenian Church, 1982).

received their name. Other sons of Shem were Arphaxad, Lud, Elam, and Aram, who is the father of the Arameans. Although the Arameans were scattered throughout Syria and Mesopotamia, they began in southern Anatolia. Padan-Aram, or "Plain of Aram," is the area south from Harran, which is called Altınbaşak today. Harran is the place where Abram and his family started on the journey to Canaan.

It was the descendents of Aram, or the Arameans, who borrowed the simple Phoenician alphabet of shapes representing consonant sounds, transformed them into an even more efficient tool, and to our great debt, passed it on to all those with whom they came in contact. The use of Aramaic for diplomatic exchanges is referred to in 2 Kings 18:26. Aramaic script is the source of the Greek and Latin alphabets, among many others.[5]

It can be seen then that the peoples who have lived here and those who have passed across the landscape have been part of the matrix from which the nations developed, and we cannot claim full right to our heritage without acknowledging the contributions of the land and the people of Turkey from time immemorial.

When God said unto Noah, "Come thou and all thy *house* into the ark" (Genesis 7:1 KJV), the first settlement in the new world could easily have taken on the same name if the world was then replenished by the "house" of Noah. During the Middle Ages the area was known as Terra Thamanin,[6] or the "Region of Eight," referring to the eight survivors heading their family group, and we have clearly seen this suggested by the markings on the anchor stones and elsewhere.

The common word *Beth* means "house" in the Bible, and without the points, it is *Baith* as seen in the word *Bethel* (Genesis 35:1), and in the Greek Septuagint it is *Baith-el*. In both Chaldee and Phoenician, *Baith* or *Baitha* is the usual way the word for "house" is pronounced. It may be that in the early language of the Khaldini of Urartu, the first settlement of the house of Noah is remembered.

---

[5]E. C. Blake and A. G. Edmonds, *Biblical Sites in Turkey* (Istanbul, Turkey: Red House Press, 1982).

[6]This word actually means "eighty," something often overlooked by Ark hunters.

There is another meaning to this word besides "house," still to be found in Hebrew, and that is "egg"! This refers to the Ark. Alexander Hislop remarked, "If any be inclined to ask, how could it ever enter the minds of men to employ such an extraordinary symbol for such a purpose, the answer is first, the sacred egg of paganism is well known as the 'mundane egg,' that is, the egg in which the world was shut up."[7]

If the whole seed of mankind is shut up in what resembles an egg-shaped structure, with a shell or covering floating on the waters, it can be seen then that this egg, with the house of Noah within, contained the whole world in its bosom.

This concept of the Flood, and the Ark, or egg, in which the whole human race was shut up, as a chick is enclosed in an egg before it is hatched, can be found from Hindu fables to the dyed-and-painted eggs used in sacred festivals in China, and even up into Japan. In Dionysia, or mysteries of Bacchus, as

Typhon's Egg.

celebrated in Athens, one part of the ceremony consisted in the consecration of an egg.

THE ARK AND THE SACRED EGG

The custom of the sacred eggs hung in the temples of Egypt can be traced back through the classical poets and the mys-

---

[7]Alexander Hislop, *The Two Babylons* (Neptune, New Jersey: Loizeau Brothers, 1959).

The Sacred Egg of Heliopolis.

The Mystic Egg of Astarte.

teries of Babylon, for it begins on the banks of the Euphrates, or the river FIRAT in Turkey, near the Ark.

Hyginus the Egyptian, keeper of the Palatine library in the time of Augustus, reports, "An egg of wondrous size is said to have fallen from heaven into the river Euphrates. The fishes rolled it to the bank where, the doves having settled upon it, hatched it and out came Venus, who afterwards was called the Syrian Goddess Astarte."

One can see how this valley that runs by Bayazit can be visualized as a once torrent riverbed, and it is true that the waters carried the Ark past here to the landing place or the banks of the Akyayla range. The Flood story doves then hatched the egg, and the broken-out shell, from which all the seeds of mankind came forth, was the unexplained structure or shell-like outer covering of the Ark.

Further symbolizing the Ark is another reference calling it Typhon's Egg. I believe Typhon is Shem. He is referred to by the Babylonians as Shu, Besh, Baba, and *Bar.* It was in the Jewish book Jubilees, written in the latter half of the second century B.C.E., that I found the Ark had landed in Urartu, on a mountain named Lu-*Bar* (Jubilees 5:28).

The Jewish Midrash refers to this same mount in the Book of Noah, and even the Qumran scrolls (Apocryphon 10:12 and 12:13).

Josephus quotes the historian Nicolaus of Damascus as reporting the Ark was to be found on Bar-is, again using the name for Shem.

The Greeks knew that Shem was the Typhon of Egypt. Herodotus (484–425 B.C.E.) speaks of him as well as Plutarch in 46 A.D., where he states that after Typhon was defeated by Horus, he fled Egypt and begat two sons, Hierosolymus and Judaeus, clearly showing, he says, "the Egyptians confused their legends with the narratives of the Jews."

It would be Shem, the Melchizedek of his later years, that begat or brought into being Jerusalem and Judea.

Various writers refer to the Typhonian religion and its variants as the oldest in existence, whether in Egypt or elsewhere, and it is here that Abraham is received by Melchizedek, king of Salem and priest of the most high God (El Elyon).

For the Ark to be representing Typhon's Egg is of course understandable, but who is Ishtar?

I believe it is the paganizing of Noah's wife. The ancients held that everything good and beneficent to mankind came through the Mundane Egg. In a variant Egyptian story, this egg proceeded from the mouth of God, and in the biblical account the Ark came into being by the direction of God. But in the Chaldean mysteries, all blessings to the human race which the Ark contained in its bosom were held to issue from Astarte, the mother of all living and benefactress to the world.

Two thousand years before the Christian era, the Egg of Ishtar figured prominently in rites where sacred bread was offered. The Book of Jeremiah the prophet mentions, "The children gather wood, the fathers kindle fire and the women knead their dough, to make cakes for the Queen of Heaven."

This ritual passed into Christendom through the early Church, where today these cakes are eaten on the festival of Astarte as hot cross buns, the emblem *T* for Tammuz looked upon as the cross on Good Friday. The dyed eggs of Pasch or Easter Sunday hold quite a different meaning today.

Therefore, it should not be surprising to find the word *East* preceding the name *Bayazit,* for East Egg refers to the object in the hills above the town, journey's end for pious pilgrims of Ishtar seeking talismans for amulets from the Great Egg itself. There, abandoned to the ages, lay the natron-washed white shell of KPR, the covering that had been applied to the reed structure of the boat, now deteriorated from within – a great hollow shell with collapsed floors fallen to the depths below.

Noah's Ark was the original Egg of Easter.

THE WIVES OF NOAH

In the commonly held biblical interpretation of the Flood story we are told there were but eight survivors: ". . . wherein few, that is, *eight* souls were saved by water" (1 Peter 3:20 KJV author's italics).

Other sources claim more were saved and some claim less, as the Greek account that only Noah and his wife, Deucalion, and Pyrrha survived.[8] Reference to the tomb of Noah's mother in Marand, and his sister in Syria, as well as numerous accounts of others aboard the Ark,[9] understandably raise consternation among fundamentalist thought when Peter remarks, ". . . but protected Noah, a preacher of righteousness, and seven others" (2 Peter 2:5 NIV).

Furthermore, it goes without saying that the line of Cain was entirely wiped out in the Flood, and only the line of Seth survived. This concept raises numerous problems to then be defended. How could only four men manage a ship the size of

---

[8]*Dialogues of Plato.* In the Greek accounts there are dozens of names for the counterparts of Noah and his wife. For further listings *see* Donnelly's *Atlantis.*

[9]Sura Houd 11:39 of the Koran, "But none save a few believed with him."

Astarte, goddess with the rimmon.

the Ark? How could eight people handle the chores aboard, sustaining life? How could Ham, Shem, and Japheth, the fruit of the union of Noah and his wife, married to goodly little Sethite brides, be the progenitors of all the racial variations and colors of mankind in the new world after the Flood?

It appears among many believers that childhood concepts gleaned from picture books in their youth have become tenets of their faith. Many hold so religiously to the childish idea that Noah and his sons constructed the Ark themselves in their spare time that they have published it could have been done in a mere eighty-one years![10] In addition to innumerable other

---

[10]Tim F. LaHaye and John D. Morris, *The Ark on Ararat* (Nashville: Thomas Nelson, 1976), p. 248.

problems, authors defend and debate endless varieties of animals, or kinds, being aboard the Ark as anywhere from fifty thousand to the bare-bones minimum of fifteen hundred, in deference to the statement in Genesis 8:1KJV: "And God remembered Noah, and every living thing, and all the *cattle* that was with him in the ark" (author's italics).

Our subject is not the varieties of man "kind," for there is but one. However, within our "kind" there are quite obvious diversities in appearance that have been termed racial differences. If Ham, Shem, and Japheth were all the offspring of Noah and one wife, how did this come about? Did it happen after the Flood? Is it an evolutionary change?

I believe the answer is to be found in Genesis 5:32 KJV: "And Noah was *five hundred years old:* and Noah begat Shem, Ham, and Japheth" (author's italics).

The first thing that strikes me as unusual is the age of Noah in comparison to the fathering of children by the patriarchs who preceded him.

Seth	105	Jared	162
Enosh	90	Enoch	65
Kenan	70	Methuselah	187
Mahalalel	65	Lamech	182

To beget children at age 500 might intimate the reclusive nature of Noah in the post-Flood years, according to Sumerian literature. Noah may have been rather ascetic in life-style until learning the fate of mankind through revelation that the age would end in 120 years. In the chapter dealing with the kings before the Flood, I suggested this came about at the time he became king of the Sethites in his 480th year.

It is my interpretation that in the twenty years following the knowledge of the impending doom of humanity, Noah saw the need to preserve mankind in the strength, adaptability, and diversity of characteristics that existed in mankind in general before the Flood. He could accomplish this by having more than one wife.[11]

[11]One of Noah's wives named Waliya called him "madjnun" (insane) and stayed behind with her son Kana-can, whom the Arabs call Yam. This Arab tradition is referred to in the Houd 11:41–43. As they stood apart from the unbelievers Noah cried out to his son, but the billows rolled over them.

If we do not accept this, our only deduction from this portion of Scripture is that Ham, Shem, and Japheth were triplets. This hardly solves the problem.

I take this verse at face value. Noah begat three sons in one year, and they represented a portion of humanity *each* in its diversity. Furthermore, I propose that Noah carefully chose his sons' wives for them. Each of these possessed additional traits that collectively would produce a gene pool among the survivors' offspring, further strengthening survival and adaptability through diversity.

When I mention this scenario to others it is usually met by stuffy idealism and Christian concepts of morality that find it objectionable that Noah, perfect in his generations, would practice polygamy. Yet we are told in Genesis 4:23 KJV that Lamech, father of Tubal-cain (not to be confused with Noah's father of the same name), had two wives: "And Lamech said unto his wives, Adah and Zillah. . . ."

This suggestion is dismissed as an example of ungodliness in the line of the Cainite civilization!

When I offer that Terah, Abram's father, must have had more than one wife to enable Abram to marry his half-sister Sari (later Sarah), it is countered that one wife may have died. It is never suggested that Terah was a godly man, however, as in reality he was a pagan idol manufacturer. King David took eleven women to wife, but seemingly only as the time and situation grabbed him. His son Solomon had seven hundred wives and princesses, backed up by three hundred concubines. This usually stuns the listener long enough for me to begin describing how Adam's sons, by necessity, would need to have had incestuous relations with their sisters in order to propagate the human race. The entire subject is quickly reverted back to Noah and the possibility that I just might be right, and that only one wife saw fit to accompany him on the voyage.[12]

---

[12]Some fundamentalists' opinions are so extreme that Dr. M. R. DeHaan in his work *The Days of Noah* (Zondervan Publishing House, 1963) suggests on page 42, "Lamech was the first man in human history to break God's rule of creation, and he began a sin which culminated in the flood." Thus polygamy was the reason, in his logic, for the Deluge.

Pursuing this further, it is interesting to note that Noah's wife is never mentioned by name. In fact, in the line of Seth no woman since Eve is mentioned until Sarai, Abram's wife. For ten generations before the Flood, or 1656 years, to ten generations after the Flood, approximately 350 years, no woman is mentioned at all.

Why is this? If Noah had but one wife with him on the Ark, wouldn't she be venerated early on as next to Eve, the mother of all living? Could it be that Noah's wife who accompanied him aboard the Ark had no special relationship to the line of Seth, or through Shem, progenitor of Heber, from which came the Hebrews?

I feel this is the case. Noah's wife need not have been the mother of either Japheth or Shem, but I feel there is cause to believe she was the mother of Ham!

On the other hand, in the line of Cain we are not only told that Lamech had two wives but their names are recorded as well. Their sons' names and their occupations are also recorded. Then comes a surprise!

. . . and the sister of Tubal-cain was *Naamah.*
Genesis 4:22 KJV (author's italics)

Now I ask the reader, is this an oversight by early writers of history to record in depth the generations and immediate family structure of the line that was wiped out in the Flood, and neglect to record who was the wife of Noah? Or is Naamah Noah's wife?

Before fundamentalists hoot and holler that Noah would never have polluted his generations with intermarriage into the line of Cain, let's stop and consider if this wicked line of Cain and the godly line of Seth nonsense isn't a figment of somebody's imagination.

And the Lord said, I will destroy man whom I have created from the face of the earth . . . for it repenteth me that I have made them.
Genesis 6:7 KJV

Let us be reminded that in the entire population of the antediluvian world, only Noah found grace in the eyes of the Lord, not the entire godly line of Seth. As for the statement of Lamech, head of the line of Cain and a contemporary of Noah, we read:

> ... Hear my voice ... I have slain a man [who wounded me], and a young man [for hurting me]. If Cain shall be avenged sevenfold, truly Lamech seventy and sevenfold.
>
> Genesis 4:23, 24 KJV

This doesn't sound like a boast from a bloodthirsty tyrant but a plea from a man realizing it a sin to take a life, and crying out that the act was one of self-defense. If his act be avenged, let the avenger's act be avenged on him by God seventy-seven times, because Lamech is innocent of any wrongdoing. What fault can we find in this?

There are other inconsistencies to be found in extrabiblical sources such as the Popol Vuh which, after describing the first men and their generations, suggests that all men spoke one language and they existed in relative peace, the black men and white men together, awaiting the rising sun and praying to the heart of heaven. The question here is, how did the red Central American know anything about black men and white men?

The opinion that all Indians are red men is of course a gross misconception. The Menominees are sometimes called White Indians. In a footnote to *U.S. Explorations for a Railroad Route to the Pacific Ocean* it states that the Zuni (New Mexico) have fair skin and blue eyes with auburn hair. They claim to be full-blooded and have no tradition of intermarriage with any foreign race.

The Kaw Indians of Kansas were very dark skinned, and isolated tribes of California were found to be as black as those from New Guinea; so the question arises, if we are all descendants of Noah and his wife (one wife), why are we so diversified in color and characteristics?

The fundamentalists must then maintain the position, if holding to the concept of total annihilation of man during the Flood with the exception of Noah's immediate family, that this diversity of man has been accomplished through natural selection, outside evolutionary changes, or the diversity in

Ham, Shem, and Japheth alone. This would be a diversity that existed before the Flood, and a diversity in his own offspring that could only be the result of three wives bearing him three children, all in the same year.

While the biblical account is silent, the traditions of the Amer-Indians and the Greeks are that the races existed before the Flood. *Adam* is a Hebrew word that occurs some 560 times in Scripture applied to individuals and mankind in general as man, mankind, or earthling man. It is, however, from a root word that means, "red or ruddy." Cain, father of the Cainite civilization, was the firstborn of Adam and Eve, and in effect, the first earthling who did not owe his existence to a direct creative act by God. Although his act against his brother was an abhorrence, it was not allowable that any should punish Cain for the offense, and God put a mark upon Cain.

> And the Lord set a mark upon Cain, lest any finding him should kill him.
>
> Genesis 4:15 KJV

It is important to recognize that this mark was not a mark of punishment but a mark of protection. It was immediately recognizable by all that he was under God's protection against the act he had committed and under God's judgment, not man's judgment.

Was this mark of Cain something to immediately identify him and his offspring from his brothers and sisters and their offspring of the "red" or "ruddy" descendants of Adam?[13]

If the mark of Cain was passed on to his children in succeeding generations this would account for Lamech, seven generations later, claiming the same protection against those who would avenge his act of taking the life of a young man who had wounded him, and whom he killed in self-defense. It is my belief that Lamech still carried the mark of Cain by his skin coloration.

---

[13]The number of Adam's children, according to ancient tradition, was thirty-three sons and twenty-three daughters. Josephus, *Antiquities of the Jews*, Book I, chapter 2.

> And Cain said unto the Lord, My punishment is greater than I can
> bear. Behold, thou hast driven me out this day from the face of the
> earth; and from thy face shall I be hid. . . .
>
> Genesis 4:13, 14

If we consider numerous instances in Scripture relating to
the brightness of the face of God and those who have had
counsel near his glory, such as the experience of Moses, we
might conclude that one hidden from the face or counsel of
God would be of dark countenance.

Lamech's wife Zillah, who bore Tubal-cain and Naamah,
has a name that means, "to hide." In another sense, it means,
"shadow" or "protection."

With Noah a contemporary of Lamech (again not to be
confused with Noah's father), it is not unusual that he should
marry Naamah, daughter of the king of the Cainites. This was
a practice of peace we are all familiar with.

There was a similar act by Moses who, "drawn out" or
"saved by water," married a Cushite. This refers to the ancient
land of Cush, which extended from the Nile valley near
Aswan southward to modern Khartoum, east to the Red Sea
and west to the Libyan desert, later considered Nubia. Although some scholars consider this "Cushite bride" an Arabian, the Arabians who are popularly classed as Semites, or
sons of Shem, admit in their traditions that there are certain
Arabic peoples who are descendants of Ham. They are called
Ṣeba, Havilah, and Raamah, etc.

There are scholars who point out that there are two Shebas
(Seba) in the line of Shem and only one in the line of Ham. In
Shem's line the first is a son of Joktan. The other is one of the
two sons of Jokshan, the son of Abraham by Keturah. I hold to
my line of reasoning because, as shown earlier, Keturah is
actually the name of Hagar, who was Egyptian, and Egypt
was settled by the descendants of Ham. The first listed Sheba
of record is the son of Raamah, the son of Cush (Genesis 10:7;
1 Chronicles 1:9), who was a son of Ham. It is interesting to
note that *Raamah* is close to the name *Naamah.* Could it be that
Naamah (pleasant, delightful, sweet) is the name of Noah's
wife, sister of Tubal-cain, and mother of Ham? Even the
Ammonite wife of Solomon and mother of Rehoboam (1
Kings 14:21; 2 Chronicles 12:13) carried this name.

How is it, then, that the name *Naamah* from the line of Cain, that wicked civilization we are told by biblical scholars was completely eradicated by the Flood, was carried into then new age? Why does Ham name his son Canaan if this isn't the line continuing through the Deluge?

Cush	Mizraim	Phut	Canaan
Seba (Sheba)	Ludim		Sidon
Havilah	Anamim		Heth
Sabtah	Lehabim		Jebusite
Raamah	Naphtuhim		Amorite
Sabtechah	Pathrusim		Girgasite
Nimrod	Casluhim (Philistim)		Hivite
	Caphtorim		Arkite
Raamah			Sinite
Sheba			Arvadite
Dedan			Jemerite
			Hamathite
			Canaanites*

*All were families of Canaan.

Among the descendants of Ham we have Cush (Ethiopia), Mizraim (Egypt), Phut (Lybia), Canaan and his numerous families, including those of his son Sidon, sometimes called Zidon, or ancient Phoenicia. The Phoenician traditions continue to list the line of Cain *after* the Flood.

In a fragmented Greek text we learn that Phoenician traditions knew their goddess as Astynome (Ashtar-No'ema), whom the Greeks called Nemaun. She was a sister of the three sons of Lamech. This could only apply to Naamah, sister of Tubal-cain, Jabal, and Jubal. If the Phoenicians were from the line of Ham through Canaan and Sidon, we can understand their listing of the line of Cain and their seven patriarchs before the Flood, rather than the ten kings or the line of Seth, in their traditions.

In their records, the Phoenicians, unlike the Hebrews, list both parents whereas in Genesis the Hebrew writers refer to both only when referring to the line of Cain. The Phoenicians list Adam and Eve as Adam and Havath; the Greek is Protogonos and Aion. Cain and his wife are Qen and Qenath, or Genos and Genea in the Greek. Of the brothers Amynos and

Magos, one is undoubtedly Jabal, who tradition says taught to dwell in tents and rear herds. The Hebrew account is ". . . he was the father of such as dwell in tents, and of such as have cattle" (Genesis 4:20 KJV).

There are others, perhaps unidentifiable, the Greeks call Phos, Phur, and Phlox (light, fire, and flame), but it is recorded by the Hebrew that the artificers of brass and iron were instructed by Tubal-cain, the father of foundries. But what is most interesting is the line of Cain continues through Mishor and Cuduq. The first, called Misor by others, produces Taautos or Taut. The second, known to the Greeks as Sydyk (Sidon?), is father to Cabiri or Corybantes, instituters of navigation. Are these the Phoenicians themselves? These seafarers worshiped Bal or Balam, and again the Popol Vuh of the Americas states that after the Flood, their first home became overpopulated. People under Balam-Quitze migrated, and their language became confounded in consequence of separation.

Flavius Josephus speaks of these times:

> After this they were dispersed abroad, on account of their languages, and went out by colonies everywhere; and each colony took possession of that land which they light upon. . . . There were some also who passed over the sea in ships, and inhabited the islands.

Josephus states further that the Greeks are responsible for many a founder's name being lost to history:

> . . . they were the Greeks who became the authors of such mutations; for when, in after ages, they grew potent, they claimed to themselves the glory of antiquity–giving names to the nations that sounded well [in Greek] that they might be better understood among themselves.

So again, thanks to the Greeks, or rather in spite of the habit of changing names into sounds better understood to themselves, we find the connection with the line of Cain through Naamah and Ham to his son Canaan, Sidon, and the Phoenicians. Ashtar-No'ema is the Ishtar of Nineveh and Babylon, the Naamah of the Genesis record. The worship of Bel (Bal,

Balam) and Astarte was observed from antiquity in Britain, along with the Druids. Were they introduced by the Phoenicians trading with the tin mines in Cornwall? Here the Druids practiced the rites of Balam or Baal as well as the forty-day abstinence of Lent in the spring of the year called Ishtar-monath, or our Easter month of today. This same festival was found in pagan Mexico and related in Humboldt's *Mexican Researches*, where he states, "Three days after the vernal equinox . . . began a solemn fast of forty days in honour of the sun."

Who could doubt the Phoenician connection? That I might suggest this and my readers not attach much weight to these verbal similarities, I should remark that others have noted the early Mayas applied the names of Balam-Quitze, Balam-Agab, and Iqui-Balam to semidivine progenitors of their people. How did the Maya get these names in Central America before the coming of the first Europeans, unless they migrated from the Mediterranean basin centuries before!

There is not enough space here to continue investigations into this possible scenario, but consider it a clue that the name *Naaman* is the masculinization of the name *Naamah*. This is apparent in Catholic countries today where a daughter is named Maria, for the Virgin Mary, and the son's name becomes Mario. Naaman, a Syrian army chief (2 Kings 5) of the tenth century B.C.E., requested that Jehovah forgive him when in performance of his civil duties he bowed before Rimmon in the temple of Astarte. The connection is in both his name and the true name of the goddess queen of Babylon, and the rimmon that is a pomegranate full of seeds of the fruit. It is an emblem of the Ark in which the germs of the new creation were preserved, wherewith the world was to be sown anew with man and with beast, when the desolation of the Deluge had passed away. Naaman is simply the masculine form of the same name.

I believe there is sufficient evidence that the line of Cain was preserved through Naamah, the mother of Ham and wife of Noah, and that this "mother of all living" is the basis of Inanna to the Sumerian, Ishtar, Astarte, Isis, or whatever name and tongue she was known, or whatever reigning queen was deified in her name. She was a representative of Noah's wife, or Eve incarnate. If some should find this unacceptable, that through the doctrine of metempsychosis, which was firmly established in Babylon, Noah's wife and blood mother of the descendants of Ham, especially through Nimrod, who no doubt instigated this idolatry, could be worshiped, I have some strong medicine for the Christian reader.

For several years the vintage in Tuscany, Italy, had been almost entirely destroyed by disease. The Archbishop of Florence conceived the idea of arresting this plague by directing his prayers not to God or Astarte but to her husband.

Archbishop's Prayer to the Patriarch Noah
Popery in Turin

> Most Holy Patriarch Noah, who didst employ thyself in thy long career in cultivating the vine, and gratifying the human race with that precious beverage, which allays the thirst, restores the strength, and enlivens the spirits of us all, deign to regard our vines, which, following thine example, we cultivated hitherto; and while thou beholdest them languishing and blighted by that disastrous visitation, which, before the vintage, destroys the fruit (in severe punishment for many blasphemies and other enormous sins we have committed) have compassion on us. . . .

This is followed by a new prayer to the Queen of Heaven, as well as notification from the archbishop granting an indulgence of forty days to all who would devoutly recite the prayer. The author of the source of this rank piece of paganism remarks that "surely here is the world turned backwards!"[14]

It should be noted that scholars have always considered the carved alabaster trough from Uruk to be a vessel for watering the sacred herd of Inanna (Naamah). Yet a vessel can either be filled with water or *float* upon the waters. Therefore it could easily be conjectured that it represents the *vessel* which *contained* the animals within. That this representation of the Ark por-

---

[14]Alexander Hislop, *The Two Babylons* (Neptune, New Jersey: Loizeaux Brothers, 1959). From a prayer in the *Morning Herald,* 26 October, 1855.

Noah's wife is here depicted as the *Great Mother* loading the Ark for refurbishing the new world. Her *standards* (behind her) represent the reed stern and stem posts of the Ark's reed raft. (stone vase, Uruk)

Again these curiously shaped emblems or standards of Inanna are seen to be supporting the reed structure within. This is the enclosed portion of the Ark upon the reed raft. From the roof opening can be seen eight life forces, showing there is life sustained under the covering. (Uruk, 2900–2800 B.C.E.)

tion of the Ma-gur should be made in white stone like alabaster only further explains the Walapai Amerindian's concept of the survival ship being a great *stone* canoe, and the Egyptian "divine boat of Nu, washed [overlaid] and purified with natron" (Úáa Nu, seāb - Θá turá - Θá em ḥesmen).[15]

The fact that it was really a reed structure, overlaid or washed with KPR, a mixture that hardened like stone, is betrayed by the reed house carved on the side. While there is no need to have a watering trough with the obvious curved bow and stern, it is pictured as such because this upper portion lay within the curved bow and stern of the reed raft that supported it. The stem and sternposts are clearly depicted as well.

Within the confines of the Ark and between the standards that symbolize the reed raft, Noah, the "king" figure, feeds Inanna's beasts with branches from the tree of life. (Cylinder seals from the Jemdet-Nasr Period, Iraq)

REFLECTIONS ON A FIASCO

We have seen in the last few chapters that Christendom in general believes the Ark must be constructed of wood. Quite obviously Ron Wyatt still believes this to be true as well, unless one could take by his statements to the press that his reference to keel *timbers,* floor *timbers,* and rib *timbers*[16] means something other than wood. He has repeatedly stated this, yet to my knowledge none has been found.

---

[15]The Papyrus of Ani, Plate XXII.
[16]CBN aired this interview on August 20, 1985.

The first point John Baumgardner and I agree on contrary to Ron's opinion is that the flow in which the Ark lies is not volcanic in origin. The second is that there appears to be at present no remains of wood, petrified or otherwise.

In an interview aired August 27 on NBC's "Close-Up," the commentator began by saying, "On Close-Up this morning, the ongoing search for Noah's Ark. An article appeared in *Life* magazine twenty-five years ago reporting a five-hundred-foot-long boat-shaped form had been spotted near Mount Ararat in Turkey, the biblical landfall of the Ark. Well, several expeditions failed to produce any hard evidence, but the search goes on, most recently by American archaeologist John Baumgardner, who joins us this morning from our NBC news bureau in Tokyo. . . . Dr. Baumgardner, is it premature to say that what lies there is an ancient shipwreck?"

"I believe it is still premature," John answered, but went on to say, "We've got some exciting new evidence . . . basically it's metal detector data, which indicates an orderly pattern of metal underground in the site."

At one point in the interview, when John correctly was hesitant about describing the metal found, the interviewer said, "Well, can I fill in for you that the hypothesis is that the metal are *nails,* that it's in the formation of nails, perhaps that . . . held the planks of the boat together!"

John replied, "Yes, yes, there's a likelihood that it's either nails or spikes we're seeing."

In a previous television interview, John had said, "It is my hunch that the wood–if it is indeed a man-made *wooden* object–that the *wood has all decayed.* I regret that, but that appears to be what we are seeing. So, I'm not *too optimistic about finding wood."*

The reader can see that even three men working side by side on the same object are not in total agreement on how they are perceiving the structure and they can make conflicting statements to the public, causing much confusion.

Making matters worse, I have completely given up trying to see the structure as envisioned by Ron and returned to some earlier research observations, concluding that the Ark is not built of wood at all!

I believe the problem still exists in our minds to try and make the Ark's construction fit our preconceived ideas, fostered by our traditional impressions of what the Ark *should look like.*

Going back to the oldest source of the story, we learn that Utnapishtim was told to *tear down his reed house* and build a boat! Is it not then logical to assume that this was the material for the construction of the Ark? Will we also find in Akkadian, the language of the court in Babylon during these early periods, the true meaning of the word rendered *gopher wood* by the Hebrews?

In the New English Bible[17] the revisionists have rendered Genesis 6:14 as follows (author's italics):

> Make yourself an ark with *ribs* of *cypress;* cover it with *reeds* and coat it inside and out with pitch.

They are of course taking the middle of the road here, in my opinion, by including both reeds and wood. The term *ribs* is pure conjecture.

The same type of conjecture is found in the Koran, where shipbuilding methods of the day are to be found:

> We carried Noah in a vessel built with *planks* and *nails.*
> (The Moon) Sura Al-Qamar 54

This, too, is subject to seventh-century A.D. cultural expressions.

In the December 1985 issue of *Moody Monthly,* an article appeared by Bill Crouse, considered a senior scholar of Probe Ministries from Richardson, Texas. It was entitled "A Tale of Two Sites." In it he referred to the boat-shaped object and stated why, in his opinion, it could not be the "true" Ark of Noah. What then is the object on the other site, high on Ararat, that eyewitnesses refer to, he implies, when in actuality there is no other site on Ararat. There are just rumored sightings, none of which have ever been authenticated or found!

I decided to call Bill Crouse since I had never spoken of the

---

[17]Samuel Sandmel, ed., Oxford Study Edition, The New English Bible (New York: Oxford University Press, 1976).

Ark question to a scholar. We immediately disagreed about the shape of the thing. From his theological viewpoint, you could write off our find because it wasn't rectangular.

"Well!" I responded. "I don't understand how you can determine its shape by saying a *Tebah* has square corners! And by the way, was that a typographical error?"

He assured me that was the correct spelling.

"Gee!" I said, pulling his leg a little. "I thought Tebah was the first named son of Abraham's brother Nahor, by the concubine Reumah [Genesis 22:24], and means 'slaughterer.'"

He replied that obviously I didn't know anything about Hebrew.

It must be true. I don't understand Hebrew, or why the King James spells it *Tebah,* considered the word for the Ark, or why Strong calls the Ark a box (#8392). I thought it a rule of BaeYT and VaeYT, that when BaeYT occurred in the middle of the word, it always became VaeYT, and therefore the name for the Ark in Hebrew should be recognized as *'Tevah!*

Of course the Ark of the covenant was a box, but the Ark of Noah and the ark of reeds in which Moses floated down the Nile were *te-vah'.*

In the Greek Scriptures, however, the one term *ki-bo-tos'* is equivalent to both Hebrew terms! I think something has been lost in translation here. A box, after all, is only an *enclosure.* We are not to consider the Ark as the Hebrew *'arohn'* meaning "a coffin." The *Te-vah'* of both Moses and Noah was made of *reeds,* like a *papyrus boat!*

In Exodus 2:3 KJV (author's italics) we read, "And when she could not longer hide him, she took for him an ark of *bulrushes,* and daubed it with slime and with pitch, and put the child therein [enclosed him]; and she laid it in the *flags* by the river's brink."

The bulrushes and flags, as seen from Isaiah 19:6, are long-stemmed hollow plants, or *reeds,* which grew at the water's edge. The little ark of Moses was an Egyptian papyrus boat, a smaller version of the seagoing type we read of in Isaiah 18:2 KJV (author's italics): ". . . that sendeth ambassadors by the sea, even in *vessels of bulrushes* upon the waters, saying, Go, ye swift messengers. . . ."

Here we can see that the word *te-vah* is the same word used to convey the thought picture for Noah's Ark. This same thought is captured by the Hopi Indians of the American Southwest when they cite in their Flood legend that the survivors of the Deluge saved themselves by lashing themselves to long plants with hollow stems.

In may be, then, that this Greek misinterpretation of just what *te-vah'* meant is the root of the problem as well as the misspelling. It might be seen to the Greek as *tebah* rather than *tevah,* and weren't all boats made of wood anyway!

What I am really trying to relay to the reader is the following: Let's not get the cart before the horse. In a sense, the ark of Moses came before the Ark of Noah. First, Moses had to come into the world and be saved by his ark before he could grow to manhood and write about the saving of Noah in his day, and the *oldest* accounts say the material came from his reed house and that he built a reed boat. Genesis was not composed by a Greek, written in Greek, or related to Greek listeners. It is Hebrew, through and through, and those who base their opinions on how the Greeks see it are in error!

In the late second century B.C.E., tradition holds that seventy-two scholars met in Alexandria, Egypt, to translate the Hebrew into Greek for the Greek-speaking Jews then living there. Working independently, so the story goes, they retired to produce identical translations. This legend must be viewed as a miracle, for the idea that seventy-two scholars could ever agree on any subject is doubtful indeed. The number was later rounded out to seventy, and the Septuagint is referred to by the Roman numerals LXX. It is the Greek concept that the Ark could be in any way conceived as a box.

The early Christians had accepted the Septuagint as their own Scriptures and the Epistles, or letters sent to the early churches, were of course written in Greek. Even the Book of Hebrews was originally written in Hellenistic Greek, and the writer was familiar with the Septuagint due to numerous quotations taken from that version.

The concept of the Ark as a wooden box or a rectangular barge has in Christendom's view not changed much since those Alexandrian times. The artists of the Eastern Orthodox Church portrayed it as such, and since you can't really do much more with a simple box-shaped design, artists of the Roman Church could do little more than portray it the same.

Regardless of the major readjustment in thinking that is necessary, now that the Ark has been found and it is not in the form of a box, the ultraconservative and militant fundamentalist viewpoint of the literal acceptance of the absolute inerrancy of the translation of the Scriptures at hand . . . is like running into a brick wall!

The fortress of this viewpoint is the Institute for Creation Research (ICR), which has published many books about the Ark. It is located in El Cajon, California, and headed by Dr. Henry Morris, former professor of hydraulic engineering at Virginia Polytechnic Institute and the founder of ICR. This school of thought is the greatest promoter of this unchanged concept, updating us occasionally by stating that due to this unique rectangular design and the accepted figures in the NIV, the Ark's length of 450 feet and width of 75 feet could accommodate 569 railroad cattle cars of 2,670 cubic feet.

The now uncovered fact that due to my survey it can be seen that by God's unique design for the Ark, the boat shape, it could have contained 852 cattle cars (if one is really interested in these parallels), is not met with whoops of joy but accusations that this then could not be the Ark, or at least the *true* Ark, for I would be proving the Bible is wrong!

Henry Morris' son, John, vice president of ICR, says on the one hand that his credentials as a geologist confirm it is a natural volcanic plug in a streamlined shape, and on the other hand that if it is found to be man-made, it is the copy of the Ark built by Constantine! When I replied in wonder as to what kind of heretic Constantine could have been to have the Ark the wrong shape, material, and dimensions on the wrong mountain, and how the site of this project could have escaped the eyes and knowledge of Sultan Süleyman years later, everyone dove for cover. It was a suggestion everyone would now like to forget was ever mentioned.

As a result of the Hagopian interview (the elderly Armenian who claimed to have visited the Ark in his youth), Mr. Elfred Lee, another enthusiast for the Ararat landing, has with some artistic ability sketched what is touted as the only authentic portrayal of the Ark from an eyewitness description. His drawing is found in many publications on the Ark of Ararat, and in August 1985 I had the opportunity to buttonhole him walking down the street in Doğubayazıt.

"Tell me, Mr. Lee, the little stairway of nine steps pictured protruding from the blunt end of the Ark – was it on the bow that crashed into the greatest seas the world has ever known, or was it Hagopian's feeling that this was the stern, which may well have taken the full brunt of the waves in pushing the Ark along? And if you portrayed this stairway, still intact, why then does George Hagopian tell of his uncle piling up rocks to stand on for Georgie to reach the roof? Why not use the stairway?"

"Well, the stairway was my idea," he replied. At least Elfred can tell the truth. Cummings recites in her publication that "Elfred had done a remarkable reproduction from the notes taken as Georgie had described the ship – even *the ladder,* dangling some ten feet from the bottom of the ship" (author's italics).[18]

It must have occurred to someone that Hagopian's account of his uncle making a rock pile in the thin air of the high elevation of Ararat would have been quite a feat to accomplish in an hour or two. Even if the uncle had lifted little Georgie to his shoulders to reach the roof of the Ark, he would have required a pile of rocks some thirty-five feet high. A stairway of nine steps on a 45° angle off the end of the Ark was then seen to be in order. So much for faithful reproductions from eyewitness accounts.

Even today, in the age of electronic evangelism, we are not free from artists' impressions misrepresenting the truth and subtly molding our opinions for us.

In response to my request that they not use my photographs of the Ark on the air, the Christian network soon came up with an artistic rendering of the photograph taken by me. In August 1985, I was watching the channel when the commentator asked, "Could these be the remains of Noah's Ark?"

---

[18]Violet Cummings, *Has Anybody Really Seen Noah's Ark?* (San Diego: Creation-Life Publishers, 1982), p. 223.

Then blurring the graceful lines of the boat-shaped site, another artist's rendition of Christendom's fixation, the rectangular Ark of Noah, was overlaid across the form to show the viewer that this was an impossibility, as the two forms plainly did not match.

This was followed by a statement that really closed the doors to further research in Turkey. "Amazing!" said the woman commentator, after interviewing John Baumgardner. "We are looking forward to learning much more about it, and with further excavations on the site. . . ." Of course Turkey's greatest fear was that we would excavate, and our permit had explicitly restricted us to surface investigations.

This statement, I discovered later, caused the concerned ministries much alarm, as well as the commentator's implications of her hopes (speaking of course for Christianity) that Turkey would give us the rights to excavate there. "Foreigners don't have any *rights* to excavate here," said the Under Minister. "We make the decisions about what goes on here in Turkey!" Of course the Turks had misunderstood the statement, but in further televised interviews with network representatives at the site, the commentator asked, "What about the reaction of the Turkish Moslem officials in the country? How have they reacted to the possible discovery of Noah's Ark, a Christian emblem, in the middle of their mountain?" This really put the lock on the gate!

It is my feeling that the Turks didn't like that statement at all. Implying that the Ark of Noah is a Christian symbol in the middle of Islam is certainly not the way to proceed with further investigations and is, in my opinion, quite an erroneous statement to begin with. If the Flood is an actual historical event and the beginnings of mankind anew in this age, isn't the Ark of Noah a cherished symbol to humanity itself? It is mentioned in more than seven Suras of the Koran and is not a Christian emblem excluding Koranic, Hebraic, or any other writings or cultures having the Flood legend.

The Ark cannot be viewed as a Christian symbol as the city of Jerusalem was to the Church during the Middle Ages. The Minister of Culture for the Republic of Turkey is in the enviable position of being the legal custodian of one of the

oldest relics of history. He must protect it from denomina-
tional and theological claims as well as religious exploitation in
general.

Sumerian version of Noah's Ark. Note how Ark is pictured with vertical
lines on sides. The same holds true with mound site.

10

Reconstructing the Ark

METAL ANALYSIS

At present, the oldest pieces of wrought iron known are two blades: a sickle found by Belzoni under the base of the Sphinx in Karnak near Thebes, and the blade found by Colonel Vyse embedded in the masonry of the Great Pyramid. There is also a portion of a crosscut saw exhumed at Nimrud by Layard, now in the British Museum. All are exceptions to what is considered the Age of Iron.

Samples of iron fittings recovered from the Ark site recall the words of Solomon:

> Is there any thing whereof it might be said, See, this is new? It hath been already of old time, which was before us.
>
> Ecclesiastes 1:10 KJV

I hurriedly opened the first-class envelope labeled "Los Alamos National Laboratory." It contained the semiquantitative analysis of the iron samples we had recovered from the Ark. The stoichiometric results were impressive, with the seven running from 60 percent through 91.84 percent FE_2O_3. The highest reading was obtained from an angular bracket.

Iron in Noah's Ark? Impossible, claim contemporary Ark hunters:

> As for the alleged cages made of iron, it is necessary to remember that this metal was discovered by the Hittites about 1500 B.C., far too late for use in Noah's Ark.[1]

---

[1]Lloyd R. Bailey, *Where Is Noah's Ark?* (Nashville: Abingdon Press, 1978.)

This unusual statement by Lloyd R. Bailey, associate professor of Old Testament at Duke Divinity School and editor for *The Interpreter's Dictionary of the Bible Supplementary Volume* is astounding in light of the Hebrew word *barzel,* translated on over sixty other occasions as "iron." Before the Flood and the building of the Ark we read in Genesis 4:22 of Tubal-cain, an instructor of every craftsman in brass and iron.

Thus one could assume this otherwise brilliant professor doesn't read or understand his own Bible!

Even the reference to brass in the KJV could be considered bronze, for Plato states that before the Flood *both* bronze and iron were in use. This would mean the sinking of Atlantis and the biblical Flood took place after 1500 B.C.E. Highly unlikely, but a necessary conclusion if we are to take the scholar's dogmatic opinion that iron could not possibly have been in use prior to that date.

A top executive from a television station once dismissed my claim of having been aboard the Ark solely on the basis that it contained iron. "Man didn't have iron then," he countered. "If your site contains that much iron, you could not possibly have been on anything built during the time of Noah!"

The term *Iron Age* is a label conveniently used by archaeologists in an attempt to divide history into neat little chronological periods identifying the dominant material used in toolmaking, but there are limitations and exceptions to this premise. I believe the key to understanding many of these out-of-place artifacts is the Mesopotamian concept that civilization was divided by the Flood, and the accomplishments of one age are not to be confused with those of another.

As an example, one could conceive of a nuclear holocaust, after which survivors might not bring the manufacture of aluminum back into common use until millennia later. This is what has caused the confusion among archaeologists when they are grubbing in the dust and silt of five thousand years, hoping to discover some traces of infant effort, some rude specimen of the age of Mizraim in which they can admire the germ that has since developed into a wonderful art. Then they break their shins against an article so perfect that it equals, if not exceeds, the supreme stretch of modern ability.

Are we to support the theory that Noah was from the age of

Neanderthals, with his knuckles dragging on the ground, and before he was cold in his grave his descendants had become so advanced in their achievements in construction and fine arts that if we possess the requisite skill today, we never attempt to emulate their accomplishments?

Were these skills brought from another age as mankind's ancient literature records? There are many clues that suggest this is the case. It has been proven beyond doubt that many of the texts comprising the Egyptian Book of the Dead were written and compiled before the period of Menes (Mizraim, son of Ham, son of Noah), the first historical king of Egypt. His reign has been variously given from 5892 B.C.E. (Lepsius) to 4455 B.C.E. (Brugsch), but as to these dates E. A. Budge, late keeper of Assyrian and Egyptian Anitiquities in the British Museum, suggests that "to fix a chronological limit for the arts and civilization of Egypt is absolutely impossible."

It would appear that someone had forged a block or slab of iron from the earliest period of the Egyptian civilization or, in my opinion, brought it *from* an antediluvian age into the present.

This artifact was found by Herutataf, son of Cheops, quite by accident in the oldest of temples. The writer of the dirge says, "I have heard the words of I-em Hotep and of Herutataf, whose many and varied writings are said and sung." I-em Hotep was the designer and architect of the Great Pyramid! The papyrus (B.M. No. 10,060) states the dirge was found

ḥer	teb	ent	bȧa	qemȧt	ȧn	em	χesbet
upon	a slab	of		iron	of the south inscribed with lapis-lazuli.		

Further mention of this event and artifact is found in both the Paris and Parma papyrus:

> He found it in his journeying to make an inspection in the temples. Strength was with him to make diligent in understanding it. He brought it as a marvellous thing to the king [Khufu or Cheops] when he saw that it was a great mystery, unseen and beheld.

There is little question that this object was *not* aerolite or siderolite, a mixture of stone and iron embedded like raisins in a cake. In other words, there is no suggestion that it was a

meteorite but a slab of iron *inlaid* with characters of precious
lapis lazuli and considered "the writing of the god himself."

Herutataf found this baffling artifact in an ancient temple of
Egypt long before the Iron Age, and no one is disputing the
antiquity of the papyrus or Professor Budge's translation?
There is no dispute with the term for iron in Genesis, or in
Plato's account of iron before the Flood, only silence on the
obvious contradictions to what is taught today.

Finding artifacts of iron such as reported by Vyse in the
Great Pyramid has led to disclaimers by archaeologists that it
was possibly an iron tool belonging to one of Vyse's own
workmen which slipped down during the course of the excavations. Of more importance is an iron deposit which was
found on a flint wand by Reisner in the Mycerinus Valley
Temple at Giza, Fourth Dynasty.[2] When this deposit was
spectrographically examined, no evidence of nickel was
found, so the iron was not of meteoric origin.

Amulets of iron and ornamental tips on "magic wands"
tend to speak of its scarcity soon after the Flood. Another
source of interesting prehistoric iron objects in Crete–probably imported curiosities, for there are no notable deposits of
iron ore on the island–are finger rings found in Mycenaean
graves built up of successive layers of different metals. Childe
describes these as "dry batteries, precursors of 'galvanic' rings
and so their magical value may rest on some basis of scientific
fact."[3]

So precious were these meaningful "bits of iron" they appeared almost sacred, as if pulled from some revered artifact.
Iron amulets have been found with silver heads in Egypt and
closer to the source, at Alaca Hüyük in Anatolia, a site that
dates back to 3000 B.C.E., where archaeologists have found an
iron pin with a gold head.

Iron nails have also appeared in Knossos with ornamental
gold heads that were held in awe by the Minoans and gold-
headed iron studs from chamber tombs at Dendra. Objects of
iron have been found that were held as such sacred relics they

---

[2] D. Dunham and W. J. Young, "An Occurrence of Iron in the Fourth Dynasty,"
Journal of Egyptian Archaeology (1942): 57, 58.
[3] G. V. Childe, *The Dawn of European Civilization,* 3rd ed., 1939.

were entirely overlaid in gold. Where did the ancients retrieve this iron before the Iron Age?

While it is generally accepted that Egypt was the last to enter the Iron Age, there seemed to be no shortage of imports! A report by Carpenter and Robertson in 1930 showed a small knife had been made by welding two pieces of metal together, the line of the weld extending along the whole length of the specimen to the point. These two different pieces were brought to approximately the same composition by carburizing. The knife had been air cooled and carburized so as to make the carbon content at the cutting edge about 0.8 percent. Brinell figures showed the hardness varied between 269 and 302. These are high figures for unquenched steel! An Egyptian ax showed hardness figures from 62 Brinell in the ferrite body to 363, 388, and finally to the very considerable hardness of 444 Brinell at the cutting edge. H. H. Coghlan considers these works of iron, brought within the range of steel with such decided skill, almost unbelievable in that such ingenious techniques were actually developed in the prehistoric period.[4]

As we move closer to the remains of the Ark in Anatolia, the abundance of these pre-Iron Age finds become more profuse. Fragments of iron at Tell Chagar Bazar in north Syria are considered from not later than 2700 B.C.E. because they were found at level Five. Again, the specimen contained no nickel and was therefore not of meteoric origin. M. E. L. Mallowan, in *Excavations at Arpachiyah,* said, "Two fragments of iron supply further proof that Habur was a very early center for working of iron in the third millennium B.C."[5] And at Tell Asmar, Iraq, Dr. H. Frankfort said, "The temple service, a closed find, to which the knife belongs, was buried at the very end of the Early Dynastic period, say between 2450 and 2350 B.C."[6]

So in reference to our Bible scholar Dr. Lloyd R. Bailey, professor at Duke Divinity School and editor of Bible dictionaries, while all this information was clearly available to him in

---

[4]H. H. Coghlan, *Notes on Prehistoric and Early Iron in the Old World* (New York: Oxford University Press, 1956).

[5]Ibid.

[6]Ibid.

1978 he still persisted in stating the metal was not "discovered" until 1500 B.C.E. Where then did it come from?[7]

As early as 1948, Claude Schaeffer was of the opinion that even these ancient objects of manufactured iron went well beyond Assyrian origin.[8] Given what has been learned from the El Amarna texts concerning the origin of iron in the fifteenth century B.C.E., and now that many objects of iron of such high antiquity have come from Asia Minor, it no longer seems prudent to refuse the paternity for the origin of iron to the Anatolians, and perhaps more particularly to the inhabitants of the *Armenian regions!*

I will go one step further and suggest that the origin of iron in this age is located at 39°26'N and 44°15'E in the Anatolian Akyayla range, in the heart of ancient Urartu. It has been stripped of its nails, pins, studs, and fittings by pilgrims of Ishtar and so treasured as to be covered with gold and entombed with their owners since earliest times. These first articles, if not forged by Tubal-cain's foundry workers, were reworked by the artificers and builders of the Ark during the early years of the new age, instructing their descendants in the skill of the old world that passed away, guarding the secret of the manufacture of iron.

The disappearance of iron after its early utilization until the end of the Ancient Bronze Period, and its apparent total eclipse during the Middle Bronze Period, is considered by metallurgists and archaeologists a very curious and interesting phenomenon. I feel it suggests the source was lost, namely, the Ark was covered by the alluvial flow from the valley above.

That the Ark today clearly shows an abundance of iron, not only in fittings but in flakes within the matrix composition itself, suggests to me that the builders of the Ark used the slag of their early smelters in the tar macadam covering and cementlike mixture of the KPR, making it practically indestructible.

The process of smelting ore may actually have been practiced by the early survivors after the Flood, the fathers in-

[7]Ibid.
[8]Ibid.

structing the young in the secrets of hardening, annealing, and tempering. The ore found in the upper surface areas of Anatolia – limonite and hematite – was undoubtedly used. First it was aired and the soluble compounds washed away, then the roasting in piles of burning wood to remove the sulfur, followed by crushing the ore. Perhaps just a simple washing of the iron-rich alluvial ore of the High Caucasus was all that was required, the simple building of a smelter and forced air. While bellows-blown furnaces were used at a very early date in Egypt, there is evidence to indicate the air blast was known in Mesopotamia in the middle of the third millennium B.C.E. In any case, a natural-draft type may have been used. The proper selection of acacia and tamarisk woods, or other close-grained wood like the mimosa was important for excellent charcoal and the introduction of limestone for the flux. These woods will easily produce a temperature of 800° to 850° C. With a proper draft and the temperature raised to 1100° C, the carbon of the charcoal will burn to carbon monoxide, and this gas will rob the oxygen from the ore to form carbon dioxide. Thus it would be possible for the early metalsmiths to obtain the porous bloom to be reworked and forged into wrought iron.

As we continue to hear from the "experts" who refuse to even study the remains of the Ark based on their far-reaching bias, frequently repeated as if they were proven facts, it is important to remember how hypothetical their suppositions are. The archaeological history of the development of the iron industry will remain dark until they consider these tangible remains of the shipwreck on a mountain and take it under scientific examination as the source of oriental iron metallurgy.

THE MISNOMER GOPHER WOOD

It has been said that when it comes to a choice between the truth and the myth, give them the legend they cherish. Perhaps the most difficult evidence to accept, then, is the fact that the Ark is not constructed of wood at all.

This gopher wood, the Ark's covering, long the puzzling word that it is, has been described in various ways:

> So make yourself an ark of *cypress wood . . . coat it with pitch* inside and out.
>
>   Oxford NIV Scofield Study Bible, author's italics

> Make yourself an ark out of *wood from a resinous tree . . .* and you must *cover it* inside and outside *with tar.*
>
>   New World Bible Translation Committee, author's italics

> Make yourself an ark with *ribs of cypress; cover it with reeds* and *coat it* inside and out *with tar.*
>
>   New English Bible, author's italics

Extrabiblical sources consider other species of wood the gopher wood of Genesis. "Built of *pine wood,* made watertight with bitumen," or from other Hebrew folklore, "Plant a *teak-wood* tree, wait twenty years for it to mature, and cut it into planking," and even the "tall plants with hollow stems," of the Hopi Indians and the camphor wood of the Asians have been rebutted by the eyewitness accounts furnished by Violet Cummings' research:

> The wood used throughout was *oleander . . .* everything was heavily painted with a waxlike paint.
>
>   The Roskovitsky account, *New Eden* magazine, author's italics

Some preferred to play it safe by not actually identifying its species, assuming everyone knew what it was: "There was an Englishman among them . . . and he saw that it was made of the ancient gopher wood of Scripture, which, as everyone knows, grows only on the plains of the Euphrates . . . which was painted brown" (Turkish commissioner's report of 1883).

While my attempt to put forth the truth of the matter on both the misnomer gopher wood and its covering may be simple to understand, it most likely will be over the heads of those who hold most dear their childhood memories of Noah and his sawmill from their Sunday-school days.

That I, too, was suffering from well-intentioned instructors of fundamentalist thought and the inerrancy of the Scriptures well past my Christian grammar-school days and my short stint at Wheaton College Academy, was quite evident in the guilt I suppressed in my later years in doubting this portion of the Bible. During my time in the merchant marine I could see this gopher wood Ark concept bringing a new horror to the voyage of Noah and the peril of the sea.

As a shipmaster, I was haunted by the reality that the longest wooden ships that were ever built, the six-masted schooners from 1900 through 1909, convinced the builders that 300 feet was the absolute limit for the fiber stress of this material. Ships approaching this figure deformed through hogging and sagging to where they visibly undulated over the waves. They were constantly in need of pumping and had to be strapped in iron to keep them together. In the end John Rockwell, the designer of this class of vessel, was forced to admit that wooden boat building had reached its limit. The ships were used only for short hauls and the coast trade, since they were considered unsafe for deep water. The 329-foot *Wyoming* needed another 186 feet to meet the Ark's requirement.

Yet biblical scholars continued to insist on maintaining their predecessors' concepts to the point they believed somehow by building it rectangular, it would survive the greatest catastrophic deluge with a little tar to keep it together. Some authors even suggest that this square-cornered rectangular chest, since it was not fashioned for motion, would not go anyplace. One could assume by this reasoning that if all ships had blunt ends and square corners, when disabled without propulsion they would rock up and down and never get blown ashore! That a nonpowered vessel in a hurricane sea could maintain its geographical position for months at a time, as envisioned by these authors because the Ark was not designed to "go anyplace," is unrealistic at best.

The basic construction of the Ark was not wood. It was not constructed of cypress, wood from a resinous tree, oleander, teakwood, or pine.

I would submit that the only wood used in the construction of the Ark were the hogging-truss support poles under compression of the longitudinal standing rigging and the beams and floorboards, all of which will prove to be cedarwood. The hull and roof were made of *reeds*. The secret to the Ark's survival, however, is its covering, and the allegorical connotations of this covering have intrigued commentators for centuries.

To many believers, the Ark is a Christ figure as a vessel of refuge. Those who are under the covering are safe within, and the judgment on the world does not affect them.

The Hebrew word is *kaphar,* and it is used over one hundred times in Scripture. Although translators have managed to rake up over twenty assorted English alternatives from which to choose, they appear reluctant to use its literal meaning, which is simply, "cover." *Kaphar* has been translated as the following (Genesis 6:14, author's italics):

> . . . and you must *cover* it inside and outside with *tar.*[9]
> . . . and *coat* it with *pitch* inside and out.[10]
> . . . and shalt *pitch* it within and without with *pitch.*[11]

This is conjecture. Neither the noun *pitch* nor the verb *to pitch* is to be found in the Hebrew, nor is coat, or tar. I was very disturbed to find this but happy that others were upset, too. One author was in a rage: "It's just another case of clerical bungling ecclesiastical translators being unable to resist the temptation to interpret what they thought the word might imply, rather than translate what it actually says."[12] I agree with this author that the word most certainly never means, "pitch" but "covering," and his statement "Gopher wood? What that is no one knows, they only guess," is in line with my thinking. Unfortunately, he eventually slips into error by stating, "The Ark itself was a vast structure of timber . . . nor was it boat-shaped."

To render this verse simply, "Cover it inside and outside with cover, or cover it with cover," may not appear to make sense, but I believe this is a valid literal translation that will enlighten us as we move along.

In Strong's opinion,[13] the word *kâphar* (kaw-far' #3722) is a primary root meaning, "to cover." From this same root we

---

[9]New World Translation of the Holy Scriptures (New York: Watchtower, 1984).

[10]Oxford New International Version Scofield Study Bible (New York: Oxford University Press, 1984).

[11]Authorized King James Version (New York: Oxford University Press, 1967).

[12]John Metcalfe, *Noah and the Flood* (Buckinghamshire: John Metcalfe Publishing Trust, 1976).

[13]James Strong, *Abingdon's Strong's Exhaustive Concordance* (Nashville: Abingdon Press, 1986).

also find another very similar word, *kâphâr* (kaw-fawr', #3723) in the Hebrew, used to describe a village or community of persons protected by walls.

Thus we can see at this juncture, the Ark was not an open-decked boat but one covered with protective walls. The community was not *in* the floating structure but *upon* the reed boat protected by a covering. This agrees with the Sanskrit description of the Ark as a *raft*.

In clarification of this is the Hebrew word *kephîyr* (kef-eer', #3715) meaning, "covered in by walls," and thus *protected*, as in #3723.

It would be helpful at this point to remind the reader that the Ezra script carried no points, that is, vowels for pronunciation, but only the consonants. We come now to another word, *kôpher* (ko'-fer, #3724), derived from #3723, with both words carrying with them not only a covering wall of protection but also that the wall itself is protected with a protective covering of *bitumen!*

Here it must be stated I find these preceding words very close to the Akkadian KPR, which we will discuss shortly. Consider that there were early records of the patriarchs written before the Flood. These were carried aboard and added to soon after disembarking. They were most likely clay tablets with ideographic glyphs impressed upon them. There could be differing narratives such as the record of Japheth and that of Shem concerning the Flood account that would cause future scholars to propose scribal and priestly meddling, resulting in more than one account of the Flood within the text compiled by Moses.

In the succeeding generations, the tablets became not only updated and added to but revised into the language of the times and eventually into cuneiform characters. These words, Semitic in origin, passed from the Chaldean of Abram into the Aramaic of these keepers of the tablets and generations of their forefathers. These early copyist scribes may have chosen to retain archaic words or supplant them with those in more common use and understanding. It would not be unseemly to include popular Akkadian words if the Hebrew equivalent had not been established.

Thus when Moses compiled these records into the book of

the beginnings, it is not as if the term interpreted today as *gopher wood* was written by Noah in Hebrew.

We then come to Strong's opinion of the mysterious word *gôpher* (go'-fer, #1613), wherein he admits it is probably from the unused root meaning, "to house in," then makes an unexpected giant leap of credibility and, succumbing to peer pressure, states it is *cypress!*

It is a frightening thing to disagree with James Strong (S.T.D., LL.D.) as the meanings of the Hebrew words from the KJV rarely if ever are found to be defective in his concordance. However, I am not alone in disagreement. Two of the greatest Hebrew scholars the world has ever known, August Dillman (1823–1894), author of *Die Genesis,* and Paul Anton De Lagarde (1827–1891), in two works, *Semitica,* i.64 and *Symmicta,* ii.93, take issue with this interpretation.

To them it is most certainly a foreign word. They believe it is not the original word but inferred from the word *gophrîyth* (gof-reeth') or "brimstone." This has been assigned number 1614 in Strong's concordance, which he then suggests is probably the feminine of gôpher! Here I feel that Strong is really reaching, and apparently this is the reason many consider gopher wood as wood from a *resinous tree.* Strong, again assuming this to be cypress (for he can obviously see the connection, as have Dillman and Lagarde), suggests the flammable *resin* of cypress is as flammable as sulfuric brimstone.

It is here that the "resinous tree" interpretation really falls apart as this word means a mixture of pumice and *bitumen,* practically an asphalt cement, and is found in the Akkadian in the three-root consonant KPR.

To help the reader follow my line of reasoning, we are all familiar with the story in Genesis 19:24 KJV concerning the destruction of the cities Sodom and Gomorrah: "Then the Lord rained upon Sodom and upon Gomorrah brimstone and fire from the Lord out of heaven."

These two cities, now believed to be covered by the Dead Sea, our planet's lowest elevation below sea level, were apparently struck by earthquake and volcanic magma that blew out of a fissure sulfuric and *bituminous* in nature. It then rained back down upon the cities in total destruction. This brimstone may have rained from heaven but did not issue from the heavens. It is the same word used in Isaiah 30:33, ". . . like a stream of brimstone, doth kindle it."

In other words we are speaking of lava, which in one state is in a liquid form, flowing like a stream, then solidifies into stone. That this could be considered bituminous as well as sulfuric is related in Genesis 14:10 KJV prior to the destruction of these cities, where we read that the area, so low in elevation, actually had bitumen bubbling to the surface.

> And the vale of Siddim was full of slimepits; and the kings of Sodom and Gomorrah fled, and fell there; and they that remained fled to the mountain.

This slime or bitumen recovered from slimepits was used as mortar in Genesis 11:3: ". . . stone, and slime had they for mortar," and is the material used to cover the ark of bulrushes of Moses.

Strong lists this word as #2564 and in Hebrew *chêmâr* (kahy-mawr), bitumen, *as rising to the surface.*

Where then is the resin of the resinous wood? It is a figment of the imagination. Trees don't bleed sulfuric bitumen and resin does not bubble out of the ground. Gopher wood is bunk, pure and simple! What the Akkadian word means, and it was not unusual to find Akkadian root words being bandied about in Egypt during Moses' time as we use café and soufflé today, is a mixture of pumice, bitumen, and natron. The KPR of Mesopotamia is still being shipped by Italian businessmen as a commodity from the island of Santorini to the mainland to be pressed into building blocks. It is lava or brimstone, the same material that was barged to Egypt from Santorini, where it was processed and shipped to Panama to be used as cement in holding the banks of the canal.

As we move along, we will begin to see that the Ark's covering was its secret of protection, and the actual identification of its true substance was lost in its more relevant allegorical meaning.

In the allegorical sense, translating this word *kaphar* into "tar" or "pitch" totally nullifies its spiritual meaning. For there is mystery in the nature of this covering. It is the covering of atonement that served as protection over Noah from the impending judgment upon the world.

It signifies the same covering of the blood of the sacrificial lamb that stood between the firstborn and the angel of death during the Passover of Egypt.

". . . and when I see the blood, I will pass over you."

It is the blood that maketh *cover* for your souls, emphasizes God, and this concept of atonement by blood to cover the sins of the transgressor is absolutely central to salvation in the Holy Scriptures.

The word *kaphar* is interpreted in most of the twenty alternatives as "atonement." If in over seventy cases it is sacrificial blood that is said to cover as an atonement or bring about reconciliation, the altar obviously was "covered," but not with tar or tree sap! In the same sense the Ark was not covered with blood. The covering seen as an atonement against judgment, and those under the "covering" in a state of reconciliation because of the atonement, is beautiful and mean-ingful in its relationship to the believer but is not telling us the material we should expect to find literally covering the Ark.

In one fragmented cuneiform script, Utnapishtim relates to Gilgamesh, "I smeared it with pitch inside, and bitumen without." It is interesting to note that the Sumerian and Akkadian writers knew the difference.

One modern writer misses the point when he records the observation that today *bitumen* bubbles up through crevices in the rocks near the modern city of Hit on the Euphrates and that in ancient times clay bricks were cemented together with this *resinous* substance. This is important. There is a difference between a petroleum product and vegetable product. Some writers do not make the distinction. When scholars inter-preting words meaning "bituminous" suggest they mean res-inous trees, red flags should be going up to challenge that assumption.

Why would this Sumerian account stress the distinction between bitumen and resin? One reason is, of course, that a petroleum product within the confines of the Ark might be harmful or dangerous. Aside from Kiyara pitch, used as an antiseptic to cure skin diseases of camels since ancient times and still in use today, bitumen on the Ark seems more desirable on the outside, with a vegetable resin inside preserving the flooring and support poles. The wood used within the Ark according to Mesopotamian accounts is cedar, not cypress.

If bitumen was used without on the covering, I perceive the resin used within served functions other than protection against moisture. It was not used to make anything watertight but was a vegetable substance used in making varnishes and medicines. There are gums such as ammoniac used in making sedatives, as well as asafetida and gamboge. Perhaps the ammoniac is the mysterious amomum sought after by the early pilgrims for medicinal purposes as well as charms in its solidified amberlike form, for talismans against evil. Undoubtedly of great value, perhaps it could only now be found within the remains of the Ark, a substance produced from a source that no longer existed in the new age.

In the Egyptian Book of the Dead, the Papyrus of Ani gives a hieroglypic account of unguents carried aboard the divine boat of Nu, and it is not difficult to consider it a disinfectant as well. The common household liquid pine cleaner contains 30 percent gum spirits. Certain gum resins have been used in fumigation when burned, and balsam fir sap has been used as an antiseptic.

Another tempting suggestion is that the aromatic fumes may have had a sedative or calming effect upon the animals during their early periods of confinement. But as to the Ark being mode completely of a resinous wood, the evidence points to *reeds*.

When I reported my findings to my colleagues, they were aghast that I should make such a suggestion. It was probably more difficult to get them to consider this than to take the Ark off Ararat. Yet the term *gopher wood* is used only once in the sixty-six books of the Bible, covering some fifteen hundred years of written text. It was definitely not an ancient common household word! *Strong's Exhaustive Concordance* has it heading the top of the list for over ninety instances where it is said to be the common everyday word for wood, but what did the letters really look like in the original script of Moses?

If one realizes that on many occasions a script is recopied because the old manuscript has become worn in time and reading, and the rendering becomes difficult due to its poor condition, an error in transmission is possible. The copyist may have just assumed the first portion of the word said "tree" (*ates*).

Remember, too, that this may have occurred in the Ezra script before the points had been added, and if a portion of the third letter had flaked off, the word could easily have had the original meaning "to shape or form." This word is *aw-tsab'*. If it was then followed by the word *gophrîyth* (gof-reeth'), or brimstone, it would carry with it quite another meaning and would in fact illuminate us as to the actual material covering the Ark. It would suggest that the mysterious covering for the Ark was a cement and bituminous substance that was shaped and formed over the entire boat as a protective covering. There is no such word in the Hebrew meaning "gôpher." It is only half a word. It is a scribal error and a mistake.

The word *'âtsab* means "shape" or "fashion," as a potter fashions a vessel. In Job 10:8, "Thy hands shaped me." And in Jeremiah 22:28, "Is he a vessel in which is no pleasure?" (masculine noun). In the verb form as in Job, the KJV has it as, "Thine hands have made me and fashioned me together round about."

If the root of this word means, "to fashion or shape," could this not be referring to the Akkadian word KPR and all the Hebrew connotations implied in the rendering of Hebrew, meaning a mixture of bituminous brimstone in a liquid state, shaping it over a covering, or covering the Ark with *kôpher* or *kâphâr,* where it then solidified into a cementlike protective covering? Or perhaps simply, "Make me an ark shaped and formed with a covering!"

This is only my attempt to try to resolve what the term *gopher wood* meant in the original, for what I have found, contrary to my colleagues' opinions, are the remains of a reed boat covered with cement, which then appeared as a clay vessel.

Thus the Persian legends called it "Varuna's House of Clay," with the abundance of this decomposed material at the site looking like a clay upswelling in the shape of a boat.

This would also account for why an Amerindian tribe calls it a stone canoe, and the Japanese legend describes it as a stone and camphor wood boat. And it is what caused me, upon locating the deck support beams, to suggest in awe to Dr. Baumgardner, "Did Noah build a ferrocement boat?"

Its broken covering may have resembled the cracked shell of the Egg of Ishtar as it slowly decomposed through the ages as related by the Egyptian, Hyginus, the Mundane Egg. Again the Papyrus of Ani (Plate XXII, line 20), the boat of Nu is said to be the color *green* (reeds?), for the divine chiefs. *Make a heaven of stars* washed and purified with natron and incense. If this Egyptian hieroglyphic text with the interlinear transliteration of "ȧri pet ent sebu" can be read as well, "make a heavenly vault" or "a canopy like heaven" over the boat, then perhaps the Egyptians, too, are referring to the covering or enclosure over the reed boat of Nu, which was then washed and purified with natron.

Natron is an important part of the composition of this mixture. It is in fact a catalyst in the hardening process. The cementlike mixture could turn as hard as stone if not for the bitumen, for the pumice, silicon, alumina, calcium, manganese, *natron,* and copper that was shaped over the reeds would quickly set up. The alumina is chemically activated by adding the soda (natron and lime), forming an aluminate of sodium, which reacts with the sodium silicate to form a zeolite, or feldspathoide, a natural cement. This accounts for Wyatt finding manganese nodules of amazing purity at the site, 80.64 percent. It is not used for ballast but was carried aboard as part of the ingredient for this quick-set cement.

The Egyptian *turȧ-Θȧ,* meaning, "purified," carries with it the same allegorical sense of *kaphar* in terms of an atonement *shed* or *washed* over *(seȧb-Θȧ,* in the Egyptian) purifying the believer, and the incense referring to the gum resin within!

Thus the full meaning of the word KPR in both its composition and spiritual meaning was known to Moses, who was raised in the house of Pharaoh and schooled in all the knowledge and wisdom of the Egyptians, which was then related in his writing of Genesis. The ark of Moses, in which he was placed as a babe, was a papyrus reed boat with a covering of protection, an enclosure (the Greek *kibotos*) covered with a symbolic *kaphar* of slime and pitch (Exodus 2:3), a perfect description of the Ark of Noah, which preceded Moses' ark.

As Noah, following God's divine commandments, shaped

and fashioned the Ark to the saving of himself and his house, so Moses, following God's design for his people, shaped and molded the Israelites, carrying them through the parted waters safely to the new land.

ári	pet	ent	sebu	seāb - θá	turá - θá
Make	a heaven	of	stars	washed	and	purified

em	hesmen	em	neter senθer
with	natron [and]	with	incense.

The concept of a solid reed raft covered with a bituminous mixture of cement usually evokes smiles from my listeners. It surprises some to discover that there are numerous types of cement weighing from 35 to 115 pounds per cubic foot. These lighter types of air-entrained cement can actually float if they contain foaming agents of aluminum powder and lightweight aggregates such as natural deposits of pumice (nature's Styrofoam) scoria, perlite, or volcanic cinders.

This is not to say that the KPR had to be light enough to float as the bitumen admixture did, for the reed raft itself displaces the water to accomplish this. Concrete of the expanded slag type can weigh 75 pounds and up, but shale and clay types slightly less.

Unfortunately those scientists visiting the site at earlier dates were geologists rather than geochemists. What they failed to realize was that what they considered a clay upswelling was in actuality decomposed cement! As a hydrated paste, the binder of KPR governs in large part the properties of the covering of the Ark. For practical purposes, this may be expressed as consisting of four major compounds of C_3A, C_3S, BC_2S, and C_1AF. Bedding compound found within the angle bracket of wrought iron suggested cement of the clinker type made up of Al_2O_3, FE_2O_3, and SIO_2 and a calcareous material of 91.39 percent (CAO). The small quantities of iron ore (2.55 percent in this sample) were added to the mix to obtain the desired clinker composition. The clinker contains small amounts of MGO (usually limited to 5 percent), with one sample showing a minimal 4.32 percent. The Al_2O_3 and MGO are the main substituents in the C_3S.

That the ancients were capable of producing cement, and in fact highly advanced in agglomerating stone, was brought out recently in the fifth annual edition (Yıl 5 Sayı 18/19) of *Arkeoloji Ve Sanat*. An article by Professor Braidwood of the University of Chicago's Oriental Institute and Halet Çambel describes their findings at ÇAYÖNÜ, a site next to a tributary stream of the Tigris in a pleasant valley on the lower slopes of the eastern Tauros mountains in eastern Turkey. Excavations showed a most remarkable achievement in the villagers' mastery of the art of building—a terrazzo floor, a process heretofore known only from much later times. Implications of the cultural advance found at this site cannot be paralleled anywhere in southwestern Asia with wheat, barley, and certain pulses under cultivation and dogs, sheep, goats, pigs, and cattle taken into domestication. The village dates to about 7250 to 6750 B.C.E.

Discoveries of the ancients' abilities in agglomerating stone and the forming of cement have been led in the scientific world by Dr. Joseph Davidovits of the Geopolymer Institute, Saint Quentin, France. In the course of his research, Dr. Davidovits has rediscovered (and patented) a long-forgotten technique for making stone.

Davidovits has buttressed, with incontestable evidence, his convictions that the facing stones of the pyramids were never carved but were molded on the spot. It is then easy to explain the remarkable and unequaled precision with which the facing stones were apparently placed. It is farewell to rollers, lasers, and antigravity when the science of antiquity is stripped of its occult and esoteric connotations. The stone has turned out to be man-made, and who does he deem responsible for these innovations? None other than Imhotep, the inventor of genius, whom I consider Shem. I highly recommend *The Pyramids: An Enigma Solved* to my readers.[14]

---

[14] Joseph Davidovits and Margie Morris, *The Pyramids: An Enigma Solved* (New York: Hippocrene Books, Inc., 1988).

A SHIP OF REEDS

We must conceive of the Ark as being made up of two components, that which contained the living, and that which provided the flotation for the living. These two components, stacked one atop the other, is what has caused the ancients to describe it as being many stories higher than the biblical account. Moses described only the portion under the covering that contained the living.

We begin at the lower flotation portion, or the raft. There is a suggestion from the text of the Epic of Gilgamesh that it was built in the ground and supported by earthworks (Tablet XI, line 53). We may also recall that the "Word God," Lord Ea, drew the plan upon the ground. The personage who planned the Ark and thereby gave Noah the means of escape is the same personage who is the creator of all things in the Sumerian accounts as well as the Bible.

We begin then by digging a shallow pit some five hundred feet in length. It needn't be too wide to begin with but with a mound of dirt about twenty-six feet wide and two hundred feet long in the forward center section of the pit.

Aboveground we begin with about ten reeds, fifteen feet in length. From the impressions of the reeds found at the site, they appear to have been roughly triangular in shape, rather than round, and about three inches to the side. They may have been stouter at the base and of course smaller in diameter toward their tops, but the size of the reed is unimportant other than to say they were quite a large species of reed.

These would be wrapped in a bundle and bound tightly for the first five feet. Then a little more than halfway in, twelve reeds would be inserted into the bundle and bound. Then fourteen and so on, until as the bundle of reeds gained length, like a rope, we would have progressed from a distance of some one hundred feet on the centerline from the pit. Upon approaching it we stay to the edge, continuing building up the reed pontoon. By the time we have arrived at the middle of the hole, we already have the bundle 357.5 feet long. Remember, we are not yet in the hole but along the edge. Reversing our procedure of adding reeds, which has increased the diameter of the pontoon to 8.5 feet, we now continue toward the stern, decreasing the diameter until we have reached a point almost 100 feet from the pit with a rope of reeds almost 700 feet in length. We build a second pontoon exactly the same down the other side of the pit.

With both completed, our labor force now digs away the embankment, allowing the reed bundle to rope its way down into the hole by its own weight, curving down into the pit at the ends and around the mound. We did not want the pit to be too wide for we wanted the weight of the reeds to force the bundles tightly alongside to be lashed together. This would be done by digging tunnels under the pontoons to pass lines.

The ends still laying outside the pit that are smaller in diameter and more manageable are under a natural strain to continue the fore and aft curve of the portion coming out of the pit. We will assist them by raising them up with large gin poles until they fall back in on themselves, steadied by guy lines of course, until they have completed the natural curve. The only curve that is truly natural is the inward curve of a wave when it breaks. With the bows of the Ark on this curve, and the length of the Ark in inches (6180), the ratio of the curve itself, I would be lacking in imagination to not propose that the curve of the upswept stem and stern were the same.

With both of the original "form" bundles lashed tightly together, and with loose lines having been passed between them off to either side for lashing the next segments onto the first, work stops long enough on the second set of pontoons to celebrate. Perhaps the wind banner on Inanna's standards found on Sumerian clay tablets which I envision as representing these reed stem and stern posts are in remembrance of this occasion (*see* page 245).

The pit is widened to receive the next segments and slid in the same way, with the tunnels extended and the loose lines for the next as well as the second layer that will be laid atop. Nothing can be left out; even the lines, heavily tarred, for attaching the hogging-truss pennants, are fastened deep within the bundles and led up through each succeeding layer.

The King of the Sethites was providing work for every craftsman and artisan in the land. Those who grew reeds suitable for the construction received the land forevermore. The woodsmen who cut the timber were not only paid for it but also received in return the king's oxen that pulled it to the site. The Ark, regardless of what his contemporaries thought of the idea itself, was the greatest make-work program in the old world. The work proceeded quickly and the form of the hull was finally shaped within the pit itself, the excavated earth forming a barrier like a hillside aboveground.

The earthworks supported the form and Noah relates, "I laid out the contours, drew it all" (XI, 59), and the work progressed harmoniously, oblivious to the danger at hand.

> I butchered bulls for the people,
> and killed sheep every day.
> Drink beer, oil and wine
> I gave the workmen to swill as if it were the water of a river, so that
> they made festival as if it were the days of the New Year's.
>
> XI, 70–74

With the majestic silhouette of the end posts against the rising sun, they appeared as the slender neck of a waterfowl and the tail of a cock within the mound as the workers now began to construct storage bins, water cells, and compartments of KPR coated with white natron to receive the seed for the planting and the roots of sustenance, all sealed for the voyage into the unknown and replanting in the new world.

Large stones with flat surfaces had been carefully placed at exacting intervals upon which the stout cedar poles were stood and held into position by guy lines. The additional rows of reeds were layered upward and around the poles and storage cells to complete the main deck. These poles, which may have numbered as many as 117, were placed upright, perhaps extending sixty feet above the main deck at the center and gradually decreasing in height and angled toward the bow and the stern. From large straps that were lashed to the bundles during construction and extended up through the deck at the stem and stern just behind the large upsweeps were attached heavy flaxen pennants. These extended to almost half the vessel's length as they were laid over the top of the poles, where they almost met at the center.

Here, a platform was raised for the workers to run a line through the ends of the eye on both pennants, and continuing this passing of the line through the eyes, it was finished off as an endless myriad of loops through which a stout wooden pole of some ten feet was struck. When turned by the workers it twisted the loop, shortening the distance between the eyes of the pennants, bringing them together in tension (a Spanish windlass). There were at least twenty-six pennants totaling thirteen lines running from stem to stern over the poles. This platform was retained and during the voyage the pennants were kept taut as a weekly routine.

It can now be seen that the hogging-truss support poles were acting as a suspension bridge in reverse, as they held the raft in tension. The hogging stress would occur in the hull as it became supported by water, which would tend to place tension on the pennants as the ends wanted to drop. This is because they did not displace water.

These poles were most likely placed along the athwartship lines noted in the survey. They would be in rows quite close together at the bow and stern, and spaced further apart toward the center. The uppermost deck appears to have had fourteen reed bundles, side by side. The outermost lines were one and fifteen, with the thirteen longitudinal lines within running stem to stern. It is along these lines that the support-pole footings are noticeable.

These are the poles spoken of by Utnapishtim in Tablet XI, line 64: "I checked the poles, and laid in all that was necessary." Checking the poles would be something Noah would be doing throughout the entire voyage.

Within these poles Noah laid three decks. This strengthened the standing rigging and it slowly became a rigid lattice-like framework that he was now dividing into three stories — the lower, second, and third. Josephus describes it as four stories, but it is not the contradiction supposed if he included the main deck. There were no cattle on the main deck during the early portion of the voyage, although it is conceivable that certain areas of it were open for exercising animals during the time the vessel was at rest, perhaps, and select periods of calm.

Noah most certainly used the Ark for sheltering the domestic variety of animals after it landed, and there is the possibility too that the lower portion of reeds under the

capped-over and cemented main deck were partially consumed as fodder for the cattle during the time the earth
renewed itself. Much of the raft could have been consumed
after the voyage for animal subsistence, as this deck was
opened to get at the seed and root cells below.

I do not conceive of this main deck as having much head-
room. It may have been rather low, perhaps only 8.5 feet, for
in reality it was a drain. Contrary to the design of vessels
today, it was not crowned to direct the waters to the side but
was lower in the center. Animal waste drained down from
above to the centerline and from the main deck drained into
the hull pool and the sea.

In constructing the craft, the entire area over and above the
open deck of the reed raft was covered, enclosing the hogging-
truss support poles of cedar, within which the upper three
decks were fastened, in my opinion, with iron straps and pins.
These formed natural cubicles, firmly restraining the movement of cattle and beast which, if they were allowed to mill
about, would virtually cause a cargo shift and possibly capsize
the boat. One can imagine the damage a six-ton beast could do
if allowed to roam free in a stable, as these pens are so
conceived by the experts before me – it could be more destruc-
tive than a rolling bronze cannon on a gun deck below, for
here the cargo was above.

The form this covering, or roof, may have taken has not
been the subject of much speculation. Everyone conceives of it
as flat since Morris proposed his design with just enough cant
to let the water roll off or the seas roll over, which was quite
likely with *his* shape for the Ark. Photos in numerous publications showing this design being sea-trialed in a wave-
generating test tank are most unconvincing and appear as a
piece of 4′ × 6′ some 40 inches long being tossed about like
overboard dunnage. Morris, who appears to be more versed in
geology than sea savvy, would have the overhanging eaves
and his roof torn off on the first sizable swell if it didn't float
upside down first. Eyewitness accounts of Hagopian and
renderings by the artist Elfred Lee have reinstalled this roof and
idea. Genesis 8:13 *plainly states it was removed!*

The phrase found in the Gilgamesh account (Tablet XI),

"Cover it with a roof as the abyss is covered," could use some revision. The word *abyss* is one of the few Akkadian words that has come down to us that is still useful in our vocabulary today. If one uses the word for the sea, or more logically, the sea bottom, then the water covering the abyss would be considered flat; therefore the roof would be flat. I do not think this is the subject of the sentence. The abyss, in my view, is the abyss within the raft, or the pit down the centerline in the forward section. This was to be covered by a roof for reasons of ventilation.

First, let me say that a flat roof would need more support from the underside to hold it up then an arched roof that would be self-supporting. In my illustration of the ZOHAR, which all rabbis found difficult to explain with the exception of Abba Ben Kahana, I envision it as running down the centerline of the exposed ridgepole for the total length of the covering. This opening, giving light from above, was the "skylight" as interpreted by the rabbi, but even Kahana was unaware of its multiple purpose. The water as well rained in, playing a very important role for the sanitation conditions throughout the voyage. This opening is to be calculated as follows:

"In a cubit shalt thou finish it above" refers to the ridgepole, or apex of the roofline. The reed covering extended up the sides of the vaultlike roof until even with a point that was exactly one cubit, or 20.6 inches from the very top. Three times this figure gives the horizontal distance to the top of the covering on both sides of the roof, or 61.80 inches. This figure times phi (1.6180) gives a golden rectangle of 5.15 × 8.33 feet, and 61.8 such openings running down the apex exposes 514.7 feet of the uppermost portion of the vessel from the Arabic root meaning "the back of the beast." These figures give an area for the ZOHAR of approximately 2650 square feet. This is one-half the area of the hull pool that is found within the central forward section of the raft, the dimensions of which are approximately 26.5 × 200 (5300 square feet).

Within this pool, an incompressible piston of water rises in a 5-foot following sea, compressing 26,500 cubic feet of air above the piston and exhausting out the ZOHAR. As the Ark is lifted up on the crest of the wave, the water piston falls 5 feet, drawing in the fresh air. As it plunges into the trough, it repeats this ventilating action. Since this period of time from crest to trough to crest takes approximately twelve seconds, five cycles are completed in a minute, three hundred cycles in an hour. It requires only eighty-five cycles to completely replenish the 2,275,630 cubic feet of air space under the roof covering, which this system would accomplish eighty-five times during a twenty-four-hour period.

During a more inclement period of the Deluge, we might expect the sea conditions to be worse, in which case this system of ventilation would improve. With no movement of the vessel at all, however, this system would not be functioning, thus necessitating the removal of the covering. We read in Genesis 8:13 KJV "And Noah removed the covering of the ark, and looked, and, behold, the face of the ground was dry." Once the vessel was grounded, the covering had to be opened.

Upon building and loading the Ark, a large portion of the side of this covering was open. When it was closed and sealed from the outside, meaning of course that the door did not open inward (Genesis 7:16 KJV), " . . . and the Lord shut him in," it was airtight except for the ZOHAR and the scuppers at the main deck. Before we discuss their purpose, and leave this thought of the door, let me explain that because this door was well above the main deck of the raft, and the top of the raft had a freeboard equal to its draft of 25.75 feet (15 cubits), there was no possibility for seawater to exert any force upon this door. The door was "in the side thereof," meaning the roof covering. This is the reason we don't hear of the door again, or of it being opened at the command of God to "go forth from the ark" (8:16).

The section of the roof containing the door that was sealed was now an integral part of the roof itself, and was removed with the covering.

The scuppers previously mentioned are alluded to in Utnapishtim's discourse in Tablet XI, column ii, line 63: "I struck water plugs into it." The water plugs were in place to restrict entry by small creatures that could get at the food supplies inside, or unwanted guests who might climb aboard after the door was closed.

The freeing ports were important for different phases of the trip. The ZOHAR presented such a large opening for the rain that during the initial period before lift-off, the hull pool became flooded before the vessel came afloat. This was desired as the main deck, now flooded, ballasted the vessel down, preventing the Ark from becoming lively on the ground in the rising water. From my salvage experience, I am impressed that Noah was aware of the proper procedure of removing a vessel from a strand in rough seas. This period of time also allowed for ballasting trim tanks. With the main deck awash, the plugs were removed, gushing water out the scuppers along the main deck at the sides. The vessel raised itself quickly from the landscape. Once the bottom of the hull pool was clear of the ground the water left on the main deck quickly fled to the drain and the Ark leaped free of the earth on its tethers.

With the decks free and the Ark rising, it was soon tugging on the lines holding it to the old world. When the lines were cut, the Ark was under way.

The Gilgamesh story, the earliest of which dates back to 2600 B.C.E., continues with the narrative of Noah: "I opened the bowl of ointment and applied it to my hands."

The Ark was completed. He had loaded into the boat:

> All I had of silver I loaded,
> all I had of gold I loaded,
> all I had of the seed of all living creatures I loaded;
> I made all my kin and family go into the boat.
> The animals of the fields, the beasts of the field,
> the children of all the craftsmen I drove aboard.
>
> XI, 80–86

"Shamash had set the time for me . . . enter the boat and close your gate . . . . To look at that day filled me with terror, I went into the Ark and closed the gate."

Noah was undoubtedly saddened by the fact that so few came with him. One man, apparently a dear friend and worker, would not listen to Noah's warning. He was Puzur-Amuru, the shipbuilder. To him he left his palace with all its goods. We can be assured his riches were short-lived.

It would appear by the rest of the text that the day and the time of Shamash had brought more than rain. Regardless of the skeptics, I will say I feel very deeply that it was a planetary catastrophe that befell the earth.

With the rain pouring in through the ZOHAR, the water on the main deck was diverted in sections to capture it for drinking water in the vaults below, which were now un- plugged to receive it. During the period of rain these were replenished, and as God had forewarned that the rain would last for forty days, these were undoubtedly topped off on the thirty-ninth day. Trim tanks were also replenished as the dwindling supplies were lightening the vessel. The action of the rain passing through the centerline of the Ark and diverted at points to wash down the cells on the upper decks made sanitation possible without the help of human labor. After the rain, in rough seas the scuppers would be opened to allow splash-in on the main deck, assisting in cleaning the residue from the cargo and washing it into the hull pool or drain. In rough weather the action of the sea in the hull pool made the fresh-air venting system work better. When the sea was more moderate, these scuppers would be closed.

Since wet dust doesn't fly, during the rain the air seemed to be clearer. Now that it had stopped, peering up from the main deck to the ZOHAR above, there always appeared to be something suspended in the suffused sunlight that bathed the Ark's innards on its trek eastward. With the gentle rolling of the Ark from sunrise through sunset we might expect that for the most part, the decks were subjected to enough sunlight for the crew to perform their duties.

Is it any wonder then that the same word used for the skylight of the Ark is the name of the commentary on the Kabbalistic level of interpretation based on the forty-nine laws?[15] For surely, the ZOHAR is "enlightenment from above"!

The earliest Sumerian accounts coincide with these thoughts:

> I set up incense vessels
> Seven by seven [49]
> On heaped up reeds
> And used cedarwood
> With incense . . . .

---

[15]There are actually forty-nine laws, but because several are run together and complement each other, they are generally referred to as the forty-two laws.

The above description of Noah's first sacrifice in the new world meets all the requirements for the materials used in the construction of the Ark.

NAVIGATIONAL AIDS

No outfitting of a vessel would be complete without onboard navigational systems. As discussed previously, a steering sweep oar may have been lowered through the hull pool of the raft, directing the Ark to its grounding point soon after cutting the drogue stones free of the Ark.

We saw how these stones, with their flat surface area against the water, created a drag, slowing the vessel's forward momentum in the following seas and effectively preventing the Ark from slipping sideways into a broaching situation. In calmer waters, the stones hung deep, reaching into the depths, sounding for the bottom, and warning of obstructions below.

But the Ark had more systems aboard to warn of impending danger. It had keen eyes scanning the waters close at hand, and a long-range radar system that could peer over the horizon and to landfalls beyond.

The first system mentioned in the Flood account worked at short range, giving an audio alarm and a bearing to the danger at hand.

It was the raven.

The King James account translates this bird as a raven, while the cuneiform texts give us the common crow, but no matter; the raven is considered a larger cousin in the crow family.

In the Genesis account, it is the raven that is first mentioned as going forth from the Ark. Prior to its release it was loose[16] inside, performing general cleanup operations after the cattle, while other species carefully scoured the animals clean of ticks and vermin. It is estimated that a single crow in a season can eat nineteen bushels of insects on an average-size farm. No doubt the raven was eating well aboard the Ark. Everyone

---

[16]The tso'har was for light and ventilation. A latticework arrangement confined birds within and possibly out of the upper portion altogether.

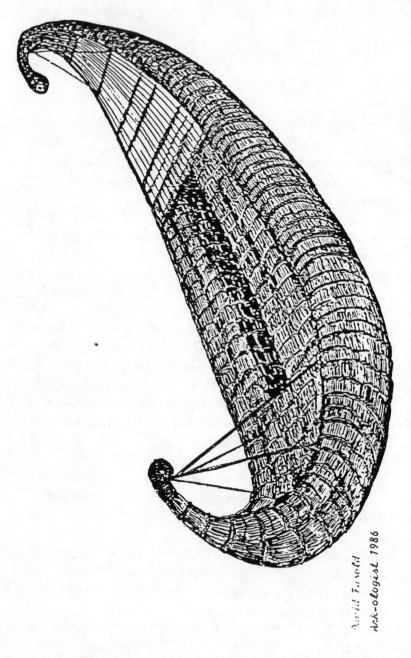

David Fasold
Ark-ologist 1986

The Ark was a composite structure. The support raft.

284

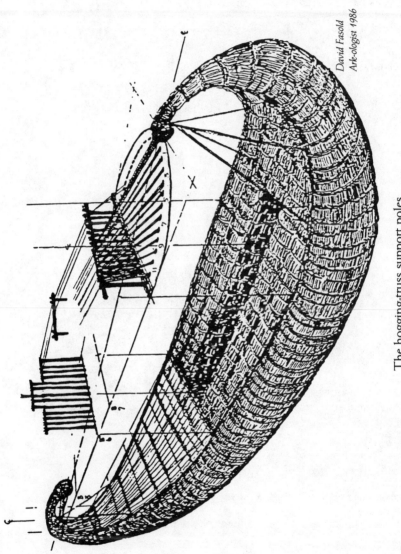

David Fasold
Ark-ologist 1986

The hogging-truss support poles.

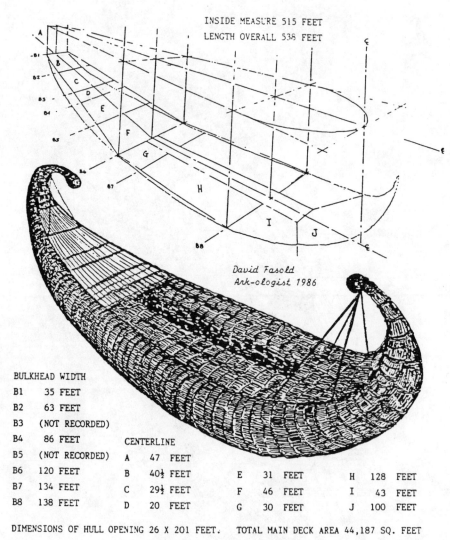

INSIDE MEASURE 515 FEET
LENGTH OVERALL 538 FEET

David Fasold
Ark-ologist 1986

BULKHEAD WIDTH								
B1	35 FEET							
B2	63 FEET							
B3	(NOT RECORDED)							
B4	86 FEET	CENTERLINE						
B5	(NOT RECORDED)	A	47 FEET					
B6	120 FEET	B	40½ FEET	E	31 FEET	H	128 FEET
B7	134 FEET	C	29½ FEET	F	46 FEET	I	43 FEET
B8	138 FEET	D	20 FEET	G	30 FEET	J	100 FEET

DIMENSIONS OF HULL OPENING 26 X 201 FEET.   TOTAL MAIN DECK AREA 44,187 SQ. FEET

Dimensions of the Ark.

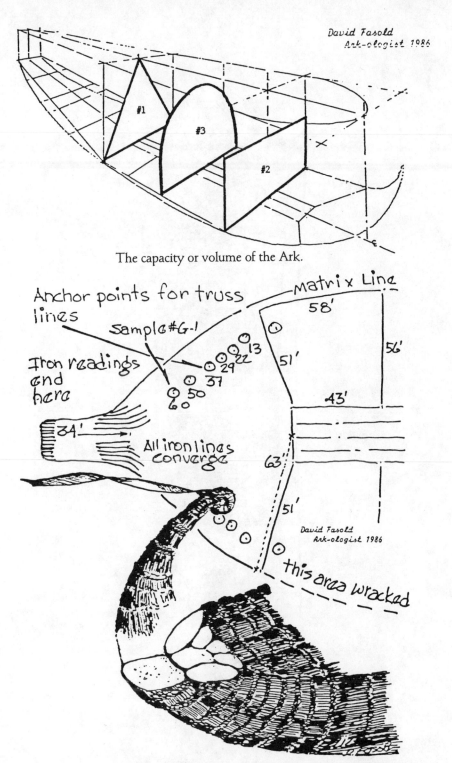

David Fasold
Ark-ologist 1986

#1

#3

#2

×

The capacity or volume of the Ark.

Anchor points for truss lines

Sample#G-1

Matrix Line

58'

56'

Iron readings and here

51'

13
22
29
37
50
60

43'

34'

All iron lines converge

63'

51'

David Fasold
Ark-ologist 1986

this area wracked

A cutaway view of the bow shows source of extension forward of the curve.

287

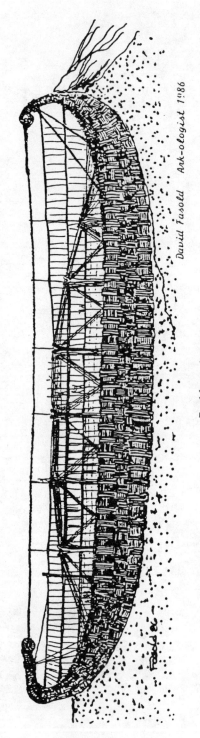

David Fasold   Ark-ologist 1:86

Building the Ark.

288

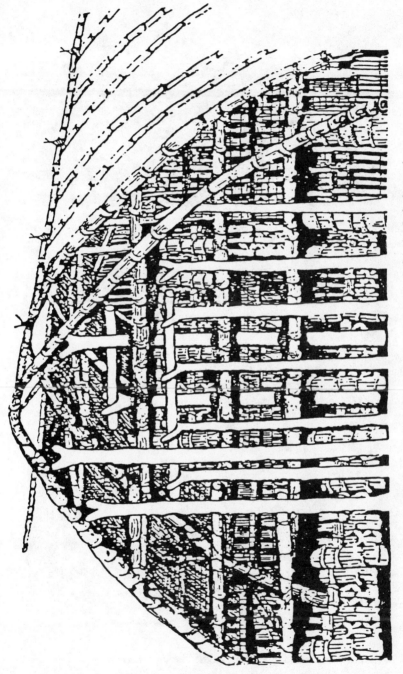

Inside the Ark. The hogging-truss framework for the 3 decks within.

The *tso'har* (ZOHAR). Past authorities translate this as "window," as the word relates to light.

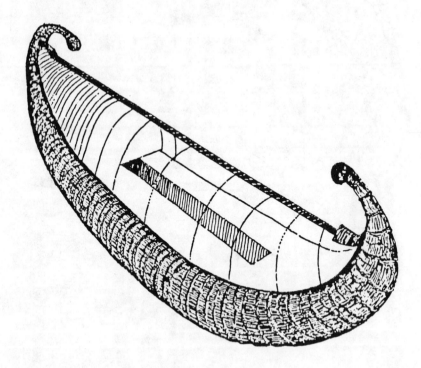

With total area of roof opening at 2,650 square feet, hull pool is 5300 square feet for overpressure of 2 to 1.

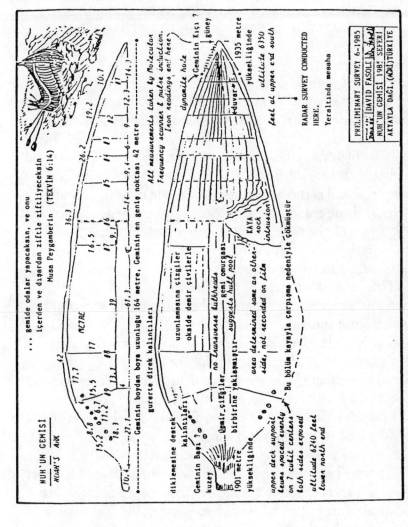

In late 1985 I prepared a 23-page report in Turkish for the concerned ministries of the Republic of Turkey.

performed his task, and there was much work to be done. But now that the rain had stopped, the raven had a new mission to perform:

> And it came to pass at the end of forty days, that Noah opened the window[17] of the ark which he had made: And he sent forth a raven, which went forth to and fro, until the waters were dried up from off the earth.
>
> Genesis 8:6, 7 KJV

As mentioned in chapter 2, with the commonly accepted chronological order of events found in today's authorized version, with the Ark at rest, the crow actually had no function to perform, and neither did the dove. As I expressed earlier, I feel the bird sequence correctly belongs in Genesis chapter 7 and is the correct relation to the original account by Moses. If the reader can consider my hypothesis correct, we are now enlightened as to the true mission of the raven, or crow, rather than wallow in the pitiful allegorical conclusions of biblical scholars of the past.

This "end of forty days" was the forty days of rain, and the window opening was slightly above the roofline facing forward. Since the Ark was being driven by wind and sea, this area was well protected and allowed Noah to scan the horizon with little effort almost a full 360 degrees. All the remarks about the situation at hand found in Genesis chapter 7 are direct observations by Noah from this vantage point.[18]

I perceive the Ark's draft and freeboard to be equal for a perfect GM of stability and trim, 15 cubits to the main deck (25.75 feet) and the height above the main deck to the roofline 77.25 feet. Thus the height of eye above the surface at 103 feet gives Noah a distance to the horizon of 15.5 miles (13.4 nautical), encompassing within his range of vision an area of 188.7 square statute miles of ocean surface. A lot of water, and

---

[17]I have shown the position of this window that was opened after the forty days of rain in the illustration referring to the *tso'har*. It is in the after portion of the roof, below the overhanging stern.

[18]Otherwise, how could he have known this if the window was not opened until after the Ark had come to rest, in chapter 8?

in my merchant marine days we used to add, "And just the top of it!"

The factual account by actual observation given in Genesis 7 is now in line with the Babylonian text, much earlier than Moses':

> The storm was over and the rain of destruction had ceased. I looked forth. I called aloud over the waters . . . . The sunlight suffused[19] my countenance. I was dazzled and sank down weeping, and the tears streamed over my face. EVERYWHERE I LOOKED I SAW WATER!

The going forth "to and fro" is the clue to the mission of the crow and why he was released first. Pompous preachers delight in drivel about the crow's thieving nature, alluding to its color in connection with all sorts of nonsensical symbolism, suggesting he failed in his duties and was replaced by the dove.

Nothing could be further from the truth. The crow is a clever and fearless bird. To go "to and fro" was his function and duty. Should his keen eye detect something close at hand, be it flotsam of interest one finds at sea where land is just over the horizon or something posing a danger to navigation, the observer standing watch at the window hearing the crow's shrill cry at lift-off from the roof of the Ark could direct his attention to the bearing of the straight course "as the crow flies" toward his objective. The crow did not return to Noah *into* the Ark, for *the crow was the Ark's keen-eyed lookout.*

The poor crow. I often think of him standing in the bows, maligned by scholars who never went to sea. He never came back inside. Never left his post. No doubt he was even fed on the job, the watch stander scattering grain upon the soft tarred roof and the crow eating his daily ration with a watchful eye to the sea.

A *Farmer's Bulletin* suggests coating seed grain with coal tar as crows will pass by a field of corn sprouts because of their inherent dislike of the flavor. I wonder if the U.S. Department of Agriculture has a clue as to why!

---

[19]Possibly another indicator of the Ark's direction of travel. The window of the Ark's conning point would obviously face ahead, protected from the weather. The early sun dazzled him. The Ark was heading east.

But the dove is a different story. Everyone admires the dove. Of the more than 650 species of the common European rock pigeon, we always have symbolized before us the pure white dove, a picture of goodness and peace with the olive branch in her beak. Indeed her return was a celebrated event, but her importance no more than her friend and fellow traveler. Together they accomplished their missions for the benefit of all aboard the Ark.

Not wanting to destroy our illusions, the Sumerian account suggests a swallow. The Akkadian agrees with the Hebrew, but the favorite among the ancients was the tough little "homer" capable of speeds almost twice that of the crow, for which a distance of two hundred miles is considered a short race.

Records show they were used by the ancient Egyptians and the Persians in carrying messages. In Greece they carried the news of the Olympic Game victories to the different cities, and the Romans used them for military purposes as the Europeans were still doing in the Franco-Prussian War.

The pigeon was Noah's long-range radar. The Ark was under way and making way. What lay ahead? The pigeon's duty then was to fly straight ahead of the Ark, on the wind current, not to the side or astern but ahead, to the new lands and the new earth and the new age of man.

Noah would carefully time her flight. Should the dove return in two hours with mud on her feet, it would indicate there was land some fifty miles ahead, or thirty-five miles over the horizon. We can actually determine the Ark's speed of drift by the time intervals between the sending out of the dove. In both cases it was a period of seven days. This indicates Noah considered his rate of drift constant. We can also surmise the following: If the pigeon's flight time was four hours, and she returned with clean feet, indicating there had been no point of touchdown, the distance traveled ahead of the Ark had been fifteen miles to the horizon plus another eighty-five miles. At a speed of fifty miles per hour, the round trip was two hundred miles. If Noah waited seven days before her next flight, that would account for a drift rate of little more than fourteen miles a day before Noah calculated he was over the spot where the dove had been seven days prior to her turnaround point.[20]

I found this quite surprising. I had assumed the Ark's geographical movement to have been greater. This indicates the pool system and the drogues were really working, or the seas were not that bad after all. Possibly the violence of the event was limited for the most part to the first forty days. Should the seas have been faster, I could envision Noah sending forth the dove more often.

At any rate, we can appreciate Noah's apprehension when the dove overstayed her flight time on that second release. I imagine him restlessly pacing the deck, the fifth hour becoming the eighth, the bird long overdue. I can see him mumbling to himself and the crow, "Don't look at me, Mr. Raven, watch for the pigeon," and the joy of seeing it in the failing light of day, high in the eastern sky, her wings beating rapid and strong from her hours of rest upon the new earth, as the crow lifted off to greet her return:

> The dove came in to him in the evening; and, lo, in her mouth was an olive leaf pluckt off: so Noah knew that the waters were abated from off the earth.
>
> Genesis 8:11 KJV

The lamplight was scant within the Ark and the phosphorescence of the churning waters within the hull pool cast a glow upon the face of the patriarch. Nets were being drawn up through the opening from the sea full of fish which by day had rested under the shade of the raft. Now the light from within attracted a species that actually burst through the surface and landed upon the deck inside, where they were gathered up in abundance to supplement the animals' rations.

The gentle heaving of the raft in the motion of the sea caused the water within the confines of the pool to raise an incompressible piston of water, expelling the stale air through the *tso'har* above where Noah now directed his eyes.

The stars in the heavens shone brightly down through the roof as the Ark was lifted from the trough and crested the

---

[20]Since the raven's duties were during the daylight hours only and the distance to the horizon from the height of eye at 103 feet is 15 miles, the Ark covered only 7 miles during the period of darkness, allowing a safe period of rest.

wave. The crisp night air felt cool against his face as it was drawn within by the falling water of the pool. The Ark breathed in its design as if alive. It *was* alive, and so were they. The Ark had passed safely through death and destruction. Those within the Ark had been saved by the covering and had passed through the judgment unharmed.

The patriarch twirled the olive stem gently between his fingers. God had remembered him and every living thing that was with him in the Ark.

THE TRACK OF THE ARK

We can see by the seven days that elapsed between the sending forth of the dove from the Ark on repeated occasions the suggestion of a drift rate of fourteen miles per twenty-four-hour day, or a speed of just over half a mile an hour over the bottom. This indeed seems quite slow for the Ark, but using the pigeon's flight more often than this appears to have been unnecessary.

From the narrative which relates that the Flood occurred on the patriarch's seventeenth day, second month of his six hundred years to the seventh month, seventeenth day, when the Ark came to a halt on her drogue stones, a period of 150 days has elapsed. In Genesis 7:17 and 18, a mariner will find a subtle difference between these similar verses. The text looks repetitive but it is not being redundant. Verse 17 states the Ark was lifted above the earth by the waters, but it may have remained tethered to the landscape. How much time elapsed before Noah deemed it safe to get under way is not made clear, but eventually the water's height was sufficient for the Ark's tether or cable made fast to the earth to be chopped loose: "And Uragal parted the anchor cable" (Babylonian text). Verse 18 then tells us the Ark is under way for, " . . . the ark went upon the face of the waters."

If we conclude this occurred within a short period of time, and the Ark's drift speed remained constant throughout the entire period of 150 days, the overall voyage covered a distance of 2010 nautical miles (13.4 × 150 days).

We can clearly see that the Ark entered the landing site area from the west. We could assume that it made a curved track from Shurippak some 550 miles to the south by east, but that needn't have been the case.

Some texts consider this the lift-off site, such as the Weld Prism of Nur-Ninsubur (Larsa, 2170 B.C.E.), and home of their Flood hero, Zinsuddu. The Sîn-leqi-unninnî version (composed in the Middle Babylonian Period 1600–1000 B.C.E.) says the same of its Utnapishtim. The account of Berosus states Xisouthros was to bury all writings at Sippar and according to the poem of Erra, this city was not completely destroyed by the Flood. The name *Sippar* means "The Sun City," but there are other place names that mean close to the same, as for instance Beth-Shemesh and the Egyptian On or Annu. We needn't take for granted that the lift-off site of the Ark is even still above water after the tectonic upheaval after the Flood.

If we consider it implausible that the anchor stone brought to Ankara could be a trophy of war with the Egyptians, and instead consider it identified with the other drogue stones of the Ark further to the east on approximately the same latitude, then we might extend this track line to the west for the distance made in the 150 days. This would bring us to a point near the islands of Baleares (Palma, Spain), just below Barcelona. Needless to say, even these portions of land may not have been part of the antediluvian landscape.

I feel it safe to consider that during the Deluge Period of the Flood (the forty days of rain) the Ark may have been making better speed.

Our figures were based on the dove's flight of four hours. I am not an expert on carrier or racing pigeons, much less the abilities of antediluvian species of doves, but if a sustained flight of twelve hours (sunrise to sunset) is possible, then we might revise our figures of the Ark's speed to 1.78 knots and a distance covered in 150 to almost 6,500 miles. This could have put the Ark's departure point in the mid-Atlantic or beyond.

There is an interesting story concerning the Azores that has haunted historians since the islands were discovered by the Portuguese. They found them devoid of inhabitants, yet there were signs someone had been there before them. On the island of Corvo, the Portuguese found a statue *facing westward* and *pointing across the sea.* While being taken down for shipment to the king of Portugal, the statue was either broken or disassembled for transportation. Records show that the pieces eventually reached the mainland, but apparently they were never reassembled and subsequently were lost.

Charles Berlitz,[21] grandson of Maximillian Berlitz, founder of the Berlitz language schools, is an archival researcher, historian, and author who speaks twenty-five languages and is considered one of the fifteen best-known linguists in the world. While researching in Portugal, he was quite startled to find the statue being referred to as *Caté* or *Catés!* For in the language of Quechua, the tongue of the Inca Empire of South America, *Catí* means "THAT WAY"!

The Portuguese have long considered that *Atlantida* existed west of their shores.

The Iberian peoples of southern Spain considered it the Canary Islands, farther to the south, west of Africa. To their recollection, this had been *Atalaya,* or a portion of that long-lost civilization.

Considering Velikovsky's observation, that should a pole shift have occurred due to the earth's rotation, waves of translation would have moved eastward because of inertia and *poleward* because of the recession of the waters from the equatorial bulge where they are held by the rotation of the earth. This would allow for a curved track from the Ark site leading back across the Mediterranean and the Atlas Mountains of

---

[21]Charles Berlitz, *Atlantis, the Eighth Continent* (New York: Fawcett Crest, 1984).

present-day Morocco to a point near the Cape Verde Plateau. If this line were continued, it would cross Brazil to Bolivia, and if the breakup of landmass occurred at the time of the Flood, the distance between these points may not have been as great as it is today.

Quite frankly, I must admit that in the past I was hampered by viewing the Flood story soley from a biblical standpoint and it was only relatively recently that I came to investigate the subject from the texts of Sumer and Babylon. In the course of my maritime career and interest in the Ark, I became aware that some oceanographers viewed anyone considering the existence of Atlantis under the sea or elsewhere with amusement, and showed considerable intolerance of my interest in the Flood story as well.

I had never thought of Noah's voyage as the "escape from Atlantis" because I had never read any works on the subject until after the Ark was discovered. Rather than finding these authors "on the fringe," I was quite surprised to find among them congressmen and world-renowned linguists and philologists, all serious researchers whose works achieved remarkable breadth and depth of scholarship.

I am now forced to reconsider my previous biased opinion and see the future full of surprises, yet no more so than did Heracleitus, 500 B.C.E., who came to realize that "because it is sometimes so unbelievable, the truth escapes becoming known."

IN SEARCH OF A PRE-FLOOD CITY

The Gateway to the Sun stands as one solid megalithic structure on the Bolivian Altiplano in the ruins of a dead city built before the Flood. It is called pre-Columbian today. There are serious questions concerning its origin, and some bold explorers have suggested it is pre-Inca, but few have gone so far as to say it is pre-Flood.

It stands desolate in a region that could never have supported its population on a plain between the western and eastern Cordilleras, south of Lake Titicaca.

Here in the Andes at latitude 16°33' south is an enigma that defies explanation. The city is at an elevation of 12,500 feet, where stone terraces rise up 2,500 feet above the city and in some places higher still under the eternal snow line of 18,400 feet on the slopes of Mount Illimani, second highest mountain in the Western hemisphere (22,578 feet).

And here is the paradox the academic community would have us believe. According to man's oldest written records, impressed on clay tablets recovered by eminent archaeologists and on view for all the world to see in the British Museum and at the University of Pennsylvania Museum, there was a cataclysmic event, unparalleled in the history of man, that resulted in a flood and the almost total extinction of mankind.

Using the technique of inverted population doublings, it can be proven mathematically that mankind could not reach the present population figures in less than fifty-three hundred years. This places the Flood close to 3300 B.C.E., and the beginning of this "fourth age" according to Mayan dates, 3313 B.C.E.

Thus, without this event that nearly destroyed the world, mankind today would be literally standing shoulder to shoulder on top of graveyards, should we believe man has existed for four hundred thousand years. This worldwide remembrance of the Flood found in almost every culture is a myth, according to these pompous scholars, and any thought to the contrary by amateurs with anthropological interests are trespassing in specialized fields.

I am referring here to an enlightening meeting with editors and archaeologists of the National Geographic Society. According to them, regardless of any evidence to the contrary, there can be no ship at 6,300 feet on the slopes of a mountain in eastern Turkey, but we are to believe that pre-Columbians were growing maize in South America under the snow at 18,400 feet, 1,400 feet higher than the very peak of Ararat.

If the view held by modern geologists today is that mountain building is a slow process that can only be noticeable in minute changes requiring hundreds and thousands of years, then the city of Tiahuanaco is over a million years old!

Sir Clemen Markham posed these questions to the scholarly world in 1910 when he challenged the president of the Royal Geographical Society, Leonard Darwin, that the city could have been built at such an elevation. Darwin surmised the only possibility was that perhaps the mountain had risen since the city was built, assuming the Andes were some two to three thousand feet lower at one time. This hardly solves the complexities of the problem.

Velikovsky points out that analysis of Lake Titicaca and other lakes on the plateau suggest they were once at sea level, having salt beds and chemical compositions similar to those of the ocean far below. Alexander Agassiz was surprised to find the existence of ocean crustaceous fauna at the bottom of Titicaca as early as 1875 and reported his unusual findings in proceedings of the American Academy of Arts and Sciences the following year.

The most astounding revelation was yet to come. Excavations suggested that the inhabitants of the city had *drowned!* Lyell, in *Principles of Geology,* was quick to combat this mounting evidence by offering a theory that perhaps a large lake on the Altiplano had burst its barrier and the cascading waters caused the aborigines to create the myth of the universal Flood.

Carrying this pitiful theory and biased opinion by one of the gods of evolutionary thought one step further, we might assume these aborigines were swept by the lake's floodwaters across the world to Mesopotamia and relayed the event to the Sumerians, who then dutifully recorded it!

This is why today one finds beautifully illustrated coffee table publications like *Mysteries of the Ancient Americas* explaining to people with *Reader's Digest* mentalities that Tiahuanaco is a puzzling relic of the past. Just what is so puzzling is not discussed.[22]

Tiahuanaco has been thrust up an incredible 12,500 feet.

The most profound studies of the ruins can be found in four volumes of *Tihuanacu*,[23] *the Cradle of American Man* by Professor Arthur Posnansky (1874–1946), chief archaeologist for Bolivian antiquities at La Paz, and published by the Ministerio de Educacion.

At an elevation where exertion would cause nausea or

---

[22]Published by Reader's Digest Association, Inc., New York, 1986, p. 229.

[23]Variously spelled *aca, acu,* or *aco,* the Bolivian government's official spelling is now Tihanaku.

altitude sickness in the rarefied air and heart attacks in the oxygen-poor eight pounds per square inch atmosphere lay a metropolis constructed of stone blocks weighing one hundred to two hundred tons each that have been transported distances from thirty to ninety miles.

The companions of Pizarro were stunned. Cieca de Leon records gateways hewn from solid stone thirty feet long and fifteen feet high and pivoting.

These are great edifices with doors, windows, posts, sills, and thresholds all hewn from solid stone. At Cuelap, to the north, are more remarkable ruins of a wall of interlocking blocks running 3,600 feet long, 560 feet broad, and 150 feet high, the summit of which supported the second structure 600 by 500 feet and equal in height. Inside, the rooms and cells had been used as tombs by the Incas. There was an aqueduct system that ran for 450 miles and roads of pulverized stone mixed with lime and bituminous cement.

Did the Asian migrants who crossed the land bridge build this city? The archaeologists today would have us believe the Incas did, yet in the time of the conquistadors, the natives clearly intimated they had not, stating that no man's eyes had ever seen the city when it did not lay in ruins. It was, they said, "built in the dark time of man's history," and they had merely built upon it and used what they had found. Certainly the faces portrayed on the megaliths and statues of the dead city were not Asian or Inca but portrayed with long faces and beards.

Thus with Pizzaro's meager force of 168 men, the Incas surrendered to the return of Viracocha's people, returning to reclaim their ancient city from the past.

A dead city and a drowned people. While the Incas buried their dead in the remains of palaces, the original inhabitants, along with their animals and debris of daily life, lay buried in gullies that had become mass graves. They rested there, covered by the silt of the waters that had swept them away. Tiahuanaco did not come to an end by disease or war but by the cataclysmic event of the Flood that inundated the entire civilization which lay submerged for months until upthrust by tectonic upheaval in a new oblation of the equatorial zone.

Here is the proof that this is the remains of a city from

another time. The calendar of Tiahuanaco shows a startling parallel to my observation that the Genesis Flood account suggests a shorter year. According to Bellamy's exhaustive investigations on the "time measuring system of the oldest civilization in the world,"[24] the petroglyphs record an orbiting satellite, the distance of which was 5.9 terrestrial radii from the earth, that made 447 revolutions around the earth in a year comprised of only 290 days! A later calendric base on the Great Idol of Tiahuanaco shows this increased to 449 revolutions in a year of 291.2 days, and apparently the people living in that age were becoming quite concerned about it! Most assuredly these startling records do not belong to anything from our era but from a time before the Flood.

How could a drowned city exist at an elevation of 12,500 feet? The Bible gives the simple answer in the Book of Psalms.

WHERE HAVE ALL THE FLOODWATERS GONE?

The Psalms are believed to have been written circa 1000 B.C.E., and a clue to the ancients' understanding of the events occurring during the Flood are to be found in chapter 104, verses 5–9 KJV:

> Who laid the foundations of the earth, that it should not be removed for ever. Thou coveredst it with the deep as with a garment: the waters stood above the mountains. At thy rebuke they fled; at the voice of thy thunder they hastened away. They go up by the mountains; they go down by the valleys unto the place which thou hast founded for them. Thou hast set a bound that they may not pass over; that they turn not again to cover the earth.

It should first be mentioned that in my youth, I longed for a translation in modern-day English to get away from the language of Shakespeare and went for the newer paraphrased versions. To my dismay, I found them pitifully rendered into having David describe that water ran downhill. David's state-

---

[24]Hans Schindler Bellamy, *The Calendar of Tiahuanaco* (London: Faber & Faber Ltd., 1956).

ments are more profound than the revisionists give him credit for.

It is clear that the above statement refers to the Flood of Noah: "that they turn not again to cover the earth." Should David be referring instead to the time in Genesis 1, then it is most certainly false, as the waters did cover the earth *again,* during the Flood.

David is no doubt referring to God's promise or covenant that "neither shall there any more be a flood to destroy the earth" (Genesis 9:11 KJV).

The first statement concerning the foundations of the earth has long been a puzzle to readers, as well as a similar reference in the Book of Job (ca. 1660 B.C.E.), where in chapter 38, verses 2–4 (KJV), we read of the Lord's interrogation of Job:

> Who is this that darkeneth counsel by words without knowledge? Gird up now thy loins like a man; for I will demand of thee, and answer thou me. Where wast thou when I laid the foundations of the earth? declare, if thou hast understanding.

The world learned of these "foundations of the earth" fairly recently when new measurements of satellite orbits showed that the earth was not as previously thought. There appeared to be a foundation to the earth which consisted of four corners—a tetrahedron! The pointy corners are not very pronounced. It is still true that the earth is roughly spherical, but there are four bumps protruding from the surface, each several thousands of square miles in area, distributed like the corners of a tetrahedron as a foundation shape within the earth itself.

They are 220 feet higher than if the earth were a perfect sphere; on the other hand, the low areas in between are 253 feet lower than they should be. The top of the pyramid is Ireland, and the three corners of the base are north of New Guinea, south of Africa, and west of Peru.

This produces a rough pear-shaped effect, and the equator turns out to be egg shaped. The measurements were made by scientists at the Johns Hopkins Applied Physics Laboratory in Silver Spring, Md., under a navy grant. Thus, terms such as the *four corners of the earth* and *its foundations,* used by the ancients, were verified in 1968. That the earth was ever considered by

ancient astronomers of Egypt, Babylon, China, or even Tiahuanaco as anything other than roughly spherical with flat-
tened poles is not even scholarly debate. In fact, the Church
throughout the Middle Ages was largely responsible for this
flat-earth concept.

The next reference King David makes to the Flood of Noah
and the earth is when he writes that God "coveredst it with the
deep." The *it* of course is the earth, and "the waters stood
above the mountains."

This does not mean the waters attained such a height that
Mount Everest was covered by the floodwaters, but since the
peak of Mount Everest is covered with diatomaceous earth as
well as bones of fish and shells of clams and snails under the
snow, it means only that the seafloor has been raised up into a
mountain peak. Lake Van at 5,400 feet above sea level, containing a species of North Atlantic herring, and Lake Urmia
(Rezaiye), at 4,022 feet, are bitter seas. These are southwest
and south respectively from the site of the Ark's elevation of
6,350 feet. North, in Soviet Armenia, is Gökçe gölü at 6,233
feet, while to the east is the great Caspian Sea, at minus 91 feet.

It is undeniable that geological terms for the layering of
strata assume these were formed horizontally. Such descriptions as beds, crusts, and sedimentary layers all refer to this
when at perhaps 3.7 to 4 billion years ago the young earth
cooled and water vapor condensed and remained in its liquid
form on the planet's surface. When uneven cooling and con-
tractions of the earth's surface caused depressions, the water
gathered to these places, exposing the dry land. Thus the
questions as to where the floodwaters came from will only
trouble those who hold extreme views as to the fixity of
oceans and continental levels.

The water always was here, that is to say, within our
atmosphere, and the forty-day rain should be considered only
a drop in the bucket. It is generally agreed by scientists that
should the surface of the earth be flat, the water would stand
over 7,900 feet or one and a half miles deep.

All that would be required for a flood of major proportions
is tectonic upheavals, a lowering and raising of the earth's crust
during some short period of time, creating new ocean basins
and elevating portions of old ocean bottoms above the surface,

trapping inland seas in depressions. Mountain ranges would be formed through overthrusts and subduction of plates and folds in the strata where the plates met in compression.

In the first chapter of Genesis we see that even after the division of the waters into that which was on the earth and that which was above, or in the atmosphere, the dry land still had not appeared. The release of this water from the "windows of heaven," then, is not what inundated the land to the point that it was covered. The dry land did not appear until after the gathering together of the waters onto one place (Genesis 1:9).

Many people see the phrase "unto one place" and consider that there was one ocean or sea. Isolated from this was one landmass projecting above the surface of the water. This single landmass has been called by various names and is believed to have broken up either before or after the Flood. This could be the case but doesn't have to be so, as the word *seas* is in the plural form. The term *one place* could logically be assumed to be an *elevation*. In other words, anything above this place or above sea level, the water will eventually tend to seek its own level or place and gather together unto itself. That is why I feel the term *waters* is also stated in the plural in verse ten. All waters above sea level tend to run down to where they gather together.

The next thing we must clear up in our thinking is that the Ark landed at 6,350 feet. The Ark did not land at that elevation! The boat went aground in 25.75 feet of water (the 15 cubits draft). Since elevation is determined by sea level, the whole concept of elevations and how high the water reached during the time of the Flood is moot. It is all relative. It could be that toward the end of the Flood the entire Anatolian plateau raised up. This is what is so nonsensical about the Ark on Ararat Only group. Anyone making a study of the drainage patterns around the rather recent volcanic cone of Ararat is struck by the absence of scours and the ancient courses from the watershed already established, as if Ararat is a late arriver on the scene.

What made the waters return from off the earth? (Genesis 8:3). If the earth's rotation was halted or if the surface of the earth already had been slowed to such an extent by the surface friction of the water in enormous tidal bulges, and the magma under the plates continued at a different rate of speed, upheavals would result. When the earth continued the roll, or shifted its axis position, the surface would experience a tremendous velocity of wind: "God made a wind to pass over the earth, and the waters assuaged" (Genesis 8:1).

The newly positioned equatorial zone would now tend to become oblate by centrifugal force of the liguid magma under the crust, at the same time creating a void under the poles that would collapse. One can imagine the sound of tectonic plates grinding and overriding, building the topography of the cleansed new world. Considering that sound travels through water at a greater speed than air, the thundering must have been heard through the hull of the Ark as voids were created for the new ocean basins, and the new mountain chains were thrust to the surface. Noah does not record seeing this in his circular sphere of observation but knew at this date in his life aboard the Ark it was the turning point or topping of the waters of the Flood. He refers only to the wind. Then the waters began to subside.

King David continues to describe the Flood:

> At thy rebuke they [the waters] fled; at the *voice of thy thunder* they hastened away.
>
> Psalms 104:7 KJV

As the mountains thrust to the surface, displacing the waters, and the new ocean basins were formed by equal depressions elsewhere on the earth, the waters gathered together "unto the place which thou hast founded for them."

New coastlines and land barriers were formed, limiting their extent:

> Thou hast set a bound that they may not pass over; that they turn not again to cover the earth.
>
> Psalms 104:9 KJV

The people of that "age that was" perished in the Flood. Tiahuanaco, built at sea level, was inundated and its inhabitants drowned. The "heavens that were of old," mentioned by Peter, stand as mute testimony to "the age that passed away" upon their stone calendars high on the Altiplano of Bolivia to this day. There is no need to probe the depths of the oceans for Plato's lost civilization, for here the remnants of Cainite civilization were thrust to a higher elevation after the Flood by the westward movement of the Andean plate meeting the Pacific plate, causing a fold.

Charles Darwin, in his travels to South America in 1834–35, found the former surf line of the raised beaches at Valparaiso, Chile, now at thirteen hundred feet. He was more impressed that seashells at this altitude were not even decayed, a clear indication of a recent upthrust.

Immanuel Velikovsky relates that at present it is the common view the Andes were created not so much by compression of the strata as by magma, or molten rock, invading the strata and lifting them. The Andes abound in exceedingly high and enormous volcanoes.

Darwin recorded in his Journal of Researches,[25] while high in the Andes looking down on the plain of Argentina, that it required little geological practice to see that the shores of the Atlantic had been driven back some seven hundred miles and at some time in the past the bed of the ocean had risen and formed a chain of mountains more than seven thousand feet high! He would have been surprised to find how extremely young the Cordillera of the Andes are!

After the Flood, the migrants came in search of the drowned civilization. It appears that many made the crossings. Apparently Uru-pa and the peoples of Amayra and Ur (or perhaps Ur-uk) made it in great Ma-Gurs of reeds. Here they met the Asians who had crossed the natural bridge, assimilated, and stayed, bringing the story of the Flood and the survivors with them to the new world.

Some never made it across the Atlantic. Others were lost on the coast, and if we are to believe the anthropologists who tell us that of the twenty-two hundred Indian languages found in the Americas, some never made it through the jungles of the Mato Grosso, for it is here we find, according to those who have made a life's study of linguistics in the new world, the oldest root language of all. The Nambicuaras of the southern

---

[25]Voyages of the HMS *Beagle*. March 30, 1835, entry.

Mato Grosso may have one of the oldest surviving tongues of any native group in the hemisphere, suggesting that their ancestors were among the earliest arrivals in the Americas.[26]

It seems strange to find the earliest arrivers here so close to the belt that runs across the continent from the modern-day city of Recife on the Atlantic coast, the closest point of land to Africa and the Pillars of Hercules, through the Mato Grosso toward the last vestiges of the past world and the ruins of Tiahuanaco. Strange, too, that the Tupians who live along the coast possess a "grandfather cult" that led various members of their group to make continuous protracted migrations in search of a happier existence in another country, the land of their grandfathers.[27] It is not clear from the information collected if this land extended westward toward the pre-Flood cities or if they had given up, perhaps afraid to continue past the sixteen-hundred-mile venture into the Mato Grosso and yearned to return to Mesopotamia. The anthropologists call this a search for a mythical country!

Was this the mythical country that caused the naming of Brazil? Charles Berlitz[28] points out that legends in western Europe before the discovery of America told of a land across the unexplored Atlantic where iron was in common use and abundance. When this land was actually discovered, it was only natural that the legendary name *Brazil* be given to it.

Berlitz recognized the root consonants B-R-Z-L meant *iron* in both Hebrew and Aramaic (bar-zel). Centuries later it became evident that Brazil possessed the largest iron ore deposits in the world.

Recent discoveries on the west shore of Lake Titicaca show that at some time in the far past the ancients worked magnificent iron mines at Ancoriames. Notice that the Bolivian anthropologists were rather careful to not suggest these mining operations were carried on by the Incas but by the "ancients." Were these operations then carried out before the

---

[26]Alvin M. Josephy, Jr., *Indian Heritage of America* (New York: Alfred A. Knopf, Inc., 1974), p. 276.

[27]Ibid., p. 264.

[28]Berlitz, *Atlantis.*

Inca civilization came into being, perhaps by those early voyagers to the new world, or should we now say those returning to the land of their grandfathers?

The question arises, were they worked before the Flood? Tubal-cain was a Cainite. Were they alone the traders in this commodity and would Noah have been required to form an alliance through marriage with Naamah, Tubal-cain's sister, to procure the abundance of iron found within the Ark's structure?

I noted in a previous chapter that the line of Cain continues after the Flood according to the traditions of the Phoenicians. We have also seen the words *Bal* and *Balim* mysteriously appearing in the Mayan language. We know that Phoenician merchants sailed great vessels across the Mediterranean through the Strait of Gibraltar and up the western coast of Europe, trading in metals and specifically in Cornwall tin.

Harvard University Department of Archaeology has found five locations within the continental United States where early merchants had colonies among the Indians at least twenty-five hundred years ago. Michigan's Upper Peninsula prehistoric mining (copper) civilization is considered by the Smithsonian Institution one of the important unsolved problems in North American archaeology. A professor of metallurgical engineering at Michigan Tech stated that material found in the prehistoric mining pits dated back to two thousand years B.C.[29] The University of Chicago dated copper implements found at Oconto, Wisconsin, as over five thousand years old, most probably originating from Michigan's Isle Royale pits.

Could these early voyagers have been the Mediterranean Phoenicians? I believe the Phoenicians were only the descendants of the ancient voyagers suggested by Thor Heyerdahl.[30]

Heyerdahl correctly suggests these ancients sailed their great ships of reeds out of the Persian Gulf, around Africa, and beyond to become castaways on the South American coasts, assimilating with the Asian stock who arrived there via the land bridge. The tribes are still called the Aymara and Uru Indians by the city-states of Mesopotamia that sent them off.

---

[29]Dr. R. W. Drier, December 13, 1953.

[30]T. Heyerdahl, *The Tigris Expedition* (New York: Doubleday & Co., 1981).

It may have been Uru-pa, the brother of Yima, from the Persian legends, who led the first voyage of discovery.

Herodotus (484–425 B.C.E.) states that these ancient voyagers, "who formerly dwelt on the shores of the Erythaean Sea," (Persian Gulf and Indian Ocean), were the forefathers of the Mediterranean Phoenicians who, "having migrated to the Mediterranean, settled in these parts which they now inhabit, and began at once, they say, to adventure on long voyages."

The Phoenician traders had far-flung colonies well beyond the Pillars of Hercules (Gibraltar), and we are not apt to find a record of them. These were "trade secrets," and their routes and destinations were guarded jealously. It would appear they traded with the Indians of the east coast of the Americas or at least had explored the coastal regions known today as Rhode Island and Maine. In time, the extent of these "long voyages" mentioned by Herodotus will be accepted, but for now the great maritime feats of the ancients are overshadowed by the more recent and accredited (re)discovery of the new (?) lands by Columbus.

11

The Ark Revealed at Last

THE RADAR IMAGE

There was a quiet knock at the door. "Let's hit it, pilgrim," Ron said in a hushed tone from the hallway.

"Right, be out in a flash," I replied happily. This was to be the day we had waited for, the culmination of all our attempts to get the graphic proof that the Ark was inside the mound itself. I had been awake for hours going over our decision of the night before.

"Look," Ron said, "the Turks told me in Washington that they were not issuing any permits this year for the site. It's strictly off limits to foreigners. But because our permit from last year was curtailed due to martial law, it is being reinstated for the remaining twenty days. They wouldn't have informed us of this if they didn't want us to do the scan and give them the results." He paused briefly. "At least someone over here does," he said. "Then in Ankara, you were with me when I confirmed the permit was waiting for us in Ağrı, right?"

"Right!" I answered.

"And again when we arrived in Erzurum at the hotel, Baki-bey had called ahead to the police chief in Ağrı, and again it was confirmed that the permit was all in order for us to make the survey."

"Yes, but when we arrived there was a rider pasted to the back of the permit that said NO ELECTRONICS," I interjected.

"Yeah, I know," said Ron, moving on quickly to his plan. "We can only take the Turks at their word. They wouldn't have made us come this far to change their minds. The police said they'd straighten it out with a call to Ankara. The min-

312

istry cannot authorize people to make a subsurface radar scan and not consider that electronics. We have to give them that much credit, don't you think?

"Now," his hands clapping together in self-agreement, "in anticipation of just taking the Turks at their word, and it *is good,* you know, we just move out early and test the equipment on the site in their best interest, and at our expense, to see if we'll be able to perform as expected when the okay arrives in the afternoon."

"Yes," I answered. "How do we know the dielectric constant of the subsurface material is even conducive to penetration? It might be saturated with water. Maybe the graphic recorder didn't even survive the trip. We really ought to check it out on the site first to see if it even works, before we put them to a lot of trouble."

"That's just what I was thinking!" grinned Ron approvingly. The rider was probably left over from 1985 when martial law was in effect. You can't have a valid radar scan permit saying no electronics!

"Merhaba," said Dilaver sleepily as he passed through the door to take the two transit cases down to the taxi.

"Hello, Dilaver. This one stays," I said, laying my hand on the large 300 MHz antenna. We wouldn't be needing that, I thought, until we really started punching down to locate the bottom of the Ark. There would be plenty to reach with the smaller 500 MHz unit, and it was more easily transportable. We'd use the big one tomorrow.

I headed for the dining room with my canteen and found the waiter busily cleaning up from the night before. It had been a great party. The Altinbaş Rakı had flowed freely among the Paris-to-Peking cross-country truckers and the Iranians, who were happy to be across the border. Turkey was a tolerant republic, a secular Moselm country that even had a law against calling a non-Moslem an "infidel." The Turks had the freedom to take a drink if they liked. They rarely seemed to abuse the privilege and if moderation turned to excess they just seemed to get happier, not abusive. Rakı was for social drinking among friends, and the French songs and Iranian toasts could be heard through the late hours till I had finally drifted off.

"Good morning," I said, heading for the kitchen. "Gün aydın," came a sleepy response. The hot water was not yet boiled and I hated the thought of starting out without tea. Ron's forays were always a bit impetuous, followed by a later "Darn it, I forgot to bring the whatever." It was always a hungry trek with Ron.

"Is there any tea yet?" I asked.

"Eh!"

"Tea, Çay . . . ne zaman hazır olacak?"

A shout came up the stairwell. "Hey fella, let's go, we're all loaded up and ready. Let's get this doomsday team on the road. We want to get the testing done early so we have plenty of time to pick up the permit this afternoon."

We piled into Dilaver's Renault, warmed up and ready to hit the freedom of the open road. With a "İnşallah," we were off to Telçeker and the guard post which undoubtedly was expecting our arrival. Dawn was just breaking over the cone of Little Ararat, and we raced the ascending sun to our goal. To be the first to look within the confines of the Ark in over a million days would truly be a day to remember.

The blues and yellows of the fields came alive in the morning sun, accented here and there with a burst of red poppy.

"It's going to be a beautiful day, Ron!" I said as we turned off after the bridge and onto the road through the fields toward the foothills.

"Yeah! this should do it, this should be the proof," Ron said with a sigh.

"How much you want to bet if the scan looks good, before we're through explaining the evidence they'll be asking for something else? I'm telling you, Ron, Christendom just isn't accepting this site as the Ark. Either that or the others have made so many false claims the world's just tired of hearing about it."

"Well, maybe it's just because they didn't find it," Ron said.

"Or worse than that," I said, "they were on it and missed it. Quite a bitter pill to swallow!"

Our optimism faded as we approached the tin-roofed stone building at the entrance to the road through the mountains. The doorway faced south and in the shadows of the aspens, long in the morning sun, perhaps the guard couldn't see well through the windows of the car or just assumed we were villagers from Üzengili, returning early after a night on the town. The equipment covered the back window of the hatchback and we were really loaded down. I'd have thought the guard might come out for a look.

"He might want to make a call to Ağrı and check it out with the police first," I said, anticipating a delay.

We crept slowly by the guard shack. Dilaver rolled down the window and softly tooted his horn, watching for a response from the guard and a signal to stop.

The soldier stood in the doorway with the machine pistol slung over his shoulder, his right index finger on the trigger guard and his left forearm resting on the barrel. He made neither a move nor a sign of protest, then gave a slight wave of the hand.

Dilaver gestured in response to our admittance and we accelerated for the grade and the hills and the Ark.

The road was being widened, and Dilaver drove slowly from one unfinished grade to the other past the big D9 Cat tractor off to the side. "Kenan Evrin," said Dilaver.

"The president?" said Ron. "The president is opening the site to tourism?" This was really a good sign. At least someone was taking the site seriously.

We rolled to a stop at a bend in the road where we could look down on the Ark. I grabbed my binoculars, and looking down I could see a lone figure standing in the very center of the wreck. I focused in on one adult and a very large dog.

"No sheep, no shepherd!" I exclaimed. "They're getting serious, Ron. They've got a guard posted right on the Ark itself!"

Someone else was up and around. It was little Jawa Selman, a boy of about ten. He was standing on a knoll singing to himself and the rising sun at the top of his lungs and swinging a smoke pot of hot tea. We quickly recruited him to carry another bundle for us, while Dilaver grabbed one seventy-pound transit case and Ron the other. I grabbed the car battery, cameras, frequency generator, and antenna, and we all trekked off down the hill to the flow below us.

It was probably the hardest mile I ever walked, down the

sloping hills and the rocks wet with dew. The earthquake fissures had to be crossed with caution, all the gear broken down and set on the edge. Then we had to lower ourselves into the crack, transfer the equipment to the other side, and climb out again.

Little Jawa needed help, too, so I was the last aboard the Ark. Ron was standing there watching me climb in when I saw the blur of the dog's attack. "Ron, look out!" was all I had time to say.

If there was ever a hound from hell, it was a Kurdish sheep dog. These dogs weren't even afraid of bears, much less foreign intruders. Ron sidestepped him just in time. The dog's lunge had been downhill, and he tumbled a bit to get on his feet again for the second pass. When these animals don't even bark, they're really after you.

Ron was now uphill with two rocks in his hand. He let fly with a close miss, and the fight was on. The dog, with the hair raised on his back, was as high as Ron's elbow. Everyone dropped his gear and ran, shouting. The guard, too, was coming downhill toward us. Everything was confusion. Finally the beast slunk away and everyone was pretty flushed.

The animal was soon brought under control by his master and we looked the situation over. The dog had never bothered Dilaver. Was it because he was Turk? Dilaver had actually been far enough ahead to be talking with the guard. Why was Ron singled out for attack? The guard pointed to a cleft in the rocks near the port side, where the dog had returned to her den of pups!

"Gee, Ron! I thought you were dead meat," I said. "I never saw a dog go for anyone like that before in my life!" No one could say the Ark wasn't well protected.

Even the guard, a policeman from the village who knew us from the trip before, was a little standoffish. He was small, but size doesn't mean much in Turkey. He had a look in his eye that could chill you to the bone. I gave him a formal greeting with a kiss on both cheeks.

Dilaver told the guard our intentions of the day and our need for men to carry our gear back after the test. We would be needing a full crew tomorrow to conduct the entire survey.

"We'll just say a little prayer that something comes out of this," said Ron, unsnapping the transit case.

"Yeah!" I said. "Let's get this doomsday team cracking!"

The first thing was to confirm our exact position for the scan. With the frequency generator heating up the iron in the Ark, we had two quick cups of tea, just to be polite. It was part of the unspoken apology for the dog's attack.

With a walk athwartship, I got the readings on the iron lines I assumed were from walls or beams under the earth that had fittings in them. I placed stakes in the ground over them. Then I moved up to where I found twenty-six lines rather than thirteen and perceived I was at the bulkhead or athwartship (transverse) wall.

I marked this and proceeded uphill with a tape measure.

"Now to the stern," I said.

"Or the bow," Ron corrected me. It was our standing disagreement. "Or the high end, whatever," he continued, mumbling to himself.

The tape stretched from the bulkhead to the stern for a distance of 87 feet. "Okay!" I said. "That's wall number two." Actually I had measured this earlier as 87.5 feet, but I had noticed that someone had drilled a hole in the center of the sternpost to get a sample for analysis, then filled it with slurry to make a bench mark, so I measured from there.

I moved twelve feet uphill again and set a stake in the ground. The transit line would be made exactly seventy-five feet down from the stern. The tape was not stretched tight to the walls, which would have given a distance of less than sixty feet, but was allowed to fall slack on the ground and follow the contours of the earth to give me the distance of antenna travel. The graphic recorder would now print out a scan equal to a distance of sixty-nine feet.

"I should first determine the dielectric constant, Ron." I could see he was getting impatient. "I can do that by throwing the transit case cover tied on a rope over the outside wall, then shooting through the wall and picking up the interface on the recorder, and determine what kind of penetration we're getting. We should get a nice picture from the metal straps on the cover. Then by measuring the width of the wall, I'll be able to determine the depth of our scan interface."

"Can that wait until tomorrow?" Ron said. He was really anxious to get on with it. "I'd just like to get moving and get out of here. I've got to keep my appointment in Ağrı with the police chief. Just a sample. Just enough to see if it works."

"Ron?" I said slowly, "we *do* have permission to do this, do we not? I mean, I never went into the police station with you. I watched the car. We really do have a permit to do this, don't we?"

"Sure, sure we do. I'm just anxious to get back to the hotel. I don't feel very well, that's all."

Ron didn't look very good. Maybe the dog's attack had shook him up a bit and that would be understandable. I didn't want anyone having heart trouble out here. The altitude could have quite an effect on you when you weren't used to it. I wasn't feeling so hot myself.

"Okay, okay!" I said. "We can do that, but if we see anything, it might be difficult to determine the depth. I mean, is the Ark's structure three feet or nine feet under us?"

"Just whatever we can get," said Ron, looking nervously over his shoulder to the roadway above.

I had prepared months for this. Actually it had been almost a year ago that I had made the first attempt to scan the Ark, and I spent a year before that just thinking of the equipment that would be needed. I was sure the Ark had been buried somewhere. If it had been buried or nearly so during the Persian era, I could expect to find it so, somewhere in these hills walking Berosus' line. Now perhaps this would be the last line I would have to walk to prove it. Dilaver was on the inner western wall, poised for the word. I started the video camera on the tripod and framed the graphic recorder. Ron stepped back and framed in Dilaver for the first pass. All was in readiness. "Tamom! Dilaver!"

The instrument was set at sixty nanoseconds, with a shallow setting at 11:45, center at 11:15, and deep at 11:15 at a hundred lines per inch and a scan speed of thirty-two per second.

Dilaver walked a cautious and steady line, hitting the event marker as he passed each stake, for a distance of sixty-nine feet of antenna travel to the eastern wall, then pressed the event marker again and held it down until the instrument shut itself off.

We all drew close to the graphic recorder in silence. Even the Kurds who had arrived on the site from the village pressed for the advantage to see. There were about eight of us now, all peering down into the depths of the Ark's infrastructure far below.

There were a total of fifteen walls. The thirteen that had shown on the frequency generator could now be seen to fall within the western and eastern bulwarks. They went down over the entire length of the paper into its interior. At slightly less than what might be three feet under the surface, the walls or posts extended upward from a *floor!*

The picture was so clear that the end sections of the flooring could be seen as square blocks segmented together between the walls. I counted six of these beam ends separating the space between them.

RESHIT REMEMBERED

The early run to the site, the tension of not knowing if the radar would penetrate the soil or indeed still be working after its arduous trip to Turkey, was taking its toll on Ron. After thirty minutes of actual tests he was ready to pack it in. It was obvious he was not feeling well and I really think the dog attack and the heavy gear in the rarefied air had been excitement enough for the first morning. We would return to the Sim-er Hotel, where Ron could rest up for the long drive ahead.

We returned with two of the villagers. They were Mustafa Eraslan, an elder, and Nuri Sarihan, the mutar of Üzengili. I had expressed the desire to visit the village to the east and climb to the uppermost escarpment to check out another theory. Because this area was really in the wilds, it would be necessary to have someone who was known along with us, and the Üzengili Köyü Muhtarı, the village mayor, was just the ticket in. This village was called Kargaconmaz, meaning "crow won't land," and we have discussed before my contention that this area and name is connected with the Ark and the Flood story.

The quest of our voluntary pilgrimage would be the very top of an escarpment called Ziyaret Mount, which meant just

that. Why would anyone want to climb up there? It appeared
to be adjoining the other mount of interest called Yiğityatağı,
the "hero's bed" or abode of the heroes. If they were connected, perhaps it was a place where many curious persons
such as myself had made a voluntary pilgrimage to the abode
of the heroes of old and to the high place (Al Judi) where the
remains of the altar made by Utnapishtim could be found amid
relics of visitors of the past, where at one time in history, they
were able to look down upon the Ark.

It was an important location to investigate, more important
than I realized, for that day I was destined to meet a figure in
the story of the Ark whom no one could ever find. I would be
the first Ark hunter to meet him face-to-face and hear for the
first time the incredible story of the appearance of the true Ark.
It would totally negate the spurious claims of others and bring
one more false Ararat sighting crashing down on the heads of
my doubting contemporaries.

After a leisurely breakfast, we left Ron and again headed
east toward the Iranian border checkpoint, passing the Ark site
and moving on to the village of Kargaconmaz. We were able
to gain elevation for some distance until finally the road was
washed out to such an extent that it narrowed down to where
even Dilaver's little Renault was too wide. He stopped just
about the time I was ready to jump out and walk, before we all
slid off the road and into the canyon below.

"No problem," said Dilaver, laughing heartily at one of the
few English phrases he used for occasions such as this.

"That's just about as far as I'll go," I replied, wiping my
brow and gingerly stepping out on the safe side. Dilaver
looked out his driver's side and decided it best to back down the
ledge a bit before getting out. Mustafa and Nuri made a hurried
exit from the crazy Turk's "taksi" and joined me, huddled
against the embankment. The wheels were blocked with
stones and we proceeded to get our gear out and prepare for the
ascent.

This is not to say the climb could be compared in any way
to the difficulties encountered by my friends who climb Ararat, looming majestically from the plains to my right, but it
was still a steep grade. Actually, the angle of repose may have
been the same or greater, but at least here the end was in sight.

After three rest stops, I was beginning to have doubts in my ability to reach the top, and Dilaver was feeling it too. I was thinking that after what we had been through that morning, it might have been a poor plan to attempt this jaunt so soon.

I was quite surprised, upon reaching the next rise, to find donkeys and goats with an encampment of Kurds. The lady who first saw us was not shocked for long. With a warbling cry of hysteria, she let fly with a rock in my direction.

Nuri walked over and calmed her down, explaining who we were. They seemed to be laughing and recognized each other. I kept my distance. Then he called up to Mustafa and in a rattle of words, I heard the name *Reshit!*

In a flash everything connected. The Ark, the boat-shaped formation, the north slope. Everyone on this mountain was family. The prevalent familes were Selman, Eraslan, Özer, and Sarihan, and I literally shouted out, "Reshit Sarihan!"

Everyone stared, then Nuri smiled in surprise and said, "Evet, Sarihan," pointing to himself and then to the woman. Yes, they were related.

"And Reshit Sarihan, where is he?" I said in Turkish. After a few moments Nuri replied, "Doğubayazıt!"

It was a timely excuse to call off the climb. It was most important to locate Reshit while I had the assistance of Dilaver and the taxi, for soon Ron would have to be heading to Ağrı.

From what I could gather from Dilaver, Reshit was from Üzengili but now lived in town. He had family everywhere, so he occasionally stayed at both places and enjoyed spending his time leisurely tending his sheep on the heights during the summer months, living in a tent. But at the moment he was in Doğubayazıt. After thirty-eight years of mystery, was this the Reshit I was looking for?

After a few false locations, Dilaver was hot on Reshit's trail and suggested we go have something to eat and we'd all meet at the Ararat Hotel lobby later. He would bring Reshit to us. In an off-the-beaten-track local kabob I enjoyed feeling very Turk, rubbing shoulders with the farmers of the village. They eyed me curiously, obviously wondering why I was in the company of such esteemed elders.

His full name was Ali Oğlu Reşit Sarihan. He was a rather shy, quiet gentleman of sixty, the type who would be likely to smile politely, yet must be prodded to talk. When he did, it would be direct but in a hushed, private manner. First the weathered cracks at the edges of his eyes would smile, preceding his warm response. Every word was from his heart.

Reshit was, as they say in Turkish, *nazik,* polite and charming. His features were of the harsh land. He was slightly balding, with the ever-present mustache of his homeland. There was the faint hint of a smile. He searched my face closely, so I leaned closer across the table as we waited for tea and the interpreter to arrive. I could restrain myself no longer and whispered, "Nuh'un Gemisi."

He took a long draw on his cigarette and a look of relief lit up his face as if to say, *Finally . . . you came.* He leaned back to recount the years he had waited to tell his story.

There were nine persons in attendance and the video was set up. The police had questioned at the front desk the purpose of the interview. Apparently they were satisfied it was not a political issue being discussed but archaeological interests. The interpreter was a desk clerk from the hotel, Najarti Atish, who was very fluent in languages.

The word seemed to have spread quickly that I had located someone of importance to the Ark, for we were soon joined by well-known guides of Ararat, Abdullah Turan (son of another famous guide of the peaks, Ahmet Turan), Halis Çeven, Yesil Gözlü, and another helpful gentleman in the import-export business named Mustafa Yavus, (whose English had a hint of a Hindu accent from his many years in India), and also, of course, the elders of Üzengili.

The entire documented interview lasted exactly fifty-nine minutes and fifty seconds, the highlights of which were the following:

"That place was in nineteen hundred forty-eight a field, yes, for sheep, it was a field. I was in that time age twenty-two years, but that time there was a *deprem,* an earthquake. But with very strong earthquake been there, it been like ship, but not very quickly – time, time."

"What month was this, September or November?" I asked, remembering the newspaper account from Cummings' story.

"It was the fifth month."

"Was it the end of the month or the beginning?" I prodded.

"That time been, all the villagers remember very well, the middle of the fifth month. But not very quickly, slowly. The earthquake always been there, yes, very soft earth. And he see before, nineteen hundred and forty-eight, that time he thinking it's a kind, uh, a *mu'cize* kind."

"Natural formation?" I questioned.

"No, not natural, *mu'cize* [miracle] yes! he thinking that time. Then, second time, nineteen hundred fifty-one, same picture like this, it starts same this, this view," Reshit related. So it would appear that after some three years, it started to fall apart.

"And then what happened?" I said, with everyone moving in closely. "In 1948, after the earthquake, what did the people think when they saw the boat and did it ruin the village? And was the village named Naşar before?"

"Yes!"

"And did they change the name of the village then to Üzengili?"

"Yes!"

"And does the name *Naşar*[1] mean 'to present a sacrifice'?"

"Yes, yes, a sacrifice!" the interpreter answered.

"Well then, didn't the villagers living in Naşar, the place of the sacrifice, on Mahşer slope or "The Last Judgment" – or perhaps it is Mahşur for Mahşur Günü, meaning, "raised from the dead" or "Resurrection day" – didn't they find it strange that such a thing should occur there?" I said.

This caused quite a stir, and I was left out of the conversation for some time as they all debated the possibilities. Mustafa said he was quite taken back that someone not really speaking the language would suggest such a thing, and I let it continue, ordering another round of tea.

It was time for Dilaver to leave. He must bring Ron to the police station in Ağrı, so we continued while he went for the permit.

"No, it didn't [ruin the village]. They took their house to the other place far from the mountain, have you seen it? Have you been there? Everybody thinking, it's not normally, it's the ship

---

[1] *New Redhouse Turkish-English Dictionary* (Istanbul: Redhouse, 1984). Nezir (Neşir) p. 884, Nezire (Neşire) p. 884.

of the Nuh being there, it's very interesting, they all thinking that."

"Well, if the villagers called the peak of the mountain Al Judi [Cudi] couldn't they connect the two, seeing that the Koran says the Ark of Noah landed on Al Judi?" I asked. This again started a long conversation, and I heard Ararat (Ağrı Dağ) and Hagopian's name mentioned several times by the climbers.

"The top of the mountain is called Al Judi because it is high up but not Ararat. He is very sorry he has not the true answer to your question, also couldn't read any Koran, so he doesn't know about it. He says, I know that when the earthquake came in our village, I remember that day very well, all the people remember, it *wasn't normal,* it was a very *interesting* earthquake. That time, all the people thinking it's the ship of the Nuh, but some of them said no! It can't be true, about that, the ship must be on top of Mount Ararat, why would it be here. Some of them thinking that, but Reshit thought, no! it's the ship of the Nuh, and then he just be quiet about that, until you ask him again right now."

"Well," I said, "Reshit and I might still be the only ones to believe it is the ship of Noah, but I believe in Reshit, and so we are like brothers."

When this was relayed to Reshit, I felt the bond that was formed between us in his laugh and his smile. He explained more to the interpreter.

"Now some people think that, when you people went in there, it can be the ship of Nuh, if it can't be, why those people going in there, now all the people thinking it must be true, and so Reshit is now very happy to talk with you."

We discussed many things—the plant that grew only at the Ark site, the historical significance of the place name of the villages, the escarpments all tying into the Flood story. As the group slowly broke up and I said good-bye to Reshit, who agreed to meet again that night for dinner, I began realizing the *revelatory* statements he had made.

When I saw Ron that night, he was brokenhearted. "They did it again," he said. "The permit is off. The area is now closed to foreigners. You can look for Noah's Ark anywhere but at our site."

"Really bad news," I said, trying not to sound too cheerful. "Maybe dinner in town tonight might cheer you up before we head back. We have a special dinner guest for our last night."

"Who's that?" Ron asked.

"We're only thirty-eight years late to meet the man who first saw Noah's Ark. God revealed it in his timing," I said. "Reshit!"

THE RESURRECTION OF THE ARK

Soon after my return home from Turkey, I could not restrain myself from calling Eryl Cummings to tell him the good news about locating Reshit. Violet answered the phone. After listening to my story there was a brief silence. "Wrong Reshit," she replied, and would hear no more of it.

I had mistakenly hoped she would delight in the mystery being solved. I cannot share in her optimism that in the same year on two different mountains in sight of each other, two farmers named Reshit found the Ark in different locations and reported it, yet had never met.

I should have anticipated this reaction. Cummings, author of several books on the search for the Ark, has concentrated to a great extent on Armenian legends. These stories, though interesting reading for the uninitiated, were just the right admixture of "gee whizzims" to make your garden grow.

Under the Armenian myth category, or "old legends die hard," came tales of how the Ark could be seen as a small black speck against the snow. But this was only when the weather and the season were "just right," of course. The traveler could be either amused or enthralled, depending on his gullibility. He could be shown the site of the Garden of Eden and the tomb of the patriarch Noah at the foot of the mountain nearby.

He had seen an ancient vinestock, still bearing grapes, that had been planted by Noah himself. All this and more was reported by James Bryce in his notes of 1876 on the "Transcaucasia and Ararat."

The pilgrim in search of truth might even be encouraged by the villagers of Arghuri to make the climb after being shown the trunk of an ancient willow that had sprung from a plank of the Ark and, after all, hadn't the wise men stood on the peak before the birth of our Lord anxiously awaiting his star to appear? If these three had made the descent to Jerusalem, couldn't he make the climb to the top as well and see the Ark for himself? This could perhaps throw a wrench into the gears of the rumor mill, so other schemes were employed to keep the relic trekkers off their sacred mountain. Hippolytus relates the best of them:

> . . . whose summit no one has ever been able to reach on account of the violence of the winds and the storms which always prevail there. And if anyone attempts to ascend it, there are demons that rush upon him, and cast him down headlong from the ridge of the mountains into the plain, so that he dies there.

Couldn't someone be found to prevail? Faustus of Byzantium wrote of a fourth-century Bishop of Nisibis who wasn't afraid. Enter Saint Jacob, who in his eagerness to locate the Ark on Ararat, was kneeling in prayer when an angel was sent to give him a commandment from God to stop looking for the Ark on Ararat. Whether this should be taken as insight by today's Ark hunters, or just Jacob's excuse for not completing the climb, in the last case it had the desired effect. To actually see the Ark close at hand was against God's will, so the traveler must be content with something less. Many have been content with much less than the Ark itself. Friedrich Parrot in 1829 and Carveth Wells in his 1932 journey to Ararat wrote they had seen a piece of wood from the Ark at the Armenian Christian Monastery at Echmiadzin. Many today expect nothing more. I suggest that those so inclined visit Echmiadzin, ask to see as well the piece of the cross and the spear that was thrust into the side of Jesus. The monks will tell you how the spear was brought to the church by none other than Saint Thaddeus himself.

But Thaddeus, it might be implored by the pilgrim, was a first-century disciple of Jesus? How could that be when by tradition the monastery wasn't founded until A.D. 302? The answer is roughly translatable as, "It has always been thus, my son."

More recent accounts, however, have not failed to charm the reader. In all fairness, it should be mentioned that just because one is of Armenian descent today does not mean he is responsible for or believes in the eyewitness accounts of Haji Yearam and Georgie Hagopian.

Although these two Bayazit bumpkins may not have sown the original seed plots of centuries ago, they dressed the ground for the authors of taller tales to come.

These stories grow well in the fertile soil of the rural southwest. The latest eyewitness account, which has since dropped to second place in the yarn-spinning contest due to a new contender from Canada, is that of Ed Davis, who is described by the author of his tale, Dr. Don Shockey, as the first American to view Noah's Ark.[2]

Violet Cummings has succeeded in relating these pieces of wishful thinking in the most optimistic light and is mostly responsible for the ongoing search of Ararat itself. Both Eryl and Violet are good researchers but both, in my opinion, have failed to be judgmental. All the stories of the Ark on Ararat obviously cannot be true. They are conflicting in both description and location, in lakes, on ledges, under glaciers, and intact, broken in two pieces, then three, and together again. There must be a fleet of ships on Ararat, and no one has ever produced a photograph of any of them. The story of Reshit, however, the one that made sense, had eluded them for the following reasons:

To be the true Ark, it must be a rectangular barge as described by Hagopian. With this in mind, it's a wonder they've gotten so much mileage out of the Roskovitsky whopper. It is related as fact by both Cummings and Noorbergen, even though by now, both must recognize it as a complete fabrication by Benjamin Allen, secretary of the Sacred History Research Expedition (SHRE) for the fund-raising campaigns of the early 1940s.

In those days it was described as submarine shape with a whaleback deck and three stubby little masts to carry just enough sail to keep it headed into the wind. Then came Reshit; the article describing his find in 1948 said, "The contour of the earth indicated the invisible part of the object

---

[2]Dr. Don Shockey, *The Painful Mountain* (Fresno, California: Pioneer Publishing, 1986).

was shaped like a ship . . . Reshit insisted it was not a simple rock formation."

It's hard to understand Cummings not making the connection after Vandeman blasted the sides out of his "rock formation" in 1960. Even though Reshit had never been found, the clues remained. Reshit's discovery was made two-thirds of the way up the mountain. If Ararat is the first mountain to come to mind, then 12,300 feet is two-thirds up from the valley floor.

Here is where we find the Frenchman Navarra justifying his claim of being on Reshit's site, skating on thin ice by describing a huge shadow with the gently inward curving lines of a ship beneath his feet.

In a letter dated January 29, 1960, from Bordeaux, the Frenchman explains to Eryl Cummings that Reshit's discovery in 1948 was on the northeast face and very close to his own discovery of 1955. How people can make these claims having never found Reshit is a mystery, but now even Eryl appears puzzled, and he states, "It is over this point that the mystery of Navarra really begins."

For now Navarra is leading his explorers for the Ark to the north*west*. The solution is simple. Navarra has heard Reshit's find was on the northwest slope, and indeed it was, but Navarra is lost because he's on the wrong mountain. The clue should be obvious that Reshit wasn't on Ararat by his statement: "There is no folklore there about the Ark."

Two-thirds of the way up Vandeman and Noorbergen's mountain was sixty-three hundred feet and the boat-shaped object! Had anyone at the time made the connection and asked if Reshit was from this area? Obviously not. Reshit might even have been in the crowd watching them set the charges.

Word spread fast in Doğubayazıt, and the climbing guides kept filtering in as I set up the public interview, hiding nothing. Reshit was a bit taken back by the policemen in attendance and may in fact have been apprehensive about what this American was going to charge him with. The Ararat guides hung on every word Reshit said. It must be remembered that this story broke some thirty-eight years ago and to many of the guides the elusive Reshit was a will-o'-the-wisp, someone their fathers occasionally spoke about but who was now lost in the haze of history and nowhere to be found. Perhaps he had been laid to rest in some village on the north side of Ararat, his Ark's location buried with him.

Now with the information at hand that the Ark had been revealed by an earthquake in the middle of the fifth month of 1948, attempts were made to nail down the exact day and the hour.

In further investigations I was informed by correspondence from Turkey:

> As you have inquired, I do not know the exact date of the May 1948 deprem, as I have tried to learn from our area's elderly. The deprem occurred in mid-May, but I do not know the exact day and the time. In this case, I regret not providing the information.

A computer search revealed some interesting data from quakes to hit the area affecting the Ark at a later date, but I was unable to recover any data prior to 1978. This is still of some interest to the site.

THE 1978 DAMAGE

The first earthquake occurred on February 6, 16:06 local time.

The second earthquake occurred on February 7, 00:48 local time, and was the strongest. Distance from the Ark was 11 nautical miles, 2.5 miles closer than the first jolt, and 23.2 km closer to the surface. We can discount the third quake, which occurred only seconds later and at a much greater distance.

Earthquake number four, however, was quite strong at 3.7 and 28 nautical miles away. This occurred at 10:57 local time on November 25. It was earthquake number four that pushed the Ark out of the ground even further. The earthquake of mid-May 1948, which originally uncovered the structure in the field of Reshit, needs additional data collected. It is interesting to note again that Berosus, in a letter to Antiochus I in the year 281 B.C.E., gives the same date for the Flood, mid-May or May 15.

It was my pleasure to be a guest of the Honorable Tahir Elhan, introduced to me through Madame Gülek, wife of the well-known statesman and lecturer Kasım Gülek, in Ankara on April 12, 1985. It was at this time I learned that the quake of 1978 was considered an abnormal experience, as earthquakes go. "I was there at the time, you know," said Judge Elhan. "The event was preceded by the sky turning *silver!* Everyone was out in the streets, looking up at the strange phenomenon, when the quake struck. That is the reason for so few injuries. They were all outside."

"But Tahir bey," I said. "Can an astronomical event be connected with a geological event?"

"I understand your question," he replied. "That is what bothered me!"

During my investigations I met with persons who had experienced the same event in Doğubayazıt. All agreed it was true, the sky appeared to turn silver before the earthquake hit.

But wait! Didn't Reshit say there was something strange about this earthquake? Isn't it strange that no one in Doğubayazıt even knew of the event, less than ten miles away, until told by the villagers? Remember, there was no damage to the village in 1948. The quake in 1978 is what caused the damage and the fissures at the Ark site.

The villagers were no strangers to earthquakes in this faulted region of Turkey. This earthquake was described as most interesting, "not normal," and a *mu'cize!* A miracle.[3]

The Ark was upthrust from the crypt of time as a sign for this generation, from the field of "raised from the dead" (*mahşur*).[4]

The earth has resurrected a sign of the end times from the slopes of "The last judgment" (*mahşer*).[5]

It hangs there now, wounded by the unbelievers, impaled through the side, rejected by those very ones who made it the object of their search.

They are left behind now. The search for the Ark is over. In June 1987, the Turkish ministers officiated at the site with the presentation of a blood sacrifice at the ground-breaking ceremony for the first building of a $2.4 million tourist venture.

---

[3] *New Redhouse Turkish-English Dictionary* (Istanbul, Turkey: Redhouse, 1984), p. 787.
[4] Ibid., p. 723.
[5] Ibid., p. 723.

Test pits have been dug, but the Turks, to avoid religious exploitation, are not revealing their findings. The area is now a national park and under constant attention and guard.

The Atatürk University of Erzurum began cautious core-drilling operations in July 1988. While visiting the site with Dr. John Baumgardner and Professor Salih Bayraktutan in November 1987, we followed the sign from the bottom of the hill that said NU'HUN GEMISI. It was placed there by the Minister of Culture.

At the new viewing center at the top of the hill, overlooking the Ark, we met an old friend. It was the village elder who was always peering into my face with the same question: "Is it Noah's Ark?" That was a question we both settled long ago, and we never made mention of it as we sat there together on the hill sipping tea. We were both quite satisfied, I think.

Soon, when the Turks are ready, it will be made public to the world on their time and terms, which is perhaps as it should be. Then the others will return making claims as to who was first to recognize it and vie for the position of who was greatest among them. In this debate I will take no part, for I consider it an undeserved blessing to have beheld it in my place in time. I knew it immediately as the vessel of my past generations' salvation the day I climbed inside. There is a new Ark and a covering to protect us from the judgment to come . . . and there is still room within. Will I see you there, and may I welcome you aboard someday?

The ancient world at the time of Noah. Arrows indicate migration paths of his descendants.